THE RAIDERS

Robin Neillands is a writer and journalist, a
frequent contributor to national newspapers
and magazines, and the author of over forty
books. In recent years he has turned to writing
novels and military history. His previous
books in this series have included one on the
Special Air Service Regiment, and *By Sea and
Land: The Story of the Royal Marines Commandos (1942–82)*. During the 1950s he
served with 45 Commando in 3 Commando
Brigade. He now lives in Buckinghamshire and
Spain.

THE RAIDERS

THE ARMY COMMANDOS
1940–1946

Robin Neillands

FONTANA/Collins

First published by George Weidenfeld &
Nicolson Ltd 1989

First published in 1990 by Fontana Paperbacks
8 Grafton Street, London W1X 3LA

Copyright © Robin Neillands 1989

Printed and bound in Great Britain by
William Collins Sons & Co. Ltd, Glasgow

This one is for Bob, Terry, Harry
and Daisy, and all the members
of 'Harry's Club'.

They performed whatsoever the King commanded

SAMUEL II

CONTENTS

'You have to keep going, no matter what. You have to maintain the advance. You see it in the cinema, don't you? A man falls and everyone gathers round or goes to ground. You couldn't do that in battle, you have to keep going. If you let the men stop or go to ground, it's hard to get them going again, so you press on, take the position, kill the enemy. Then you can take care of the prisoners and the wounded, ours and theirs. That's the only way to do it and it saves lives in the end.'

Major Leslie Callf, MC & Bar – No. 9 Commando
Past President, The Commando Association

ACKNOWLEDGEMENTS

My thanks go first to Henry Brown of No. 1 Commando, Secretary of the Commando Association, with my best wishes for his retirement, and best wishes also to his successor, Ron Youngman. Henry published a letter in the *Commando Newsletter* calling for contributions and provided me with a list of names and addresses. He also told those members who enquired about this project that I was 'all right'. Commando soldiers have learned to be cautious. My thanks must then go to all the Commando soldiers who sent in their stories, and with those thanks my apologies for those parts I could not use – it was all useful, as background or as a check to other stories. The contributors are all mentioned in the text but some particular thanks are still due to those who were tireless in offering assistance and whose enthusiasm kept me going. Thanks, therefore, to Brigadier Peter Young, DSO, MC, of 3 Commando and 3 Commando Brigade, for his help with this book and with *By Sea and Land*, the story of the Royal Marine Commandos; to Major Leslie Callf, MC, and Captain Harry Lucas of 9 Commando, for their friendly advice, their fascinating contributions and permission to quote from copyright material in their own history of 9 Commando; to Colonel Philip Pritchard of 6 Commando, who wrote from Australia, sending his massive and carefully researched history of his troop in north-western Europe. Other people who were tireless in sending in their recollections include 'Red' Skelton of 5 Commando, Eric Groves of 2 Commando, Frank Barton of 6 Commando, RSM Cliff Bryen also of 6 Commando, with special thanks for the loan of his photograph album

ACKNOWLEDGEMENTS

and North African diary, Sergeant Terry of No. 11 (Scottish) Commando for his story of the Rommel Raid, Captain R. J. Bavister of 2 Commando, Jim Coker of 1 Commando, one of the Police draft of 1942, Des Crowden and Geoff Riley of 5 Commando, Joe Edmans of 1 Commando, Charles Hustwick of Brigade Signals, who found himself on an excessive number of operations, as signallers will, Ted Kelly of 2 Commando, Major G. I. Milton of 7 Commando, Ken McAllister of 2 Commando, Stan Weatherall of 6 Commando and the SBS . . . the list is endless, and my thanks to you all.

My thanks (and yours, the contributors) must also go to my secretary, Estelle Huxley, who typed draft after draft, deciphering in the process a wide variety of handwriting, some of which – she says – was almost as bad as mine; and to Terry Brown for the maps. Thanks should also go to the staff of those fine institutions, the Public Records Office, The Imperial War Museum, the National Army Museum, and the D-Day Museums at Portsmouth and Arromanches in Normandy.

To everyone who has helped, once again my thanks, and I hope the result justifies all our efforts.

PREFACE

This is the story of the Army Commandos of the British Army, from their formation in 1940 to their disbandment in 1945–46. It should be made clear now that this is not an official nor even a recognized history. It is a collection of stories, the stories of the men who served in those units during that period, told in their own words with as few interjections from me as possible. The object of the book has been to gather together the experiences of Army Commandos who served in all the raids, landings and operational theatres during the Second World War, and present them here as a portrait of Commando soldiers at war.

I have been told that all the official histories have been written, that it all happened a very long time ago, even that in these piping times of peace, war stories are somewhat out of fashion. Perhaps this is so. Who really knows? What follows in this book is not the traditional type of military history, full of dates and figures, but stories of men, ordinary men, in the extraordinary days of war. These, I think, are still of interest, and at least some of the old soldiers seem to agree with me.

'People don't want dates any more,' said Major Leslie Callf, MC, of 9 Commando, when I went to interview him. 'What they seem to want to know is, what was it really like?'

In an attempt to show what it was like, I have gathered in these stories and here present the face of war in all its diversity ... before the battle, training, waiting, the advance and withdrawal, mistakes – plenty of those – getting wounded, becoming a prisoner, escaping. In battle or in billets, the stories conjure up a very different time, almost another age. The battlefields of the Second World War are now as empty and unremarkable as the ringing plains of Troy, but it wasn't always so. As this book reveals, the sharp end of the Second World War was a painful place to live, yet these men lived in it and came through it.

To collect these stories I approached the Commando Association, who published a request for help in their *Newsletter* and supplied a list of names. From this we sent out some 700 letters, and after a short delay, the replies began to flood in, letters, tapes, diaries, old yellowed maps, troop orders, photographs, and a surprising amount of poetry. For a while we were quite overwhelmed and as I sit here surrounded by it all, I face the daunting task of sending it back to its original owners. The rest of the book is awaiting only this preface before dispatch to the publisher.

The lay historian, writing a personal history of a battle, a war, or a campaign, is very much in the hands of his contributors. If they will not tell him what happened, he is lost, for (usually) he wasn't there. When we had the material filed into order of unit Nos. 1 to 12, it became clear that some units had been much more forthcoming than others, but while we hunted down contributors to fill a few gaps, in the main we let the contributions we received speak for the rest. After all, the Commandos themselves only wanted volunteers. As a result a number of units, notably Nos. 5, 6, 9 and 12 Commandos, plus Layforce – units whose exploits have received less attention in the past than they are due – feature here quite strongly. Given the number of units involved, the number of years covered, and the surprisingly large number of contributions which we received, it has clearly been impossible to fit in every detail of every unit during the time of their existence. I have, therefore, chosen to tell the story by campaign, bringing the units forward as they appear on stage, and in the main keeping strictly to the twelve main Commando units, although I was unable to resist some stories from the Small Scale Raiding Force and the first SBS unit, 101 Troop, raised by 6 Commando. I have also been at some pains to collect stories from the other ranks to fill in details of the battle from the viewpoint of the private soldier.

To cram in as many personal stories as possible I have eliminated all but the most basic outlines of the campaigns, and where possible let the Commandos themselves set out the original plan as well as what actually happened. This is not – nor was it ever intended to be – a blow-by-blow account of what every unit was doing throughout the Second World War. This, I repeat, is the story of Commando soldiers in that conflict, told in their own words, however halting.

What comes through is a story where the total is greater than the sum of its parts. These were ordinary men, drawn to the war from every walk of life. They were volunteers, coming forward to join units where the risk of death or injury was perceptibly higher than in their parent units, where life was hard and the training, that relentless, never-ending training, always went a little beyond the point where a man might willingly go.

And yet out of this harsh existence come great tales and a lot of gentle humour. Commando soldiers are great raconteurs. There is pride here too, pride in their units and in their comrades, living and dead, never in themselves, and a great deal of courage, that quiet, rather British kind of courage, the courage to go on, day after day, in the face of great adversity, taking whatever comes without complaint. It may be, as I was told several times by professional civilians, that war stories are now out of fashion, but is there ever a time when brave tales go totally out of fashion? Pity the time, if so.

'Cursed be he who first invented war.' Indeed, but war has the knack of bringing out the best as well as the worst in people. In this book then, is a great deal of war. But there is also much kindness, comradeship, loyalty and quiet determination. One of the great pleasures of this type of work is to meet and talk with the old Commando soldiers. In spite of the passing years, they haven't changed much, and to collect and write up their tales has been a pleasure and a privilege. As their compiler I commend them to you.

Robin Neillands
London 1989

Guerrillas, Ancient and Modern

'Now David was in a hold and said, "Oh that one
would bring me a drink from the well of Bethlehem
that is by the gate." And three mighty men went
out by night through the army of the Philistines and
took the water and brought it unto David, but he
put it from him saying, "Far be it from me that I
drink this, for is this not the blood of brave men
who went in jeopardy of their lives?"'

SAMUEL 23 V. 15–17

This is the story of the Commando soldiers of the British
Army, and the units in which they served during the
hard, long years of the Second World War, from 1940 to
1945. The story of the Army Commandos is told here as
far as possible in their own words, covering recruitment
to disbandment, and many of the conflicts, triumphs,
defeats and disasters they encountered during the years
between. After disbandment in 1946 it seemed that the
Army Commandos had blazed a glorious trail across the
military firmament and then gone for ever; but in fact the
Army Commandos live again today. Over 1,000 Army
Commandos now serve in 3 Commando Brigade, Royal
Marines, and sailed with their comrades of the Royal
Marine Commandos to retake the Falkland Islands in
1982. History has repeated itself, but then this is history's
habit.

There is nothing new about Commando operations, for
as the quotation above shows we can go back as far as the
Old Testament to trace the origins of the Commando
soldier. Guerrilla warfare has a long history. King David

harried the Philistines and the armies of Saul, and had he lived in these present times, he would surely have ordered his troops to make the classic raid on Entebbe. Down the centuries, irregular warfare has always been the way in which small countries can maintain their nation in arms against more powerful foes. This tradition is true of many nations, but especially of the British, and when British history is examined, it displays a long series of actions where amphibious warfare has played a significant part. This book should begin with a brief historical survey of amphibious assault, the chosen métier of the Commando soldier. As with all history, it is as well to begin at the beginning which, in the case of the British Isles, means Julius Caesar.

In 55 BC Caesar sailed from Gaul against the Britons, bringing his legions across the Channel in a fleet of eighty ships. They sailed all night, reaching the shores of Kent at about nine in the morning, only to find the Britons alert and in arms, galloping their war chariots across the beaches and into the surf. This warlike reception terrified the legionaries, as Caesar himself recalled, 'until the standard-bearer of the Tenth Legion threw himself into the sea and started forward with the eagle . . . when all men followed. When everyone was ashore the legions charged.' The invasion of 55 BC was repulsed, but the following year a more successful assault was launched.

Britain entered written history with a seaborne invasion and fell back into the Dark Ages under maritime attack from the Saxons, who sailed across the North Sea in their narrow ships to stave in the bulwarks of the Roman Empire during the fifth century AD. 'If there were a hundred tongues in every head,' wrote an Irish monk, 'they could not recount or retell or enumerate all we have suffered at the hands of that valiant, wrathful, purely pagan people.' In the following centuries the Saxons were followed ashore by the Danes and Normans, raiders and sea-rovers to a man. The British people therefore come from raiding, sea-roving stock.

In 1066 William the Conqueror repeated Caesar's feat, and eventually conquered most of the island, nearly 900 years before armies sailed the other way in a series of combined operations, culminating in the D-Day landings of 1944. The 'Overlord' Tapestry in the D-Day Museum at Portsmouth mirrors the scenes on the one at Bayeux. During the Hundred Years War, from 1346 to 1453, the French constantly raided the south coast of Britain, paying particular attention to the Cinque Ports of Kent and Sussex, ports charged with supplying ships for the English Navy and with conveying English armies over to France. In 1588 this navy, with the Royal galleons in the van, beat off the Spanish Armada. Philip II of Spain, who dispatched the Armada, was in no doubt regarding the difficulties of an invasion. 'The Kingdom of England is, and must always remain, strong at sea, since on this the safety of the realm chiefly depends,' he wrote. Had the Duke of Medina Sidonia managed to meet with the armies of Alexander Farnese, the Duke of Parma, as was the intention, there would still have remained the task of landing that army on a hostile shore. But English cannon and the English weather prevented even that possibility. The lesson to be drawn here is that navies are ideal for defence, but lack the ability to project their power ashore unless they possess some amphibious capacity. For a landlocked power this may not matter; for an island, an amphibious capability is essential.

In the seventeenth century, with the Royal Navy now officially in existence, a force of infantry was available for just such an amphibious role – the Duke of York and Albany's Maritime Regiment of Foot, raised in 1664. Eventually this regiment evolved into the Royal Marines. During subsequent centuries the Empire expanded, most notably when General Wolfe's army was ferried up the St

Lawrence river in Canada to storm the Heights of Abraham by night, and take the city of Quebec during the Seven Years War, a classic combined operation that added another dominion to the Crown.

'The procession of boats steered silently up the St Lawrence, the night being moonless and sufficiently dark. As they reached the landing point, the tide bore them in towards the rocks, the silence broken by a sentry's challenge:

"*Qui va là?*"

"France," answered a Highland Officer of Fraser's Regiment.

"*A quel régiment?*" countered the sentry.

"*De la Reine*," replied the Highlander, knowing that regiment mustered into Bougainville's Corps, and the boats passed on. The men disembarked at a small beach below the Anse du Foulon, at the foot of heights as steep as heights covered with trees can be, and twenty-four riflemen led the way up, followed by the rest of the advance force, while the main body waited in their boats. No sound reached the strained ears of Wolfe but the splash of a nearby waterfall and the cautious sounds from the climbers above, until at length the sound of musket shots told him the men were masters of the position. The word was given, and the men, with loud "huzzas!" leaped from the boats, and with slung muskets prepared to scale the heights. In the grey of dawn the red-coated soldiers moved quickly up and formed in order on the plateau above.'

Wolfe's landing below the Heights of Abraham was the blueprint for a dozen Commando landings in World War II, and many more such assault landings were to follow during the next century and a half.

During the Napoleonic Wars, the British received first-hand experience of what an irregular army could do. When Lord Wellington took the country's only effective field army to fight in Spain, he found that the Spanish Army could achieve very little in open battle against the French, but that the Peninsula terrain, 'where small armies are defeated and large armies starve', proved ideally suited to the activities of the Spanish *guerrilleros*. These small bands of irregulars shredded the French garrisons, cut the lines of communication, ambushed couriers and generally rendered the French position in Spain completely untenable. Meanwhile, dashing frigate captains sent in parties from the sea to cut out ships from well-garrisoned ports. No less a person than Nelson lost his arm while coming ashore during the amphibious assault on Tenerife. All this should have added up to something, but amphibious operations were still as ancillary ventures, mounted as required, with whatever forces came to hand. The main conduct of war was left to capital ships and big battalions, and the colonial campaigns and conquests of the Victorian era were not greatly concerned with amphibious operations, for by then the Empire was established. The Royal Navy ruled the waves, and the British Army, with horse and gun, could march wherever it wished.

In the early years of the present century, the scene shifted to South Africa during the Boer War of 1899–1902. After some initial successes the Boer Army found itself quite unable to defeat the ever-increasing power of the British Armies in regular engagements. But after the Boers went 'on commando' they were able to keep up the war for years, and the story of the British Commandos can be traced back directly to this point. One Boer Commando soldier, Denys Reitz, wrote a book about his life in the Boer Commandos, which inspired British soldiers some forty years later. In *Commando*, Reitz describes in some detail how small roving forces of horsemen, equipped with little more than courage, tenacity and Lee Metford rifles, staved off the assembled might of an Empire. Reitz's account of his departure for the wars would gladden any Commando soldier's heart. 'In September of 1899 . . . British troops were moving up to the Transvaal

5

and the Free State, while Boer forces were mobilizing on various fronts and we were ordered to entrain for the Natal border. The moment we heard of this, we took our rifles, fetched our horses from the stables and within ten minutes had saddled up and mounted . . . little knowing on how long and how difficult a trail this lighthearted enlistment was starting us.' (When one Boer Commando blew up an armoured train and captured the passengers, they numbered among their prisoners an officer of the 4th Hussars, serving in South Africa as a war correspondent. His name was Winston Churchill.)

The Great War, which followed shortly after the Boer War, provides two examples, one disastrous, one successful, of amphibious operations. The first was the landings at Gallipoli in the Turkish Dardanelles on 25 April 1915. The landings, by British, Australian and New Zealand forces, met with firm resistance, and were soon checked with great loss along the shore. The force maintained itself ashore until the end of the year at great cost in lives, finally being withdrawn under cover of night on 8/9 January 1916. The landings put a temporary blight on the career of Winston Churchill, then First Lord of the Admiralty, who had been in favour of this maritime attempt to outflank the Western Front and drive Turkey out of the war. Nothing was achieved and the losses among the troops were considerable: 30,000 killed, 74,000 wounded, 8,000 missing or taken prisoner. Churchill was forced to resign and from then on the British military establishment became very wary indeed of amphibious operations. Fortunately, the next amphibious operation, if smaller in scale, was much more successful in execution.

On St George's Day, 23 April 1917, a force of Royal Marines, drawn from the 4th Battalion of the Corps, carried out a raid on the Belgian port of Zeebrugge. Zeebrugge was a submarine base where the channel had to be blocked and the harbour facilities destroyed. The raid was carried out with great *élan*, the harbour was completely blocked and the Corps gained two Victoria Crosses. This landing was made under the overall command of Roger Keyes, a man who later became Admiral of the Fleet Sir Roger Keyes, GCB, KCVO, CMG, DSO, MP. In 1940 Sir Roger became the Director of Combined Operations.

This gallop through history has carried us from 55 BC to the closing years of the Great War. Peace was forced on the Central Powers by a naval blockade, by terrible losses on the Western Front, and by the entry into the war of the United States, which offered the Allies an unlimited supply of cannon fodder should the attrition continue. Successful strategy had very little to do with it. The Great War ended on 11 November 1918, and for the next twenty years the military forces of Britain quietly stagnated. Even so, a few of our characters are already on stage, notably Roger Keyes and Winston Churchill, people who had some experience of irregular warfare. From these few acorns a great tree would grow, but their time had yet to come. Given 2,000 years of history and countless examples of all that an amphibious strategy could achieve, it is somewhat surprising that Britain still saw no need for a properly trained and equipped amphibious force.

The irregular warfare covered in this book falls into two broad areas; small coastal raids and all-out amphibious assaults. Since 1664 Great Britain had, at least in theory, maintained a force designed for these two purposes, the Corps of Royal Marines, but by 1918 the Corps had all but lost its amphibious role. The duties of the Corps had become more naval than amphibious, their opportunities for shore training were limited, and their continued existence was often in doubt.

During the Great War, apart from Zeebrugge, the Corps had manned the armament on capital ships, and provided a division for the Western Front. When the Great War ended, the Corps' strength stood at 55,000 men, divided into two branches, the Royal Marine Artillery and the

Royal Marine Light Infantry. This force was swiftly reduced by demobilization to around 15,000 men, and in 1923 the two arms were amalgamated into a single Corps, the Royal Marines. The functions of the Corps were then defined by the Admiralty as 'to provide a detachment of HM ships which, while capable of manning their share of the main armament, are also trained to provide a striking force . . . *for amphibious operations, such as raids on the enemy coastline*, or for the seizure and defence of bases for the use of our own fleet'.

This seemed to offer the Corps the chance to develop the role they had demonstrated so successfully at Zeebrugge, but there is no further indication of the need to develop amphibious forces, although the problems of assault landing had been outlined by a joint Army-Navy Committee as far back as 1913. The Committee's findings had been published in *A Handbook of Combined Operations*, which laid out the problems of amphibious warfare very clearly. But just analysing the problems is not enough, and nothing was done to tackle them, provide the necessary craft or train men in amphibious techniques.

Although the Corps' amphibious role was raised again by the Madden Committee in 1924, no funds were provided for equipment, training or landing craft, and when war broke out in 1939, Britain was woefully unprepared. The problems of Combined Operations – which in practice at the time meant large-scale seaborne landings with air and naval support – had been under review for about ten years. In 1930 an Inter-Service Training and Development Centre (I-STDC) was established at Fort Cumberland in Portsmouth, commanded by a Naval Captain, L. E. H. Maund, assisted by a small Inter-Service staff, an RAF Wing Commander, a Royal Artillery Major and a Captain of the Royal Marines, J. Picton-Phillips. This last officer was killed leading 40 Commando on the Dieppe Raid in 1942. The I-STDC had three prototype landing craft to experiment with in 1930. The best of these craft had a top speed of five knots and drew four feet of water. In the next ten years, the number of landing craft available expanded to six, none of which was of a noticeably better design. On the rare occasions when there were landing exercises, the Army went ashore as in the age of sail, rowed to the beaches in the launches and cutters of the Royal Navy.

Bernard Fergusson describes an exercise on Slapton Sands in 1938: 'It had been a stinker of a night and everybody was desperately seasick. They had to wait for the weather to moderate before disembarking, an Anglo-Scottish shambles, led by the Royal Scots to cries of "Whair's Jock?" "He's doun there." "No, he's no'." Once ashore, the troops ran up the beach as hard as they could pelt. This was put down by the umpires as praiseworthy élan and by the naval officers as a desire never to set foot in a ship again.'

Ten years of prodding from the I-STDC failed to convince the War Office that landing craft or amphibious training were at all necessary, and when war broke out on 3 September 1939 and the British Expeditionary Force departed for France, the I-STDC were given short shrift. Captain Maund sent a signal to his superiors requesting instructions, and their reply was stunning. With the BEF already established on the Continent, there could be no need for amphibious or Combined Operations. The I-STDC was therefore to be shut down forthwith, the officers and men returned to their units. Even the concept of Combined Operations was promptly abandoned. But nine months later came Dunkirk.

There is a certain dichotomy in British military thinking. On the one hand, no army in the world has produced so many innovative soldiers – General Wolfe, Sir John Moore of Light Infantry fame, Lord Wellington – or been so tolerant of eccentrics – Lawrence of Arabia, Orde Wingate of the Chindits, David Stirling of the SAS – to name but a few. No army has been so willing to experiment with new methods of warfare, for example the tank, paratroops, the SAS, the Long Range Desert Group. Even such obviously eccentric units as the marvellously named Popski's Private Army were created or permitted to function by the British Army. All this is most commendable. But on the other hand every innovative soldier writes bitterly of the sheer weight of inertia that lies so heavily on the military establishment. According to 'The Book', there is, there must be, a place for everything, with everything in its place. But there is no place for people with wild ideas who want to raise private armies and go about with knives between their teeth, killing sentries. Fortunately, nothing concentrates the military mind quite so much as defeat.

Between 1 September 1939 and the spring of 1940, Hitler's armies, masters of 'lightning war' – *blitzkrieg* – rapidly overran the parts of Europe which had not already been ceded to the Nazis during the years of appeasement. During the 'Phoney War', which occupied the winter of 1939–40, after the defeat of Poland, attention shifted to the northern flank, and in particular to Denmark and Norway. Protected by the Ribbentrop-Molotov Pact, Russia first shared in the dismemberment of Poland and then began the Winter War with Finland where, much to everyone's surprise, the much larger Russian forces at first met with defeat. Numbers finally told in the end and Finland capitulated on 13 March 1940. Less than four weeks later, on 9 April, the Germans invaded Denmark and Norway. Denmark was swiftly overrun but France and Britain were able to send forces into Norway, though by any standard the Norwegian campaign was a débâcle. The Royal Navy scored some successes against the German fleet and transport ships, but a shortage of air cover plus the combined effects of the bitter winter weather, German air superiority and the *blitzkrieg*, swiftly led to a collapse of the Allied effort; the British and French soon withdrew and Norway surrendered. The story of the Norwegian campaign lies outside the scope of this book but this disaster does have two bearings on our story. Firstly, as a result of this defeat, Neville Chamberlain was forced to resign and Winston Churchill became Prime Minister. Secondly, the Independent Companies, the forerunners of the Commandos, took the field for the first time.

Five Independent Companies were sent to the Norwegian campaign because the Royal Marines, who might otherwise have been rushed north, were busy manning the guns of the fleet or serving in coastal artillery. A Royal Marines Brigade was being formed, mainly from HO (Hostilities Only) recruits, but since this was still undermanned and quite untrained the decision was taken to raise a number of small units – to be called Independent Companies – from the various divisions of the Territorial Army. With the bulk of the regular army in France with the BEF, the Territorials provided the Home Army Commands, and they proved a fruitful source of volunteers. Each brigade was directed to furnish a platoon for an Independent Company, with every battalion of that brigade providing a section. Each section was led by a lieutenant or subaltern, and the company was commanded by a major. Ten Independent Companies were formed and among their numbers were some famous future Commandos, like Major Charles Newman, later to win the VC as CO of 2 Commando at St Nazaire; Major Thomas Trevor, later of No. 1 Commando; Major Ronnie Tod, who was to lead No. 9 Commando in Italy, and many more we shall hear from in this book.

Ken McAllister was one of the original Independent Company volunteers. 'I had joined the Territorials, the Liverpool Scottish (Cameron Highlanders), in 1937. This was my father's old regiment with which he went to France in 1914. We were called up when war broke out on 3 September and moved to Woodbridge, Suffolk, in

April 1940. One Sunday church parade, the sergeant-major spoke to me, asking some very odd questions . . . "Was I in a fighting mood? . . ." and so on. Then he took about nine or ten of us aside and a captain came along to see us while the rest of the company went to church. The captain then told us we had been picked for a special unit because we appeared to be the type they wanted. "Men who would not be squeamish at seeing their mate's head blown off." Don't ask me how they could tell we wouldn't be, or indeed how anybody wouldn't be, but we all volunteered and became part of No. 4 Independent Company, the nucleus of the original Commandos. It was a small unit, with no transport. We did a bit of training at Sizewell in Suffolk, before being sent to Gourock in Scotland for embarkation, destination unknown, but which turned out to be Norway.

'This expedition proved to be nothing, and not much happened for five weeks, which was a good thing as we were more like boy scouts than soldiers. In the end we did a Dunkirk; after a forced march to Bodo, the navy took us off and back to Aberdeen. Later we were formed into a larger unit of No. 4 and No. 5 Independent Companies, which consisted of Londoners and was called No. 1 Special Service Battalion. This was soon found to be large and too unwieldy, so we were then made smaller.' Ken McAllister went eventually to No. 2 Commando.

Each Independent Company had a strength of twenty-one officers and 268 men, and the first five Independent Companies were soon in Norway, where they did sterling service, notably in the heavy fighting around Narvik. The Anglo-French forces withdrew from Norway on 8 June, and the country fell to the Nazis, but in that short campaign the British Army lost some 2,000 men.

Charles Hustwick joined 9 Independent Company from his Territorial unit, the 53 (Welsh) Division, which he joined on 2 September 1939, later being transferred to the 38th Division Signals. 'It was a Fred Karno's Army . . .

1914 signalling equipment and no wirelesses. We did have rifles, although I didn't get to fire one until April 1940. One morning, a Lieutenant Clube, ex-Artists Rifles, called for volunteers who wanted to see some action, and I was the first to step forward. Lieutenant Clube became a firm friend and later lost a leg in North Africa. We were kitted out in battledress (until then our dress had been 1914 breeches, puttees and *spurs* – no horses) and sent to St Mellons in Herefordshire. Here we met the rest, all volunteers from 38 Division, issued with two blankets and slept eight to a bell-tent. There were infantry, REs, RAMC, Ordnance, Signals, all mixed up and banded together into No. 9 Independent Company, a complete, self-supporting unit about 240 strong. We also got radio sets but they had been manufactured for the Rumanian Government and all the instructions were in Rumanian, so needless to say it took us some time to get them going. These sets had to be carried, plus our other equipment, rifle, 200 rounds of ammunition, water bottle, gas mask, entrenching tool, and any other odds and ends. When fully loaded we couldn't stand upright. Our OC, Major Siddons, DCM, had fought at Mons in 1914. He had a sabre wound on his forehead and carried an African knobkerry as his personal weapon. We became very fit indeed before embarking on the *Royal Scotsman* at Gourock. This had been a cattle boat, so we had to sweep out the cattle stalls before we could bed down. We were then told our destination – Norway. Our task – to carry out behind-the-lines warfare and interfere with the enemy lines of communication, but this was not to be. The campaign in Norway collapsed and we returned up the Clyde to Glasgow, where we were greeted like heroes. This was now about the time of Dunkirk and certain members of Nos. 6, 7, 8 and 9 Independent Companies were sent to Southampton to form No. 11 Independent Company under Major Ronnie Tod. We paraded at Southampton Football Ground, the Dell, carried out a couple of

13

raids as No. 11, and then in August No. 11 Independent Company ceased to be. We were returned to our various units and I went back to No. 9 Independent Company, then in the Scillies. There we were relieved and sent to coastal defence at Mounts Bay, and on to yet another football ground, Home Park, home of Plymouth Argyle. Then we heard that No. 9 Independent Company was to be disbanded and we could either return to our parent units or revolunteer for Special Service. The volunteers from No. 9 joined those from 2 Independent Company, who had been fighting in Norway, and became No. 1 Special Service Battalion, and with members of other Companies, mustered about 800 all ranks under Lieutenant Colonel Bill Glendinning (Welsh Regiment). Major Tom Trevor was the second-in-command. The CO was a gentleman in every respect and loved by all who served under him. Being too large, in about October 1940, No. 1 SS Battalion broke up to form No. 1 and No. 2 Commandos. I went to join the SS Brigade Signals, under Captain Clube.' Charles Hustwick has supplied copious notes on his very varied career with the Commandos and we shall meet him again.

By 24 May 1940 the German Army had pushed the British Expeditionary Force, totalling some 400,000 men, back to the Channel coast, reducing their territory to a pocket around Dunkirk, and with collapse imminent, they had to be evacuated. Eleven days later, no less than 338,000 soldiers, most of them British, had been lifted across the Channel. The country was ecstatic, but as Winston Churchill remarked at the time, 'Wars are not won by evacuations.' Even so, the rescue of the British Army from Dunkirk seemed a miracle at the time, and the bulk of the country rightly rejoiced.

Geoff Riley, later of 5 Commando, remembers leaving France. 'I was evacuated on the last boat out of St Nazaire, 19/20 June. My most vivid memory of that time is of a French boy, about fourteen years of age, who was sobbing bitterly as we marched out. He clung to me, begging me to take him with us, which I couldn't, of course, but I promised him silently that I would be back with the British Army as soon as I could.'

Suddenly the situation in Britain became serious. Just a month before, in mid-May 1940, British soldiers had been fighting on two fronts in Continental Europe, in Norway and in France. Three weeks later, the Army had been abruptly bundled off the Continent and were back on their island, leaving many good men and much valuable equipment behind. If the Germans quickly followed, a disaster seemed inevitable. Even so, there was a sense of euphoria in the air, a sense that the years of indecision were over. The country was on its own, without allies underfoot, and luckily the country had a new leader in Winston Churchill, a man who spoke the truth plainly and declared the common intention to fight on, whatever the cost. After all, the Army was back and retraining, the Home Guard – Dad's Army – was out there drilling in the parks and streets each evening and at weekends; even the children went out to gather shrapnel from the streets and gardens in the aftermath of the ever-more-frequent raids. Park and garden railings and saucepans were being collected and turned into tanks and aeroplanes. This at last was war.

Coming to the House of Commons, Churchill stated the obvious; that the Battle of France was over and the Battle of Britain was about to begin. This could not be a defensive battle; the country must display aggression and fight back. An army that has been soundly defeated will not be left alone for long to lick its wounds and gather strength; no enemy is that forgiving. Hitler's armies had passed on to capture Paris, and France had surrendered. Unless he was checked, an invasion must surely follow. For a while in 1940 the security of Britain depended on less than 1,500 young men, the trained fighter pilots of the Royal Air Force, the men of the hour, the Famous

15

Few. Crowds stood in the London streets, day after day, craning their necks to see the Royal Air Force fighters dive into the massive German bomber formations. By their sides, in those same streets, stood men who wore the uniforms of other nations, nations which had already fallen to the Nazis, providing a living daily reminder of what could happen in Britain if the German Army should ever cross the Channel.

Britain was almost alone. America would not enter the war for another year and a half, the British Empire had still to muster, and France had fallen. On the morning of 25 June 1940, the French Government was led into that same railway car at Compiègne, where the German Commanders had been made to sign the Armistice documents in 1918. Here, in their turn, the French were forced to sign the instruments of surrender, a sad moment for a proud nation. French spirits might have been a little lighter had the ministers known that just twelve hours before, a small British Commando force had landed on the shores of Occupied France.

2

Haste to the Battle,
1940–41

'Now thrive the armourers'
HENRY V: ACT I

Operation Dynamo, the evacuation to Britain of the BEF
– and a large number of French soldiers – was officially
terminated at 14.23 hrs on the afternoon of 4 June 1940.
The first step towards creating the Commandos occurred
about five hours later. On the evening of 4 June, Lieutenant Colonel Dudley Clarke, Military Assistant to General
Sir John Dill, Chief of the Imperial General Staff, was
walking home from the War Office, brooding on the
problems which currently beset the nation and, not least,
on the necessity of finding some means to strike back at
the German forces now gathering on the Channel coast.
Lieutenant Colonel Clarke had read all the books on
irregular warfare in the twentieth century, from Reitz's
Commando to Lawrence's *Seven Pillars of Wisdom* and
to these he could add his own experiences as a staff officer
serving in Palestine under the League of Nations Man-
date. There, while the British were attempting to keep
the peace between Arabs and Jews, he had seen what a
handful of fanatics could do to nullify the strength of a
full Army Corps. Might not what had been done in
Palestine be attempted now, here, on the western shores
of Europe, where a thousand miles of coast lay open to
the Royal Navy and her amphibious forces?
The snag was, of course, that there *were* no amphibious

forces. The Royal Marines who, by tradition, should have filled that role, were now hastily manning coastal defence batteries, serving the main armament on HM ships or mustering in the Royal Marines Division. 'I joined up at Deal in 1940,' records Nobby Pendrigh, later of 43 (Royal Marine) Commando. 'We were down there for four months square-bashing and a two-week weapon course. The story was that when our training was over, we would challenge the Wehrmacht to a drill contest – and win, of course.'

The story of the Royal Marine Commandos has been written in another book in this series (*By Sea and Land*), so it only remains to explain why the Corps of Royal Marines did not raise the first Commando units. The explanation is quite simple. They were not asked.

That evening, still pondering on the necessity to hit back, however feebly, at the German forces, Dudley Clarke mustered his ideas onto a single sheet of writing paper. On the following day he passed the paper through to his chief, the CIGS. The outline proposal harked back to those Boer Commando operations in South Africa forty years before. Even now, in the Europe of 1940, was it not possible that something similar might be attempted. Lightly equipped teams of men, carried across the Channel in the small ships of the Royal Navy, could still harass the enemy and give evidence of an unquenched will to fight, while demonstrating to the public at home that all was not yet lost. The risk was small, and the gains might be incalculable. Winston Churchill, on whose desk Dudley Clarke's memorandum presently arrived, could judge the worth of the suggested enterprise from his own experience. On 6 June General Dill called Dudley Clarke into his office and told him that his scheme was approved. He was to form 'Commando units' and mount a cross-Channel operation at the earliest possible moment.

The intention was to form ten Commando units, each of approximately ten troops or platoons, with a total strength of 500 men, a formation based on experience with the Independent Companies, which were to provide a basis for many early Commando units and a considerable number of their first recruits. A circular letter was sent to the Commanding Officers in all the battalions of Home Command, calling for volunteers for special service. Applicants must be trained soldiers of good physique, physically fit, able to swim and immune from air or seasickness. Personal qualities must include courage, endurance, initiative, activity, marksmanship, self-reliance and an aggressive spirit towards the conduct of the war. Volunteers must be prepared 'for longer hours, more work and less rest than other recruits to HM Forces', and 'will be trained in the military uses of scouting, able to live off the country, move unseen by night and day, being able to stalk the enemy and report on his activity.' Officers would interview prospective candidates and be satisfied that they first had the necessary moral and physical attributes for good Commando soldiers. The final strength of these volunteer Commando units was fixed at 462 men. This gave a Commando about half the establishment of a regular infantry battalion, organized in ten troops of approximately fifty men.

This call for volunteers was Winston Churchill's offer to the nation of 'blood, toil, tears and sweat' spelt out in practical terms. The response from all ranks of the Army was instantaneous and overwhelming; every soldier worth his salt rushed to volunteer. Among the first was Captain J. F. Durnford Slater, then Adjutant of the 23rd Medium and Heavy Training Regiment, Royal Artillery, stationed at Plymouth, who took the memorandum upstairs to his Commanding Officer. 'This is exactly what I want to do,' said Durnford Slater. 'Will you release me?' Durnford Slater's Colonel took a little convincing but he eventually agreed and directed Durnford Slater to write the necessary letter himself which the Colonel would then sign. It must have been an impressive missive because ten days later the reply arrived on the Colonel's desk.

> Captain J. F. Durnford Slater, RA, is appointed to raise and command No. 3 Commando in the rank of Lieutenant Colonel. Give every assistance and early release as operational role is imminent.

Since at that time Nos. 1 and 2 Commandos had yet to form, John Durnford Slater, an artillery officer, became the first Commando soldier of the war. We will meet Durnford Slater and No. 3 Commando later.

The practical result of the War Office circular was to raise ten Commando Units, drawn from the various Home Commands. Nos. 1 and 2 were raised from the Independent Companies, No. 3 from Southern Command, No. 4 from Yeomanry and Cavalry Units, Nos. 5 and 6 in the West Country, No. 7 in East Anglia, No. 8 from London District (the story goes that the officers of No. 8 Commando were recruited from the Household Division at the bar of Whites), No. 9 and No. 11 (Scottish) Commando from Scots or Highland Regiments. Major Callf recalls that No. 9 was a mixture of Scots and English troops, and when the troops were formed the officers were careful to pick first an Englishman and then a Scot, to thoroughly mix the unit. Even so, No. 9 always retained a Scots flavour, with a piper for every troop, and a black hackle on every green beret. No. 10, which it was hoped the Northern Command would raise, never found sufficient volunteers, but a year or so later, No. 10 gained life as No. 10 (Inter-Allied) Commando, with troops formed of French, Dutch, Belgian, Norwegian, Polish and Yugoslav soldiers, even from German nationals. 10 (IA) Commando never served as a unit, the troops being attached to various operational units according to their linguistic abilities.

The Army Commandos were raised entirely from volunteers, every unit selecting its own men from those who came forward. The COs selected the troop officers and the officers in turn travelled about the Commands selecting their men.

Peter Young joined 3 Commando rather as Durnford Slater was appointed to command it; by recommending himself. His unit, the 2nd Battalion, The Bedfordshire & Hertfordshire Regiment, was at Yeovil when Young was summoned for an interview, meeting 'a captain with a high-pitched voice who bore a superficial resemblance to Mr Pickwick'. This, he eventually realized, was his future CO, Durnford Slater. Other officers joining No. 3 at this time included Joe Smale of the Lancashire Fusiliers and an old crony of Durnford Slater, Lieutenant Charles Head, a Cornishman. These officers, like those from the other Commando units, were then dispatched to raise their troops. This was not an easy task, for many battalion commanders were naturally reluctant to lose their best men; not all the volunteers were entirely suitable, and the recruiting officers had different ideas on exactly what background best indicated a potential Commando soldier.

Major Milton was serving with his regiment when the call came. 'I was one of the last of the so-called gentlemen-cadets to pass through the RMA Sandhurst, and I had a regular commission. In June 1940 I was stationed in Hounslow at the depot of my regiment, the Royal Fusiliers. It was intensely boring. All we did was walk about watching the recruits receive basic training from the NCOs. Soon after Dunkirk, a notice appeared calling for volunteers for either an experimental parachute unit, or a seaborne raiding force. This seemed to me a sultan's dream, a wonderful idea. So I immediately volunteered, and the day I volunteered, I walked back to the mess for lunch and went into the ante-room, which was occupied by one other person, Dudley Lister, who was adviser on physical training to Eastern Command. He told me that he had just been appointed to command one of the new Commandos, and I said, "Well, I have just volunteered."

He said, "Well, in that case, you can be my first officer," and so I joined C Troop, No. 7 Commando, at Billericay in Essex.

'Quite soon we were sent out to interview hundreds of men in the Eastern Command who had volunteered. With another officer, I went around the units in my Singer 9, but I don't think either of us had any idea how to pick men for an enterprise of this sort. We knew that toughness would be essential, but I think that the idea of rigid, strong discipline, which is needed to fight in a co-ordinated manner, escaped us. We chose the men who stood out for having done something odd in civilian life, like one who had gone round the Horn in a Finnish sailing ship, and another who had fought in Spain in the International Brigade, and another who had been in a razorgang in Glasgow (that one) I regretted. One of our officers had served in the Gran Chaco War in Paraguay, a very strong character. When No. 7 was finally formed it contained officers and men from no less than fifty-eight separate corps and regiments of the British Army.'

Among the officers of No. 11 Commando was the fighting Ulsterman, Blair (Paddy) Mayne, who went on to win four DSOs while serving with the SAS. Gerald Bryan remembers him well. 'Blair was a natural soldier, a born fighting man. He never really settled down in the peace. When sober, a gentler, more mild-mannered man you could not wish to meet, but when drunk or in battle, he was frightening. I'm not saying he was a drunk, but he could drink a bottle of whisky in an evening before he got a glow on. He had great physical strength, and had been both a boxer and a rugby international. He was 6ft 4in tall. One night, when he had been on the bottle, he literally picked me up with one hand, clear of the ground, by the lapels of my uniform, and punched me with the other hand, sending me flying. Next day he didn't remember a thing about it. "Just tell me who did that to you,

Gerald," he said. I told him I'd walked into a door. He was a very brave man and I liked him very much.'

Peter Young has some very decided ideas about Commando soldiers. 'In the Bedfords, before the war, we had perhaps half a dozen officers who would have been accepted as officers in the heyday of the Commandos. We also had a lot who were either useless or who didn't want to be at war . . . Supplementary Reserve Officers, who had been teachers or something, and quite happy in civilian life. They didn't want to go around cutting throats. The Officer Corps in the Commandos was quite different. We only had maniacs in the Commandos really – if they weren't that way . . . well, no, I don't really mean that, but some of them were fiends, who just loved to fight. I can name half-a-dozen . . . Algy Forrester, Denis O'Flaherty . . . they were thirsty for it. It's a wonderful attitude and, of course, the soldiers will follow officers like that. The Bedfords were a very steady regiment. "Steady the Bedfords," we used to say. When the war started we had maybe 200 men in the battalion. "A" Company, which I was in, had two officers and nineteen men. It follows that we were made up with reservists, and your reservists would as soon hear the Devil as a drum. They were happy in civvy street, at home with their nice plump wives. They had settled down to their dull civilian lives, and believe me it is dull. In the Commandos I had the company of people who hated peacetime. Jack Churchill couldn't bear bloody peacetime. So, what makes for a good Commando soldier? Well, a restless nature . . . no, all sorts . . . you got all sorts. You had to know the different troops and play on them like a violin . . . their different ways, how to tweak them into action. It's an art, great fun. We had wonderful people. I was cut off in Italy for a week with only four soldiers, and they looked after me so bloody well, you know? You look after them, with a good plan and all, and they will look after you, relieve you of all fear of ambush or surprise. They'd get their shot in first. It also helps to be lucky. I am notoriously lucky and I didn't get a lot of soldiers damaged, and the sods like that . . . they stick with you. A Commando is like a club – you must keep up the membership, you mustn't squander soldiers, not at all must you do that. Breed them up into suspicious alertness, never relaxed, always on their toes. Otherwise you are no bloody use to me, as officer or man, or sergeant major . . . and I'll break your back if that's your attitude. I looked for a man who could soldier – absolutely. To pick them? You look at them, don't you? You talk to them a bit, make up your mind if he's a bullshitter or has something to contribute . . . you can tell. I was very seldom wrong. I admit to being wrong sometimes. Young soldiers are good. They have no wives or children. They follow you out of innocence – you know that. And a good old soldier is a good soldier. A bad old soldier is worse than useless.'

Durnford Slater toured the garrison towns of Southern Command to recruit his officers and gave them four days to select their men and get them to Plymouth. He preferred 'men who didn't talk too much, the quiet type of Englishman, who knew how to laugh and how to work'. According to Peter Young, 'The majority of the men (in No. 3 Commando) were reservists, many of them having served seven years with the Colours, mostly in India. Their average age was about twenty-six. They knew their weapons, had seen some fighting and wanted more of it.'

Stan Weatherall joined 6 Commando at Scarborough in mid-1940. 'I was a member of No. 1 Troop. The whole Commando was placed in civilian billets, with civvy ration cards and paid 6s. 8d. (33p) a day billeting allowance. The landladies in Scarborough were paid £1 10s. (£1.50) a week, so the lads benefited by 16s. 8d. (83p) a week, which was not to be sneezed at when a pint of beer was 6d. (2½p) and the better brands of fags 6d. for twenty. The first get-together of 1 Troop was a talk by the Troop

Commander, who said, "You will be made to suffer all manner of discomforts. Those who cannot make the grade will be RTU'd (Returned to Units) and as you are all volunteers, you can all return to your units at any time at your own request." Our training consisted of forced marches across country and field exercises on the Yorkshire Moors. Every man of the troop was certainly put to the test at Scarborough.'

Living in civvy billets was considered a great privilege, but there were occasional snags, as Geoff Riley remembers. 'Every serving man knows the cardinal rules regarding weapons and the loading of same when not in use; they must be *empty*. Being a Mountaineering Troop (No. 1) of No. 5 Commando, we were practising cliff-climbing with a bunch of us kipping up in a local guest house at Salcombe in Devon. Our Commando rules were not as restrictive in our use of weapons as we were expected to have more sense than the average soldier. One Sunday morning, a couple of us were going out to do a little practice with a Colt 45. It started to snow, so my comrade, Jock Hardy, handed me the gun and said he wasn't going. I took the pistol, and in just idling absent-mindedly cocked the gun, and as I pulled the trigger, the shout went up, "It's loaded!" Too late. With a crash the bullet hit the floor. With "Oh my God!" they all scattered, leaving me alone in the room. At that moment, a trembling landlady appeared. She had been in the kitchen below and about to make a cake. She climbed onto a chair and reached onto the shelf for the cake tin at the same time as my slug crashed in with the speed of a space rocket, knocking the tin out of her hand, then ricocheting round and round the kitchen until it smashed into the chair and left her sprawling on the floor, leaving a hole in the ceiling as big as a barrel. The chaps left the talking to me! I gently soothed her, promised all weapons would be stashed, unloaded, in the corner of the outside wash-house, which seemed to satisfy the lady. We then arrived back one night to be confronted with a hysterical lady on the verge of a complete breakdown. One of the chaps had left a cluster of hand grenades on the washer, preventing her from doing her washing. We definitely had to leave after that!'

John Wall also remembers a civvy billet incident. 'In early 1942, my troop was located in civilian billets in and around Dittisham, Devon. Next door to my billet was a farm labourer and his wife, who were billeting three Gunners. These chaps were notorious for their sleeping prowess and they held the landlady responsible if they were late on parade! However, that lady was no country simpleton, for she simply put one of her husband's ferrets in each of their beds. We could hear the screams next door!'

Volunteers of all ages came forward, as Cecil Blanch remembers. 'One character I particularly remember is Sergeant Jock Bellamy of 12 Commando. His real name was McKenzie and he took the name Bellamy from a book he read while in prison for smuggling whisky. How he ever got into the Commando was a mystery, for he was much older than the rest of us and had served in the First World War. I think he had the DCM and the Croix de Guerre. Jock was as tough as his native granite, but he had a heart of gold and a great sense of humour. When Lord Louis Mountbatten became Chief of Combined Operations, he visited 12 Commando, and during the inspection he stopped in front of Jock and said, "Another old-timer like myself, I see. How old are you, sergeant?" Jock replied, "Thirty-five, Sir." "Come on," said Lord Louis quietly, "I won't give you away." Whereupon Jock said, "Ach, well, I'll take a chance . . . thirty-five-and-a-half, Sir."'

Sidney Dann of 6 Commando also went to a great deal of trouble to join the Commandos. 'I requested an infantry regiment when my call-up came on New Year's Day 1940, and went for initial training to the Essex Regiment. Lots of tradesmen were lost in France before Dunkirk and the infantry units were scoured for tradesmen, and as I had been a butcher, I went to the RASC, then to the REME (of course), and then finally into the Catering Corps. From the beginning of my service I volunteered for everything that would get me out of cooking and into the infantry. At that time, COs could veto any application for transfer, and although I finally got before a Commando selection board, I had a lot of trouble convincing the officer that a cook could make a good Commando. I was accepted and returned to my unit to await my posting, where I was at once reduced to the ranks from full corporal by my angry CO, who did not want to lose me because I was a good scrounger and kept the officers' mess supplied with eggs and chickens from the local farms.' Sidney Dann finally got to the Commando Basic Training Centre at Achnacarry in January 1942, where his serious infantry training began.

From the formation of the Commandos in mid-1940 until the Basic Training Centre was opened, most of the initial Commando training was carried out at unit level. Alf Barker joined 5 Commando in 1940. 'The first highlight was blanco-ing my webbing three different colours in as many days. This was considered essential to wipe out stories which had appeared in the newspapers about the new "killer force". I then went to No. 12 Commando and when they were broken up later in the war, to No. 6. Apart from unit training, much of the early training was at Lochailort, and at other places like Dorlin House, which have never received full credit for all they did. Achnacarry gained all the kudos. As Heavy Weapons people, I remember the training we did at Braemar under Colonel John Hunt, later Sir John Hunt of Everest fame. In addition to ordinary training we did a lot of work with mules, packing the mortars and machine guns.' The advantage of this unit training was that it gave scope for individual initiative. Ideas could be tested at unit level

27

and if they worked they were adopted and passed around. The disadvantage was that there were considerable variations in unit standards which eventually led to the opening, in 1942, of the Basic Training Centre, based at the home of the Cameron of Lochiel, Chief of Clan Cameron at Achnacarry House near Spean Bridge in the Western Highlands. Commandos had trained in Scotland from the early days, most notably on Arran and Lochailort.

Fred Musson joined 2 Troop of No. 5 Commando at Bridlington, Yorkshire, in July 1940. 'In the early days, most of our training was done in Scotland, in the Loch Fyne and Lochailort areas. It was in Scotland that No. 5 Commando was issued with the Balmoral bonnet as the standard head-dress (until then we had all worn the one of our parent regiment), and on it we wore our own regimental cap-badges, over a green backing, with a gold-coloured hackle. For an arm-badge we had crossed fighting knives with No. 5.

'There was a lot of weapon training, night work and troop attacks. Every day we did speed marches, carrying platoon weapons, rifles, Brens, ammunition, the lot, covering five miles in fifty minutes. After weeks of training we were fit enough to do our five miles and still be fit to fight.'

John Murphy of No. 2 Commando was another early recruit. 'I joined No. 3 Independent Company in March/April 1940 and went to Norway. On our return to the UK in June 1940 we were stationed at Lochailort. We underwent some pretty hair-raising and tough training in and around Lochailort. I remember marching from Fort William to Lochailort on an unmade road and it was no joke, despite the fact we were all reasonably fit. I also remember being in the tender care of Captain Sykes and Fairbairn (ex-police officers from the Far East) for unarmed combat. Eventually, No. 3 Independent Company became part of No. 2 Commando and I was on its strength, but from

approximately August/September 1940 until about May/
June 1941, I was an NCO instructor at the Special
Training Centre, Inverlochy Castle, near Fort William,
training Polish officers.'

Cecil Blanch joined E Troop of 12 Commando in 1940.
'Our Troop Commander was Major Robert Henriques,
and our section officers were Second Lieutenants Purdon
and Brett, who were taken prisoner during the raid on St
Nazaire, and Christopher Burney, who left us early on
and joined SOE. He was captured in France in 1942, spent
eighteen months solitary in the Gestapo prison at Fresnes,
and ended up in Buchenwald concentration camp, though
he survived the war and became a banker in the City.

'Life in 12 Commando was poles apart from normal
army units. For a start, we were in our own billets – it
was like living at home. Secondly, there was no pettifog-
ging discipline. It was made plain from the start that self-
discipline was the order of the day. One was expected to
be perfectly turned out and to keep one's weapons in
perfect order, and it worked. We were not the thugs some
made us out to be and the biggest disgrace that could
befall a Commando soldier was to be RTU'd.

'Training was designed to achieve peak physical fitness,
self-reliance and skill at arms. Weapons were the ·303
Lee-Enfield rifle, the Bren light machine gun, the ·45
Thompson sub-machine gun – issued centrally as
required – and later on the Sten. Coshes, knuckle-dusters
and the fighting knife made by Wilkinson were also
issued. Route marches of up to thirty miles were regular
events, and there was plenty of night work. Physical
fitness certainly reached a very high level. In the winter
of 1940–41 B Troop of No. 12 Commando marched from
Crumlin to Londonderry, carrying full equipment, and
covered the distance of sixty-three miles in nineteen
hours.'

Cecil Blanch recalls other less successful exercises.
'One night the Section I was in was crossing a field which,

unknown to us, contained a bull. The first we knew of it was the drumming of hooves as it charged at us. The ten of us ran like hell and managed to get over or through a blackthorn hedge before it caught up with us. Talk about the pride of the army! In November 1941, when 12 Commando were at Ayr, we effected a dawn crossing of the River Doon (actually it was not very deep, about waist-deep and we could wade over) before carrying out an attack on a position in the Carrick Hills. We remained out that night, night patrolling, before marching back to Ayr in the late afternoon of the following day. It was bitterly cold and we were soaking wet, but I do not recall any of us suffering ill effects. Basically our training was similar to that of an infantry unit, but more prolonged and intense. On a march you did not fall out unless you passed out, and at the end of a march or an exercise you were not dismissed but sent over the assault course or for a spot of drill or weapon training. It was all designed to teach you that you *could* keep going and fight at the end of an arduous day, so it toughened you mentally as well.'

Geoff Riley of No. 5 Commando did some of his Commando training at Falmouth. 'During practice on the firing range, situated on the clifftop on Bodmin Moor, we were practising grenade throwing. A grenade is primed with either a four-second or a seven-second detonator, the seven-second for the distance throw, and the four-second for close, street fighting. On this particular day, we were practising throwing some forty yards onto a marker post, with the aim of making it explode on contact. To do this meant pulling the pin, letting the plunger strike home and, holding it, count up to four and throw. This was to eliminate the situation where an enemy could pick it up and throw it back at you. I was actually very good at this, dropping them onto the stick in one go, and we had been at it all day. About 16.30 hrs I took up my usual stance. "Right, off you go, Riley," said Captain Tom Addington. I took the pin out, let the plunger click, and after counting

four seconds, dropped it. Pandemonium! "Take cover
everybody!" Captain Addington yelled, at the same time
flinging me to the ground and covering me with his body.
The grenade exploded with a crash, covering us all with
dirt and rock. Nobody was hurt and the drama was over.
But was it? Suddenly Captain Addington bellowed,
"Where's Geoffrey?" My Troop OC, Geoff Rees-Jones,
was nowhere to be seen. Then we heard a faint cry coming
from over the cliff. He had actually flung himself over the
cliff, his fall broken by a bush some fifty feet down. All
we could see was his moustache. It brought a little light
relief, and Captain Tom said, "Right, I think we'll call it
a day. We're all getting tired now." No recriminations,
and I feel he saved me from serious wounds. In civvy
street he would probably have received a medal. But it
was taken as part of the job in wartime.'

Lieutenant Colonel Newman of 2 Commando set out
his requirements in a Unit Order, soon after his Commando was formed.

No. 2 Commando

SERVICE IN A COMMANDO By Lt.-Col. Newman

1. The object of Special Service is to have available
   a fully trained body of first class soldiers, ready
   for active offensive operations against an enemy
   in any part of the world.
2. Irregular warfare demands the highest standards
   of initiative, mental alertness and physical
   fitness, together with the maximum skill at
   arms. No Commando can feel confident of
   success unless all ranks are capable of thinking
   for themselves; of thinking quickly and of acting
   independently, and with sound tactical sense,
   when faced by circumstances which may be

entirely different to those which were
anticipated.
3. *Mentally*. The offensive spirit must be the
outlook of all ranks of a Commando at all times.
4. *Physically*. The highest state of physical fitness
must at all times be maintained. All ranks are
trained to cover at great speed any type of
ground for distances of five to seven miles in
fighting order.

Examples:

    (a) Fighting Order
          (seven miles in one hour [march & run]).
    (b) FSMO (Full Service Marching Order)
                          (15 miles in 4¼ hrs)
      5 miles in one hour (marching)
                          (25 miles in 8 hrs)
      9 miles in two hours (marching)
                          (35 miles in 14 hrs)

After all these distances and times, troops must
be ready, in para (a) to fight, and in para (b) to
fight after two hours' rest.
5. Cliff and mountain climbing and really difficult
slopes climbed quickly form a part of
Commando training.
6. A high degree of skill in all branches of unarmed
combat will be attained.
7. *Seamanship and Boatwork*. All ranks must be
skilled in all forms of boatwork and landing craft
whether by day or by night, as a result of which
training the sea comes to be regarded as a
natural working ground for a Commando.
8. Night sense and night confidence are essential.
All ranks will be highly trained in the use of the
compass.
9. Map reading and route memorizing form an
important part of Commando training.

10. All ranks of a Commando will be trained in semaphore, Morse and the use of W/T.

11. All ranks will have elementary knowledge of demolitions and sabotage. All ranks will be confident in the handling of all types of high explosives, Bangalore torpedoes, and be able to set up all types of booby traps.

12. A high standard of training will be maintained in all forms of street fighting, occupation of towns, putting towns into a state of defence and the overcoming of all types of obstacles, wire, rivers, high walls, etc.

13. All ranks in a Commando should be able to drive motorcycles, cars, lorries, tracked vehicles, trains and motor boats.

14. A high degree of efficiency in all forms of fieldcraft will be attained. Any man in a Commando must be able to forage for himself, cook and live under a bivouac for a considerable period.

15. All ranks are trained in first aid and will be capable of dealing with the dressing of gun-shot wounds and the carrying of the wounded.

16. These are few among the many standards of training that must be attained during service in a Commando. At all times a high standard of discipline is essential, and the constant desire by all ranks to be fitter and better trained than anyone else.

17. The normal mode of living is that the Special Service Soldier will live in a billet found by himself and fed by the billet for which he will receive 6s. 8d. per day to pay all his expenses.

18. Any falling short of the standards of training and behaviour on the part of a Special Service

Soldier will render him liable to be returned to his unit.

RSM Bryen of No. 6 Commando remembers the type of men he had in his unit. 'It was noticeable that various Commandos had a preponderance of certain nationalities. No. 1, for example, had many Welshmen, while my own unit, No. 6, had more than its share of Scotsmen. My own section nearly all came from Scotland or Tyneside, and I must confess that I would as soon live and fight with a Scotsman than any other nationality. Their happy atmosphere and shrewd sense of judgement endeared them to me, but I think it would be wrong to suggest that any one nationality made an ideal Commando. The quick-wittedness of a Cockney, the pluck of an Irishman, shrewdness of a Scotsman, tenacity of a Welshman and good nature of a Geordie would, I think, combine to make the perfect Commando.'

Lieutenant Colonel Allen, MC, recalls his men in 9 Commando: 'Like any other body of men, 9 Commando comprised a mixed bunch of all shapes and sizes, with a fair share of villains, eccentrics, and the occasional failure. Some of the men I particularly remember are my batman, Private Ellis, who announced to me on the start line before an engagement at Anzio, that he had had enough mollycoddling me and wanted to do some proper soldiering in a fighting troop. After the battle he withdrew his resignation on the grounds that despite being a batman, he had experienced quite enough fighting during the preceding twenty-four hours to satisfy him until the end of the war. Then there was the Post Corporal, "Gobi" Priest, who claimed to have marched back alone across the Gobi desert, the sole survivor of a British garrison massacred by the local infidels. "Gobi" turned up with the mail just as we were about to embark in our assault craft at Comacchio and I invited him to join me in the last boat. He accepted the offer, but never again trusted the depth of my regard for his personal safety. Among the officers, there was Mike Long (Major M. C. Long, MC, MBE) whose relaxed approach to battle was matched by his quaint preoccupation with the safety of his bagpipes and the construction of a wooden model of our favourite assault ship, HMS *Queen Emma*. I doubt if this model has yet been completed. Another long-time friend is Mike Davies (Captain M. Davies, MC, MBE) of the Coldstream Guards, a martinet with a soul. Inevitably, he was not the best-loved man in 9 Commando, but I know full well that he was respected by all ranks for his soldierly qualities. I know without doubt that every one of us recognized his valuable contribution to the survival of those of us who returned from the Wadi battle at Anzio, when he took up the rear Bren gun during the final engagement.'

While all this was going on, the Commando command structure was being set in place. On 12 June Churchill appointed Lieutenant General Sir Alan Bourne, Adjutant-General of the Royal Marines, to the post of Head of Combined Operations, or Offensive Operations as it was then called, but he held this post for only a month, until 17 July 1940, when he was replaced as Director of Combined Operations by Admiral of the Fleet Sir Roger Keyes of Zeebrugge fame, who asked General Bourne to stay on as his deputy. By then the fledgling Commandos had already tasted action.

An official British communiqué of 26 June 1940 states: 'In co-operation with the Royal Air Force, naval and military raiders carried out a reconnaissance of the enemy coast. Landings were effected, contact made with German troops and casualties inflicted before our troops withdrew without loss.'

This operation was carried out by 115 officers and men of No. 11 Independent Company under Major R. J. F. Tod. Among the party to land was Lieutenant Colonel Dudley Clarke, who had thought up the Commando idea just three weeks previously. Parties landed at four points on the French coast, between Boulogne and Berck Plage. One party advanced inland for a quarter of a mile, found nobody and withdrew. Another found itself in a seaplane anchorage and was about to attack a seaplane when, somewhat to their consternation, it took off. The third party, landing at Mirlimont Plage near Le Touquet, surprised and killed two German sentries. The last party, which included Major Tod and Lieutenant Colonel Clarke, got ashore without trouble but was surprised by the enemy during the withdrawal, and in an exchange of fire a bullet struck Lieutenant Colonel Clarke behind the ear, injuring him slightly. Three weeks later, it was the turn of No. 3 Commando.

John Durnford Slater's appointment to No. 3 Commando came through on 28 June. No. 3 Commando paraded for the first time at Plymouth just seven days later, on 5 July, and on 7 July they commenced training for a raid against the enemy-occupied island of Guernsey.

The raiding party, from H Troop of No. 3 Commando under Durnford Slater, and No. 11 Independent Company commanded by Major Ronnie Tod, embarked from Dartmouth on the destroyers HMS *Scimitar* and *Saladin*, accompanied by seven RAF air-sea rescue launches, or crash boats, which, in the absence of proper landing craft, would ship the men ashore. H-Hour, the time of landing, was set for 00.50 hrs on the night of 14/15 July.

The force sailed from Dartmouth at 18.00 hrs on Sunday 14 July, aiming to land on the Jerbourg Peninsula, where No. 3 would attack a machine-gun post and cut a wireless cable, while No. 11 Independent Company attacked the main target, the island's airfield. Matters began to go awry soon after sailing. Two of the RAF launches assigned to No. 11 dropped out with engine trouble in the Channel, and those which continued turned out to be terribly noisy. But by midnight the small force was in station off the south of Guernsey, in the loom of the land, and here the Commandos trans-shipped into the

launches, after which Durnford Slater's launch promptly
set off in the wrong direction towards the coast of Brittany. Once the compass error had been detected, the craft
put about and closed the beach by about 1.00 a.m., putting
the men ashore at high tide in several feet of water, which
drowned all the weapons. It all made for a noisy landing,
followed by a hard squelching run up a long flight of steps
to the top of the cliffs where the machine-gun post was
found empty and unmanned. No. 3 Commando wandered
about on Guernsey for an hour or so until Durnford Slater
fell over and let off his pistol, which produced a burst of
machine-gun fire from the enemy. At the re-embarkation
point, four men admitted they could not swim and had to
be left behind, but the balance of the Commando withdrew by swimming out to the boats through the surf. The
Independent Company, coming ashore in two craft also
fitted with faulty compasses, got totally lost, one boat
hitting a rock and the other landing the men on Sark.
They had done no damage to the enemy but they had
learned a few useful lessons, not least that amphibious-
ness is not half as easy as it looks.

Churchill, who was already having some difficulties
with the military hierarchy over the Commando concept,
was less than pleased with these initial raids. 'It would
be most unwise to disturb the coasts of these countries
by the kind of silly fiascos which were perpetrated at
Boulogne and Guernsey.' 'The idea of working up all
these coasts against us by pin-prick raids and fulsome
communiqués is one to be strictly avoided.'

As this book will reveal, Commando operations were
plagued throughout the war by problems with landing
craft before the men even got ashore. Landing craft broke
down, got lost, put their men on the wrong beach, failed
to turn up or ran ashore so firmly that they could not get
off again. With all their other problems, the lay reader
might suppose that these additional difficulties drove the
Commando soldiers frantic, but in fact their stories are

full of praise and support for their friends and comrades in the landing craft crews.

This is probably because the Commandos knew just how difficult a task the landing crews had. On the face of it, getting ashore onto a beach in a flat-bottomed landing craft looks simple – until you consider the situation. Commando soldiers went ashore in a wide variety of craft during the war, from two-man Folboat canoes to the large LSTs (Landing Ship Tanks). But as the war wore on, they increasingly used the ALC or LCA (Landing Craft Assault), which can serve as our example.

The LCA is a flat-bottomed craft, with the steering wheel forward and the engine room aft. She carried a crew of four – a commander, a coxswain (helmsman), a stoker who controlled the engines, and a deckhand, a general dogsbody – and had a speed of about six knots. Fully loaded, she could carry a platoon or section of thirty Commando soldiers, who sat on long thwarts below deck level during the run-in to the beach. About fifty metres offshore the craft slowed and the deckhand dropped a kedge anchor over the stern (Out Kedge!). The craft then grounded and the coxswain dropped the bow ramp and the steel doors to the passenger compartment opened (Down Ramp – Out Troops!) on which order the troops streamed ashore.

Practising with the first LCAs at Inveraray in 1941, the thirty men of Algy Forrester's F Troop from 3 Commando could get out of their craft and twenty-five yards up the beach, fully equipped and with platoon weapons, in ten seconds. Peter Young's troop held the re-embarkation record of fourteen seconds. This rapid embarkation and re-embarkation was crucial, for both craft and men were most vulnerable when beached offshore, within easy range of the beach defences, so constant practice in disembarking was essential – and still is. Discussing the disaster which struck the Welsh Guards at Bluff Cove in the Falklands War, a Commando Officer told me, 'Had you, or I, or any Commando soldier been that close to the shore, we would have been off the *Galahad*, up the beach and into cover like a rat up a drainpipe. We know, don't we, that you don't hang about offshore.'

Getting ashore looks simple; now consider the difficulties. The landing will probably be made in the dark, there is probably a sea running. The men in the first wave have to climb out over the rail into their craft, without lights and without talking, and the craft are then lowered. Subsequent waves must clamber down scrambling nets. Anyone who falls into the sea, fully loaded, will drown. Once in the water, the LCA is very low and the visibility, even in daylight, is restricted. Dropped five miles or so offshore, the coast may only be visible when the craft rises on a wave. At night, trying to find the right beach and arrive exactly at the right time to fit in with a plan, with no lights other than gunfire, can never be an easy task. Perhaps the real surprise is that the crews did not get lost or into trouble more often. In an attempt to reduce landing problems, Combined Operations established a Beach Pilotage School for landing craft crews at Tighnabruaich in Scotland later in the war.

By the end of July 1940 the Commando organization was more or less in place, but a certain amount of tinkering then followed. In October the Chiefs of Staff decreed that the Commando and the Independent Companies should be amalgamated into Special Service (SS) Battalions. The letters SS found no favour with the Commandos and John Durnford Slater, for one, refused to have anything to do with the scheme. 'Never let the term "Special Service Battalion" appear on our Orders,' he told Charlie Head. Letters addressed to the OC A Company, Special Service Battalion, were replied to by Lieutenant Colonel J. Durnford Slater, OC No. 3 Commando. After a few weeks, the War Office gave up the SS Battalion idea, but the various Commando brigades remained SS brigades until the end of 1944. The first Special Service Brigade was formed in October 1940 under the command of Brigadier J. C. Haydon, DSO, OBE, and by March 1941 this brigade consisted of eleven Commandos. Their organization had by then been altered from the unwieldy ten troops to a more handy six troops, each of three officers and sixty-two men, which fitted neatly into two of the new ALC (Assault Landing Craft – later called LCAs) which were then coming into service. One small problem which affects the lay historian at this point is the question of Commando organization, for the unit establishments were not yet homogenous, although the majority of Commandos were based on the 'fighting troop' or 'assault troop' organization and consisted of five troops plus a Heavy Weapons Troop equipped with three-inch mortars and Vickers machine guns. Each troop was divided into two sections under a subaltern and each section divided into two subsections commanded by a sergeant. Each CO had a fairly free hand within his own unit. One of the great initial attractions of Commando soldiering had been the absence of red tape, but although it was always kept to the minimum, some administrative back-up proved necessary, in spite of those early enthusiasms.

'It is the greatest job in the Army,' wrote Geoffrey Appleyard of 7 Commando and the Small Scale Raiding Force. 'No red tape, no paperwork, just operations.' When Durnford Slater commanded 2 Special Service Brigade in Italy three years later, he recalls that his Brigade Major, Brian Franks, could keep all the brigade paperwork in one pocket of his battledress. Nevertheless someone had to do the administration, see to the pay, send men on courses, indent for ammunition and supplies. Some units therefore established an Administrative Troop and most units had an Administrative Officer, and among the most notable of these was the redoubtable 'Slinger' Martin of No. 8, and later No. 3 Commando.

During this period, when most of the Commandos were concentrated in Scotland, on Arran, or around Largs, some units began to develop special sections. No. 6, for example, raised a canoe section, later called 101 Troop, which we shall meet in the Mediterranean. The original No. 2 (Para) Commando became first 11 Special Air Service Battalion and later 1 Battalion The Parachute Regiment; 12 Commando were based in Northern Ireland on internal security, while in February 1941 three Commandos, Nos. 7, 8 and 11 (Scottish) sailed for the Middle East, where they were brigaded with two small, locally raised Commando units, Nos. 50 and 52 Commandos, the whole unit being known as Layforce and coming under the command of Lieutenant Colonel Robert Laycock. We will look at the exploits of Laycock in a later chapter.

Too much training with no prospect of action will soon take the edge off any fighting unit, and by the early months of 1941 many of the original volunteers were getting very disgruntled, some even applying for return to their parent units. Raids were constantly planned and trained for, but somehow they were all cancelled, often at the last minute. Then on 4 March 1941 a real raid came along at last, when 3 and 4 Commandos were ordered to mount a full-scale operation against the Lofoten Islands.

3

Lofoten to Vaagso, 1941

'There must be a beginning of any good matter,
but the continuing to the end, until it be
thoroughly finished, yields the true glory'

SIR FRANCIS DRAKE TO WALSINGHAM
OFF CAPE ST VINCENT 1587

The Lofoten Islands lie off the north-western coast of Norway; just inside the Arctic Circle, 900 miles north of Britain. They are separated from the mainland by the wide strait of the Vestfjord, opposite the mainland ports of Bodo and Narvik, two places already known to Commando soldiers who had served in Norway with the Independent Companies. The main occupation of the islanders was – and is – fishing and the Germans were obtaining valuable supplies of herring and cod-liver oil from processing factories at four of the ports: Brettesnes, Henningsvaer, Stamsund and Svolvaer. The plan was for 3 and 4 Commandos, still mustered as Special Service Battalions, to send raiding parties against these ports, to destroy the processing plants, kill Germans, arrest Norwegian traitors and return with prisoners and volunteers for the Norwegian forces in Britain. The codeword for this raid was Operation Claymore.

The raiding force, commanded by Brigadier Haydon and escorted by five destroyers, sailed from Scapa Flow on 1 March 1941 on two converted cross-Channel ferries, the *Princess Emma* and the *Princess Beatrix*, with LCAs

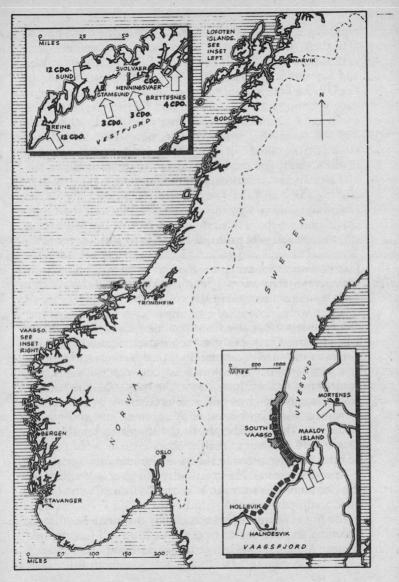

Lofoten and Vaagso

replacing lifeboats in the davits. The force consisted of 500 men drawn equally from both Commandos and demolition teams from the Royal Engineers, plus guides and interpreters drawn from Free Norwegian Forces in the UK. 3 Commando landed at Stamsund and Hennings-vaer, 4 Commando at Svolvaer and Brettesnes, both units receiving a tumultuous welcome from the local people, and the somewhat disappointing news that the islands were not occupied, although German prisoners trickled in throughout the day. The oil factories were blown up, 300 Norwegian volunteers were taken out to the waiting landing ships and the force sailed for home early in the afternoon. On the way out of harbour they met their only opposition when a German armed trawler opened fire on the convoy and was promptly sunk by the destroyer HMS *Somali*. The raid had gone like clockwork, a considerable leap forward from previous operations, proving that large-scale raids were perfectly feasible. Yet no more large-scale raids were mounted until the end of the year.

There were, however, a number of smaller operations, and between these the Commandos got on with training and refining their raiding techniques. Lieutenant Algy Forrester of No. 3 Commando introduced rocky landings and cliff assault techniques to the repertoire. As he pointed out to Durnford Slater, the more obvious landing places, sandy beaches and sheltered areas, would surely be mined, wired and covered by machine gun and mortar positions. Whatever the physical difficulties, landing onto rock-bound coasts and scaling sheer cliffs would probably be safer and also provide the vital element of surprise.

Forrester's initiative eventually led to the founding of the Commando Mountain Warfare Training Centre (a role now occupied by the Mountain and Arctic Warfare Cadre of the Royal Marines), which taught the elements of rock climbing and the basics of cliff assault to all Commando troops. Accidents were common, as Frank Barton of 6 Commando remembers. 'I must tell you about Bill Allan, a very brave man. In 1941 – we had our first casualty when rock climbing on the screes in Cumberland. Our guide was a Corporal Hunter, who was just above Bill Allan and myself, when he slipped and fell on us. Bill grabbed him and they slid down the mountain together. Bill managed to grab a bush forty feet below, but Corporal Hunter fell to his death.'

F. Farmborough of 4 Commando also recalls training accidents. 'On one occasion we had a couple of men drowned, and orders came round that everybody had to be able to swim a few yards in battle order. I can tell you it's not easy to swim in battle order. A couple of days later we paraded in battle order, thinking we were going on a forced march, instead of which we headed for Troon open-air swimming pool, single file up the ladder and jumped off the first board. Those who had to be rescued got extra training. Our troop officer, Captain Pettiward, had a long ginger moustache, and as he came to the surface, face upward, his ginger hair and moustache floated on the water. It was one of the funniest things I've ever seen. Sadly Captain Pettiward was killed at Dieppe.'

Joe Edmans, of 1 Commando, went through one of these early Commando schools. 'We came up to Scotland on the *Princess Beatrix* (little did we know we would be seeing more of this ship), and the unit was split, some at Kilwinning, some at Irvine, all in civvy billets – it was just like home from home. Quite a few courses had started and we were sent on a mountaineering course at Glencoe. My troop was the first to go and we were taught from scratch, first over small boulders, then on higher cliffs, then abseiling. When we had finished, I stayed on to instruct the other troops when they came up.'

Victor Stevenson of 12 Commando did his course near Braemar. 'The Commandant was a famous Himalayan climber called Frank Smythe, and the Chief Instructor was a Captain Hunt of the KRRC, later Sir John Hunt of Everest fame. I climbed Lochnagar with him, and I remember being bawled out by 12's CO, Lieutenant Colonel the Lord Sysonby, for thinking that the Brigade Intelligence Officer Evelyn Waugh, was an ATS officer.'

Other memorable Commando instructors during this period were two ex-officers of the Shanghai police, Fairburn and Sykes. Arthur Woodiwiss of 2 Commando passed through their hands at Inverlochy. 'They instructed in the use of the Wilkinson fighting knife, held low in the left hand at the point of balance, raising the right hand to create an opening for an upward thrust under the rib-cage. They also taught us how to break away from someone holding a pistol in our back, breaking the man's finger in the trigger guard as we turned. I also remember that No. 2 received a present from the Mayor of New York, a chest full of tommy-guns confiscated from New York gangsters by the police. These went into our general weapon pool. I remember they wouldn't fire on automatic in cold weather until the recoil pads warmed up.'

Meanwhile, the units were continuing to weed out and RTU the sick, lame and lazy. They received a stream of new recruits, even though Commando units were being presented in the Press as suicide squads or gangs of thugs. Dusty Miller of 2 Commando was one volunteer in 1941. 'Reg Tuson and I had left the Grenadier Guards at Windsor to join the Commandos, and I well remember the send-off we got from the Senior Drill Sergeant. "Miller," he said, "goodbye to you, lad ... I hate to see you die so young."' Dusty Miller and his friend were billeted on a council estate in Ayr, where the landlady's son was an engine driver, and though not liable to call-up, a keen member of the local Home Guard. Dusty Miller again: 'Within a month he was a sergeant. We used to pass on everything we learned and take him for rifle exercises, map and compass work, unarmed combat training ... he must have been the best trained Home Guard in Britain.'

'Red' Skelton of 5 Commando has another tale of

soldiers and civilians. 'We arrived at Crewe station and were standing about chatting on the platform, when I felt a thump on my back, as if someone had hit me very hard ... then I heard the bang. Corporal Ball shouted out, "Sergeant, you've been shot!" and I saw blood on the floor and found a razor-sharp cut in my uniform but not a mark on my body. That puzzled us, and the Red Caps came up and said that a civilian had been hit in the shoulder further up the platform. A soldier had been playing with his rifle, not realizing it was loaded, and pressed the trigger. The bullet had hit my steel helmet – that was the thump I felt – and ricocheted. The civilian's shoulder was a real mess, but they never found the culprit for the platform was jam-packed with troops waiting for their trains.'

In between raids and recruiting, the training went on, and Lieutenant Milton of 7 Commando has memories of his course in the Highlands. 'While the Commando was at Felixstowe, I was sent on a course to Lochailort. The course was on demolition and sabotage, and the instructors were the best I had come across since Sandhurst. Among them were Lord Lovat, later of 4 Commando; Spencer Chapman, who raided behind the Japanese lines in Malaya; one of the Stirling brothers of SAS fame; and Fairburn and Sykes, who had been in the Shanghai police. The course involved "survival" as it would now be called, but which was known then as "fieldcraft". It consisted of stalking the deer, unarmed combat from Fairburn and Sykes, and weapon training under a Colonel who handled a rifle in a way I would not have thought possible. I don't know how many shots he could get off in a minute but it was marvellous to watch, and every round hit the target. Randolph Churchill was on the course, in the same section I was in, but he left pretty quickly. I remember him being extremely and quite unnecessarily rude to one of our NCO instructors.

'After a month, for our final exercise we were given

47

small quantities of light food, including pemmican, and made a pretty colossal march across the mountains, performing various tasks on the way. I remember preparing a supposedly unused railway line for demolition, and just as we put in the detonators, there came a chug-chug-chug and a train came along and we had to rush back hurriedly and disarm the charges. The exercise ended in appalling weather at Mallaig, and we were told we could spend the night there or return to the castle. I thought I'd return to the castle and was one of a party, with two Highlanders from the 11th Scottish Commando and a sergeant, to march back down the West Highland railway line. We were very tired, almost asleep on our feet, but I remember that we marched to attention as we entered the gates of the castle. Lord Lovat seemed to be pleased with us and took us out to dinner and told us we could eat anything we wanted. All I wanted was bacon and eggs and whisky. Anyway, I enjoyed it. I returned to 7 Commando, but not once did I have the chance to practise or teach any of the things I learned at Lochailort, which I recall as being the best course I ever attended.'

On 27 October 1941 Sir Roger Keyes stepped down as Chief of Combined Operations, heading directly for the House of Commons to state his reasons to the assembled Members. 'Having been frustrated at every turn in every worthwhile offensive operation I have tried to undertake, I must endorse the Prime Minister's comments on the negative power of those who control the war machine in Whitehall.' Sir Roger was an MP, but in an attempt to silence him the War Office posted him a copy of the Official Secrets Act and sent an officer to impound his papers.

Sir Roger's problems and frustrations were not untypical. One officer commented: 'The real war, the only war worth fighting with any enthusiasm, is the one between the front line soldier and the Staff.' The Commando units had been at the sharp end of this war since their inception.

The military hierarchy dislikes private armies and new formations. Durnford Slater's 3 Commando suffered greatly from this at Plymouth where 'the Military Command looked on us with suspicion and resentment as Winston Churchill's private army – unnecessary, irregular and taking all the best men to creep about at night cutting throats.'

The Staff deployed passive resistance, even against the Commando concept. If a training area was needed, it was not available. If there was brawling in the town, the Commandos had caused it. No. 3 Commando 'left Plymouth thankfully', writes Durnford Slater. 'No one could have been more kind than the local people or more helpful than the Royal Navy, but the continual nagging and obstruction from the Army authorities was really beginning to get us down.'

The Army Command also dragged its feet over the issuing of a distinctive headgear to the Commando units. In the early years the Commandos wore their own regimental head-dress on parade and for walking out, and either steel helmets or the woollen cap-comforter for battle or training. When the green beret was first proposed, the Higher Command objected on the grounds that a variety of head-dress served to increase security and might, say, conceal the fact that a Commando unit had arrived in a coastal port for a raid across the Channel.

Ted Kelly, later a CSM in 2 Commando, remembers the early days. 'One of the oddities of Commando life was pay parade. The units had no regimental status and we were seconded to Commandos rather than posted, which did help to get rid of misfits who were simply RTU'd. Pay parades took time, as we came from every regiment in the Army and had to be paid on separate payrolls. This also had a side-effect on dress. Military conformity was considered irrelevant to the basis of our discipline, so it was common to see men going out in the evening in naval rollneck sweaters, leather jerkins and rope-soled boots. If something more formal was required, battledress with regimental forage cap fitted the bill. We were allowed to wear our regimental dress cap, but since no officer could remember which regiments we all belonged to, artistic licence soon crept in. The skull and crossbones badge of the 17th/21st Lancers looked well on the dark blue with yellow piping of the RASC dress cap, but it couldn't last.' It didn't, and the green beret replaced all this, and the popular Balmorals, at the end of 1942.

The objections to the green beret were eventually over-ruled by the Combined Operations new Chief, Lord Louis Mountbatten, who took up his appointment on 27 October 1941. A few days later, to underline the importance Churchill attached to Combined Operations, Mountbatten was appointed to high rank in all the services, as a Lieutenant General in the Army, an RAF Air Marshal, and a Royal Naval Commodore.

Between Lofoten and the next big raid on Vaagso at Christmas 1941, small raids continued, with varying success. At the end of July, Second Lieutenant Pinkney took a party from 12 Commando ashore in France near Ambleteuse, staying for an hour before returning to their boats. Norwegian troops raided Spitzbergen in August, destroying vast quantities of coal and the winding gear for local coal mines. At the end of that month, No. 5 Commando began a series of small cross-Channel raids, when on the night of 30 August they landed two parties, one at Hardelot, the other at Merlimont near Boulogne. Neither party encountered any opposition and stayed ashore for only half an hour before withdrawing. Geoff Riley was with one of these parties. 'I recall that the sea was very rough, choppy, and chucking the landing craft about a lot, and remember we were still fairly fresh at that stage and the raid was more of a probe or a recce. Anyway, when we did hit the beach, it was laced with trip-wires and in our inexperience we tripped some and sent flares all over the place. When we did make a brief contact with the enemy they went off like bats out of hell, and so did we. So we didn't take any prisoners or have a scrap but, as the OC said, "It'll all do for training, lads."'

At the end of September, No. 1 Commando went across, landing one party from No. 5 Troop under Lieutenant Scaramanga near St Vaast on the Cherbourg peninsula, and another under Captain Davies near Courseulles. Scaramanga's party cleared the beach and then bumped into a German cycle patrol, which they engaged with tommy-gun fire, killing three, before withdrawing to their landing craft. Lieutenant Scaramanga writes: 'This was perhaps the only raid that year in which actual contact was made with the enemy. We met the German patrol in the dark. They came very swiftly and silently before any plans could be made, but I had three men with tommy-guns in the van of the section, so it was all over in a second. Everything is so unpredictable when you land by night on a strange shore, but I am sure the Germans realized that they must be prepared for our raids at any time and place on a thousand miles of coast, and lost many nights sleep.' These two landings were codenamed Chopper-Deepcut, and Lieutenant Scaramanga's and Captain Davies' official reports went as follows:

Chopper-Deepcut

Force 'A', Commanded by Lieutenant G. A. SCARAMANGA, landing at POINT DE SAIRE, near ST VAAST

Having slipped the tow at 00.10 hrs/28 assault ALC and spare ALC proceeded inland at high speed until land was sighted at 00.55 hrs. After some uncertainty as to exact position, this was established

51

as being the middle of St Vaast Bay. The assault ALC was put ashore on an excellent beach at 01.35 hrs. This, being only twenty-five minutes before latest limit of withdrawal, left the patrol very little scope of action. The troops landed practically dry-shod.

It being only one hour before high tide, the width of beach was only five to ten yards. This was crossed by the patrol and a bridgehead left according to plan.

On the far side of the beach was a low wall skirting a good road running parallel to the shore. At the foot of the wall two signal cables were found; sections of these were brought back for examination.

Crossing the road and turning right, the patrol came upon a shuttered house. A brief examination revealed no occupants. Meanwhile, with the exception of the signal cables, no enemy activity of any kind had been encountered.

Time was now running short, it being 01.55 hrs. The leading scouts of the patrol, proceeding up the road for greater speed, reached a bend at the same time as a German cyclists' patrol travelling in the opposite direction. Fire was immediately opened upon the Germans with tommy-guns at point-blank range, and it is unlikely that any of them escaped serious injury. Two bodies were carried back towards the ALC, but one had to be abandoned owing to the acute need, by this time, for speed. A third body was seen sprawled in the hedge. There was no time for further search, but no Germans were seen to run away. This was a golden opportunity for taking prisoners, and I am enquiring further into the action taken.

All troops and the dead German were re-embarked at 02.10 hrs. During the withdrawal one enemy machine-gun opened fire with tracer at about 200 yards range.

No searchlights, or Very lights, were seen at any time.

It then being too late to pick up the MGB or *Prince Leopold*, the return passage was made direct to Portsmouth, where *Prince Leopold* was boarded at 16.15 hrs, 28 Sept.

The dead German was handed over to the MI9 representative, who identified him as belonging to 183 Pioneer Battalion, a new identification.

Force 'B', Commanded by Captain J. H. DAVIES, landing at COURSEULLES. (NNW of CAEN)

MGB slipped the ALCs at 00.55 hrs/28, having set them upon a course for their objective. Land was sighted at 02.10 hrs, and eighteen minutes later it became obvious that approach was being made to the centre of the town. A few white star-shells were seen to go up some miles to the eastwards, in the Luc sur Mer direction.

The town was first thought to be Courseulles, but after a brief longshore reconnaissance in the assaulting ALC it was identified by Captain Davies at St Aubin, which lies three and a half miles east of Courseulles. This identification was possible owing to a close examination of the low-oblique air photographs by Captain Davies before the operation. He recognized a conspicuous turreted house.

As was the case with Force 'A', time was now running very short, and after consultation between the Naval and Military Commanders it was decided that advantage must be taken of the fifteen minutes remaining, in spite of being at the wrong place.

The patrol therefore landed at 01.40 hrs to try to pick up a prisoner, leaving a bridgehead to protect the ALC according to plan. The town was quiet and

the only light showing was a badly blacked-out
window. As the last few men were leaving the ALC
a loud hail was heard to their left. This was thought
by some to be 'Halt', but it was followed
immediately by a burst of machine-gun fire, so may
have been a fire order.

Captain Davies ordered an assault upon the MG
post. He was confronted with a ten-foot-high
promenade-wall surmounted by the usual rail and
two coils of Dannert wire, one upon the other. As
the patrol was climbing this wall a second MG
opened fire from the right flank, followed
immediately by a blue flare and fire from a third
MG, firing at a high rate and apparently of heavier
calibre, from a second-storey window seventy to one
hundred yards to the left.

Faced with this heavy opposition and with so little
time left, Captain Davies had no option but to
withdraw his patrol to the ALC. The withdrawal was
carried out under constant fire from the three MGs
while blue flares were sent up continuously.

After the bridgehead had been called in, two of our
men were seen to be struggling in the water.
Sergeant Hewlett, with complete disregard for his
own safety, immediately dived overboard and, under
continuous and accurate fire, brought them back to
the ALC. One of them had been wounded.

Meanwhile all available fire-power from the ALC
was brought to bear upon the MG posts.

A check-up of numbers then revealed that two
men were missing. There were no bodies on the
beach, however, and although searching in the water
in the dark did not locate them, it must be presumed
that they fell in the water.

The ALC then went out fast, being hit by MG fire
repeatedly. Flares continued to go up until she was
well out to sea and quite out of range.

The MGB was found fifteen minutes later and the troops from the ALC transferred.

Portsmouth was reached at 09.50 hrs 28/9.

These operations ushered in the 'monthly raid', an attempt to get a Commando force ashore on the enemy-held coast at regular intervals. During the next months Commando units 2, 5, 9 and 12 all mounted raids across the Channel. No. 9 Commando's raid in November was a large affair, ninety men landing to attack a German coastal battery near Houlgate. The party got ashore without trouble, but due to delays and signalling errors had no time to carry out the attack. They withdrew without loss. Captain Lucas of 4 Troop 9 Commando describes this operation:

The warning order for Operation Sunstar was received early in November 1941. It was for a raid by approximately one hundred men of 9 Commando on an enemy-held coastline.

Lieutenant Colonel J. M. Saegert, RE, then commanding No. 9 Commando, decided that the task would be carried out by No. 1 Troop with elements of other Troops including whatever specialists (Signals, Demolitions, Medical etc.) might be needed. Captain Cyril Suter, OC 1 Troop, would command the raiding force, though Colonel Saegert would have overall responsibility for planning and expressed his intention of accompanying the raiders. I had just been appointed to command No. 4 Troop but, as I had been Intelligence Officer since March, and as my successor had not yet been appointed, I continued to act as IO for the purposes of this operation.

Almost immediately, the Colonel, Cyril and I went down to London for the initial briefing by Combined Operations Staff. It was made clear to us that this was to be a modest, but very positive, crack at the Normandy coastline in the area of Ouistreham at the mouth of the River Orne. Excellent aerial photographs, both vertical and oblique, showed that the open beaches of the small seaside towns in the area were quite strongly defended, with MG posts securely sited in the basements of houses on the front. We would have the support of three or four Motor Gunboats, who would be able to engage these strongpoints and enable us to get a foothold, and I had the impression that the Combined Ops people were rather keen on this scheme. It was not clear, however, what we could do when we got there, apart from creating general mayhem. Colonel Saegert preferred another target. A German battery on the high ground behind Houlgate, he thought, would be an ideal objective for a Commando raiding force of this size and type. The maps and photographs suggested that the landing could be made without opposition from anything stronger than patrols; the cliffs here were generally no more than seventy-five to one hundred feet high, and not very steep. The country behind the cliff top looked like heathland, with a good deal of scrubby cover, rather like the country round Aldershot, for example. The battery was no more than about two miles away, and it was thought that we would have a good chance – within the very narrow time limits imposed by moon, tide and their Lordships of the Admiralty – of reaching the objective, surprising its garrison, holding it while our demolition teams did a great deal of damage to the installations, and returning to catch the last boat home. We had been very firmly told that crews would have strict orders not to risk beaching their craft on a falling tide. We appreciated this – our getaway vehicles were of some interest to us too (I had, but did not declare, a special interest, as I was due to be married on 3 December).

Anyway, this was agreed, and we returned to our station in Kirkcudbright to make preparations for the raid; preliminary briefing, special training, sorting out equipment, stores and ammunition etc. Then, about 15 November, we embarked at Jamaica Quay, Glasgow, in the pre-war cross-Channel packet *Prince Leopold*, one of the first Commando landing-craft carriers. After a very rough passage through the Irish Channel we paused at Falmouth for exercises in the LCAs. I think this was the occasion when, on the insistence of the Colonel, and against the advice of the LCA Flotilla Commander, we carried out a landing exercise at night, on a beach about seven miles west of Falmouth, which involved re-embarking a little after high water. As the first returning troops approached the beach, they saw that the LCAs were apparently still afloat, about 300 yards out in the bay. They started to wade as ordered and, before the first man reached the nearest LCA, all vessels were aground – they even had dry land all round them. We marched back all the way to Falmouth just in time for breakfast and another busy day. This lesson was taken to heart by all concerned.

We then sailed to Spithead, where final plans were made for the raid. We had a very instructive and interesting session with Naval and RAF Planning Officers. The plan, which was naturally determined by naval considerations, was for *Leopold* to leave Spithead with the raiding party on board towards dusk on 22 November, and steam to a point five miles off the selected beach. Here, the raiding party would embark in four LCAs and proceed under their own power, while the parent ship returned to Spithead. Having landed the troops, the LCAs would stand off until shortly before high water, when they would come in again, pick up the returning raiders and return to Spithead. We now heard that German E-boats stationed in Ouistreham posed a possible threat both before the landing and on the way home. However, the RAF would give us very adequate cover from first light. (I believe it was a squadron of Spitfires – it certainly looked like that.) This was very comforting, though they admitted that they were hoping the German Air Force, and possibly coastal forces, would be tempted to come out and have a go at us if we annoyed them enough!

So we did that, and all went well until we were about a mile off the beach, when it became apparent that one LCA, with the Colonel and a small party on board, was no longer with us. They had lost touch in the darkness and had in fact landed some way to the east of us. They took no further part in the operation as planned. They had adventures of their own, I understand.

Fortunately most of the party, including the Troop Commander, Cyril Suter, were still together and made a happy landing on the right beach. This was where things began to go really wrong. With hindsight, I have to admit that I had made a serious misjudgement regarding the suitability of the landing place and, given the time restriction, of Houlgate as an achievable objective. Had I taken into account the geological nature of the cliffs and the effect on them of November rains, I would have given different advice. As it was, the troops attempting to scale them found themselves sinking knee-deep and more in a wet, heavy clay. This was a more severe obstacle than a much steeper cliff made of hard rock. It must have taken at least half an hour of our precious time to get all the men – and most of the boots – to the cliff top where they found another obstacle. (What follows is what Cyril told me when we got home.)

The gorse, which as the photos had shown, did have numerous paths through it if one could find them in the dark, was extremely difficult to penetrate. Indeed, by the time the whole party assembled on the other side, it was obvious to Cyril that he was not going to be able to carry out his task and return over the same obstacles, within the time limit – or anything like it. He therefore decided to cut his losses and try at least to find out something about the movement of patrols, and even perhaps intercept one and bag a prisoner or two. He went to a house and knocked on the door. To the nervous farmer's wife who asked who he was, he replied, 'The British Army.' This, he said, made quite an impression. He learned from this helpful lady that the OC of the battery was billeted in her house, and was, as usual at that time, in the Officers' Mess, but was expected back at any time. This sounded promising, and Cyril and his men set about preparing a reception for the gentleman. Unfortunately, however, Germans are not always as regular in their habits as they are sometimes made out to be, and this one was having a late night. Cyril waited as long as he dared – and much longer than was wise – then gave up and returned to the beach.

Meanwhile I was carrying out my very simple task of examining the beach area as a potential landing place for larger forces, and in particular trying to discover whether the smallish pillboxes at either end of the beach (about a mile apart) were occupied. With my batman, Ted Healey, I walked along to the westward one. As we approached we heard voices, German voices, I was sure. I believe I did have a brief dream of glory involving a hand grenade, a quick rush, a prisoner or two and a

Victoria Cross for each of us. But we only had a rifle and a pistol between us, and we had been ordered not to stir it up, so we went back to the other end of the beach, found the other pillbox empty, and returned in time to meet the main body as they struggled back down the cliff, at least half an hour late.

We had seen no sign of the LCAs since we landed. We now waited for them to appear. After what seemed a very long time – Cyril had reached the point of discussing with his brother officers whether we should go to Ouistreham and try to seize a fishing boat, or whether the time had come to scatter and try individually or in very small groups to contact the Escape Line – someone thought he heard a boat's engines. I scrambled to the top of a large white rock which had been our chief means of identifying the beach during our approach, and saw what I thought was the outline of a smallish craft. I flashed with my blued torch the agreed Morse Q signal. No reply, so I tore off the blue paper and tried again. The agreed reply was flashed back immediately, and in the same instant a machine gun opened fire on me from the cliff top. I hit the sand about twelve feet below me, and lay for a moment watching the tracer spraying off the rock where I had been standing. There was nothing we could do; one young officer, under fire for the first time, gave the historic order: 'One round rapid fire.' (He left the Commando soon after. The next time I met him was in Italy in 1944, when he had been commanding a tank troop with some distinction throughout the North African campaign.) Neither we nor the patrol on the cliff top could get at each other, so we set about swimming out to the LCA now lying about fifty yards off the beach. Some equipment was left behind, and Private Alanach was wounded in the arm – not seriously, but he was losing quite a lot of blood and so gave us some concern, especially as it was clearly going to be a long time before he received proper attention.

I think most of us went to sleep as comfortably as we could, with seventy or more in a craft designed to carry thirty men. I awoke at about 09.00, to find the LCA about five miles off Le Havre, in bright sunshine, and wallowing in quite a swell, but otherwise motionless. The steering gear had broken down. Once more I had visions of my bride waiting at the altar, and wondered if Jerry would let me ring her in time to warn the guests. Fortunately, at that moment, we spotted another craft about half a mile away making towards us. It was one of the other LCAs. Her Commander brought her alongside and, after an attempt to tow us in line had been frustrated by the heavy and increasing swell, the two vessels were lashed alongside and we proceeded, slowly but surely, towards Spithead, ninety miles away.

Morale was good, and reached its high point when the promised Spitfires or Hurries, I can't remember which, appeared high overhead and proceeded to entertain us with a fine display of aerobatics, which we were just enjoying when we heard a long burst of cannon and MG fire, and saw the water churned up all around us; a Messerschmitt had come in under our fighter cover, shot a hole through our ensign (narrowly missing Mike Long) and went away with a couple of Spits (or Hurries) on his tail. We discovered weeks later from a German Air Force report captured at Vaagso that the pilot had been awarded the Iron Cross for this exploit, so perhaps our journey was not really wasted.

By noon, cloud cover extended from horizon to horizon, our fighters had gone, and we felt rather lonely. Also the wind was rising again, and the seas were now quite big – but not breaking, fortunately. The condition of the LCAs was deteriorating too. There were no fenders on board, and the stretchers and other gear we had put between the vessels were soon ground to fragments. Before nightfall the plates were beginning to open, and holes appeared in the sides. These craft were well provided with buoyancy beneath the deck, but they were becoming waterlogged, and we were almost waist-deep in water. Poor Alanach, getting rather weak now, had to be laid on a bed of ammunition boxes built up high enough to keep him above the water. He seemed cheerful enough, but he must have been getting near the end of his tether. Just before darkness was complete, a headland was spotted about five degrees on our starboard bow. 'Culver cliff,' said our RNVR friend. 'That low line you can see to the right is the Spithead submarine defence boom. With any luck they will have spotted us while it was still light enough and send someone to meet us.' He was disappointed. The headland was Beachy Head, the 'boom' was Eastbourne beach. The compasses, which had been carefully 'swung' or calibrated for each steelclad vessel, behaved quite differently when two craft were lashed together. In fact the compass by which we were steering had something like a forty-degree error. We splashed through Beachy Head overfalls, narrowly escaped being blown out of the water by the nine-inch guns near Pevensey, and landed on the only bit of unmined beach on the south-east coast. (The gunners had obligingly used their searchlights to guide us there.) As the ramps went down the first men out came running back, shouting that we had landed back in France. It turned out that the troops holding that part of the coast were French

Canadians. In fact they and our friends in the
Coastal Battery RA gave us a wonderful reception.

We had failed, and poor Colonel Saegert lost his
command although he was in no sense to blame for
the failure. The task was an impossible one, given
the time limits obtaining. I accept that I misled him
regarding the probable conditions to be expected at
the landing place, but I have wondered how many
Battalion or Commando IOs would have consulted a
geological expert before giving the advice I did, at
that stage in the war. Truthfully, no one comes out
of this episode with any very great credit, except
perhaps the LCA Commanders who disobeyed orders
to come in and get us home, casting away their
vessels in doing so (really owing to stress of
weather); and of course the German pilot for being
such a rotten shot. He was the only one who got
decorated for his part in the adventure – quite
rightly. I got my bride, and began forty-one years of
great happiness. Private Alanach made a speedy
recovery and rejoined 4 Troop within a few weeks.

It was then the turn of 6 and 12 Commandos, who
sailed from Scapa Flow in December, to attack the town
of Floss in Norway. This raid was marred from the start
by an accident on board their assault ship, HMS *Prince
Charles*, when a primed grenade exploded, killing six
men.

C. L. G. Bryen was there when this incident took place.
'We had with us several Press cameramen whose aim was
to obtain a record of the expedition. They had filmed the
usual scenes – Commandos exercising, chaps in their
hammocks, or writing a last letter home – and it was
suggested that they should shoot a close-up of the final
weapon overhaul and grenade priming on one of the troop
decks below, and the cameras began to roll on a scene of
intense activity. A hundred men were cleaning all types

of weapons, while at a table six men were busy cleaning the Mills-type 36 grenades, passing them to the end man, who put the detonator in. One enterprising cameraman, anxious to get the grenades in focus, pulled a handful of grenades nearer, unnoticed by the men busy with their tasks, and so mixed up the primed and unprimed grenades. The number one man picked up a grenade, thinking it unprimed, and removed the safety pin and striking lever to clean it. To his horror, a small bang denoted that it was primed and the fuse was burning. He shouted and made a desperate effort to hurl the grenade through the hatch onto the empty deck above. It hit the hatchway and fell back. A Norwegian standing below the hatch caught it and hurled it again. It exploded just opposite his chest and killed six men outright, injuring eleven others. I had been watching the filming from a vantage point on a table. When I heard the shouting I dropped to the deck, too late to avoid a small piece of shrapnel, which entered my forehead. My friend also jumped and caught a largish piece of shrapnel through the palm of his right hand. I rushed my friend along the gangway to the MI Room. We were the first to arrive and I told the Naval Officer the facts, and he sent stretcher bearers and first-aid men off at the double. In a short space of time the MO's quarters were filled with dead, dying and walking wounded. I saw Captain Coke, the Commando Medical Officer, trying to blow air through a lemonade straw into the lungs of a man with a shattered chest, but he died. The speed with which the whole thing happened, transforming a happy body of men into a shambles, is a thing one cannot easily forget.'

Spirits fell further when the Naval Commander was unable to fix his position, and in the end the raid was abandoned. These raids achieved very little, but they were excellent training, and far better than any amount of practice against friendly forces. Landing in the dark, moving across ground which might be mined, a bullet in the breech of his rifle, actually setting foot on the enemy-held shore, gave the Commando soldier a touch of the real thing. What they needed now was a chance to strike at the enemy, and that chance finally arrived on Boxing Day 1941 when 3 Commando, reinforced by two troops from No. 2 Commando, plus medics and engineers from 4 and 6 Commandos, mounted a major raid against the Norwegian port of Vaagso and the offshore island of Maaloy. This raid, Operation Archery, was the first to be mounted under the new Director of Combined Operations, Captain the Lord Louis Mountbatten.

Vaagso is the first example of a truly Combined Operation, a major amphibious landing supported by air and sea forces. The naval forces, commanded by Rear-Admiral H. M. Burrough, CB, consisted of the cruiser HMS *Kenya* and elements of the 17th Destroyer Flotilla, HMS *Offa*, *Chiddingfold*, *Onslow* and *Oribi*, escorting two infantry assault ships, the HMS *Prince Charles* and *Prince Leopold*, carrying the landing force, with the submarine HMS *Tuna* sailing ahead to beam the force in to the Vaagsfjord. The RAF element consisted of ten Hampden bombers from No. 50 Squadron, tasked with laying smoke to cover the LCAs during their run-in, and bombing coastal defences. Other aircraft were directed to provide fighter protection and bomb the German fighter fields at Herdla. This Vaagso raid was in a different league from all that had gone before, not least in the opposition, for this time the Germans were present in force.

There were coastal batteries on Maaloy and along the Ulvesund strait. There were field guns, anti-aircraft batteries and machine gun posts on Maaloy and heavy guns on the island of Rugsundo, able to bring down fire on Vaagsfjord. The town of South Vaagso and the island of Maaloy were known to be garrisoned by German troops, and although their numbers were unknown, in view of the artillery defences it was anticipated that the infantry garrison would be large and well trained. The Commando force to overwhelm all this totalled fifty-one officers and 525 men drawn from 3 Commando, plus two troops of 2 Commando which Durnford Slater kept as his floating reserve.

The plan required the landing force to approach Vaagso undetected and sail up the Vaagsfjord to the Ulvesund strait which separated South Vaagso from Maaloy. Here the landing force, split into five groups, would go ashore in LCAs to capture Maaloy and South Vaagso. Meanwhile the artillery emplacements would be attacked by bombers and engaged by the six-inch guns of HMS *Kenya* and those of her destroyer escort. Once the enemy had been eliminated, the demolition parties would blow up everything of use to the Axis and the force would then withdraw.

Combined Operations rarely run to plan and so it was here. The force sailed on Christmas Eve, aiming to land next day, but bad weather forced a change of plan. Charles Hustwick, of SS Brigade Signals, was on the Vaagso raid: 'Brigade HQ was at Castle Douglas. 9 Commando were there as well, or in the area, and the local people were very kind and generous. There seemed to be no shortage of food, but this was not to last for long. At long last a real taste of action came my way. We went to Scapa Flow by way of Invergordon, sailing from there with 3 Commando on board the *Prince Charles*. We had stuffed hearts for breakfast, not very appetizing in a force seven gale, and it got up to force nine as we sailed from Scapa on Christmas Eve. What a terrible trip! Crew and troops were really ill, water and overflow from the heads was everywhere, so we put into Sullom Voe in Shetland for Christmas Day and got pumped out. Here we learned that our destination was Vaagso. We sailed on Boxing Day and a really fine show it was. Army, Navy, RAF all worked together. In Brigade Signals the volume of traffic was really something.'

Sailing again at 16.00 hrs on Boxing Day, the battle began at 08.48 hrs on 27 December, when HMS *Kenya* illuminated Maaloy island with star shells as the aircraft swept in to drop smoke canisters and bombs. HMS *Kenya* and the destroyers then rained fire on the island, pouring more than 400 shells on to the landing area prior to the Commando sweeping ashore, then switching their fire to silence the battery on Rugsundo.

Fortunately the German garrison on Maaloy was caught completely unawares by this storm of shellfire, and the island fell without difficulty to 5 and 6 Troops of 3 Commando, led ashore by 3 Commando's Second-in-Command, Major J. M. T. F. Churchill, generally known as 'Mad Jack'. He first piped his men ashore, then put the bagpipes aside, drew his claymore, and led his men to the assault.

Maaloy was overrun in eight minutes, at the cost of one man killed – Captain Martin Linge of the Norwegian Army – and one man wounded, the redoubtable Major Churchill, who was blown up standing too close to a demolition charge and was carried back to the boats calling loudly for his bagpipes.

South Vaagso is a long straggling town, running for nearly a mile up the shore of the Ulvesund. Durnford Slater's force landed at the southern end, scaling a small cliff, and then began to fight their way from house to house up the main street. Such street fighting eats up infantry. Johnny Giles, OC of 3 Troop, was shot and killed clearing one house soon after the landing. 4 Troop lost Arthur Komrower, crushed between a rock and his landing craft, and Bill Lloyd was shot through the neck as he stepped ashore. He was to recover but his Troop Commander, Algy Forrester, was killed assaulting the German HQ in the Ulvesund Hotel, about a hundred yards up the main street. Other NCOs were killed or wounded knocking out a tank, and within twenty minutes of landing, Forrester's troop had lost all the officers and Senior NCOs and was commanded by Corporal White, who gained the DCM for his leadership that day.

The resistance turned out to be stiffer than anticipated, probably because the German garrison had received a temporary reinforcement of fifty well-trained soldiers, and as the attack faltered, Durnford Slater sent for his floating reserve and ordered Jack Churchill to send troops over from Maaloy. Peter Young arrived shortly afterwards with 6 Troop and with Sergeant George Herbert at his side, began to grenade his way up the street. The Commando began to advance steadily, winkling out enemy posts and snipers. By 13.45 hrs the battle was over, and an hour later the force withdrew.

The Vaagso raid was a great success. 3 Commando had achieved all their objectives, dealt the Germans a fierce blow, and returned to the UK with over one hundred prisoners and over seventy recruits to the Norwegian forces. The unit losses, however, had been severe for such a small, closely-knit force; twenty men had been killed, including many founder members, and fifty-seven had been wounded.

While 3 Commando were rampaging through South Vaagso and Maaloy, 12 Commando were mounting a raid on the Lofoten Islands, codenamed Operation Anklet. Sergeant Cecil Blanch was there: 'Operation Anklet was a diversionary raid in support of the raid against Vaagso.

'The main element of 12 Commando went ashore at Reine but a small party of about twenty, of whom I was one, went ashore at a small fishing hamlet called Sund. Both these landings were made early on Boxing Day and met with no opposition. We destroyed the German wireless stations and took the staffs prisoner. At Sund we also rounded up one quisling whom the Norwegians were keen to get their hands on. I believe he was the son of the local postmistress and he took off when our presence was known, but the Norwegian guides who accompanied us discovered him hiding under the bottom of a mountain hut. We remained here for two days during which time the Navy took toll of some German shipping. I saw one small ship, probably a tanker, explode in a ball of fire. We had but one small alarm when a German spotter plane flew over us. It was fired at but not hit.

'I will never forget the quiet dignity and fortitude of the Norwegian people. I also remember how bitterly cold it was. We had gone ashore in Eureka boats – fast, unarmoured motor launches – and the spray came up in ice pellets. The fjords were beautiful and the *aurora borealis* magnificent. The girls were pretty too! Once we were back on board on the first evening some of them came out in small row-boats to us and they were showered with gifts like blocks of chocolate. All in all this was not war but a holiday tour. We brought back with us some Norwegians who wished to come and, of course, the quislings and prisoners we had taken. Of the latter, one can only say they were of poor quality and I think they were glad that the war was over for them. One, who had been a prisoner of the English in World War One and who spoke some English, told me he was happy and wanted to know if he would see London. We had not undressed or had a decent wash for about a fortnight and most of us had scabies and/or body lice. For my part this was the worst discomfort I suffered. On arrival back in Scapa Flow it was a joy to be taken ashore, given a hot bath, be deloused and given fresh clothing.

'We had war correspondents with us on this raid. One of them was Gordon Holman, and on our return, two of our officers, Lieutenant Pinkney and Lieutenant Jeffries, entered Holman's cabin, took his camera film and account of the action and threw them over the side. I think they were disappointed at the lack of action, and annoyed at the photographing of the misery of the poor Norwegian people. The inflated reporting that the Commandos got in the Press was another irritant. Doubtless they were reprimanded for this and made to pay for the equipment, but when I met Gordon Holman again in the

1960s he vividly remembered the incident and was still somewhat aggrieved.'

Vaagso brought 1941, that year of mixed fortunes, to a satisfactory close, at least for those units based in the UK who were able to take part. In the Middle East though, the Commandos which made up Layforce were having a much more difficult time.

4

Layforce,
1941

'Though at first they be stoutly resisted,
yet they will as resolutely undertake the
action a second time, though it is to meet
death itself in the face.'

The English Soldier: from Lupton's
A WARLIKE TREATISE OF THE PIKE, 1642

After Dunkirk, from 1940 to 1943, the land battles against
the Axis Powers of Germany and Italy took place mainly
in the deserts of North Africa. Much of this territory had
been annexed by Italy before the war, and the British
Eighth Army, which contained strong contingents from
New Zealand, Australia and South Africa, did very well
at first against the Italian forces, inflicting defeat after
defeat, while managing to divert forces for the overthrow
of the Vichy French regime in Syria.

The main problem which faced Army Commanders on
either side during the Desert War was one of supply. The
Desert War was a highly mobile affair, fought out by
tanks and lorried infantry, and the armies advanced or
withdrew in relation to their ability to bring forward
supplies of petrol, food, ammunition and reinforcements.
This led to much to-and-fro fighting along the North
African coastline in campaigns which became known,
half-ironically, as the Benghazi Handicap. The North
African campaign also produced a surprising number of
irregular forces on the British side, notably the Long

71

Range Desert Group, and later the SAS, which carried out reconnaissance or raids behind the enemy lines by driving round their southern flank through the Great Sand Sea. With the desert on one flank and the Mediterranean on the other, there were in fact two flanks open for raiding operations, and so in February 1941 Colonel Robert Laycock embarked with Nos. 7, 8 and 11 (Scottish) Commandos in the infantry assault ships HMS *Glenearn*, *Glenroy* and *Glengyle* and sailed for the Middle East.

Lieutenant Milton sailed with 7 Commando: 'These three ships were fast merchant ships of the Glen Line, with the davits adapted to carry ALCs (Assault Landing Craft) and MLCs (Motor Landing Craft). The officers were housed in a hold below the waterline in the *Glengyle*, which we called the Altmark after the German prison ship Phillip Vian captured off Norway. We had been on these three ships for some time, sailing from Gourock to Lamlash Bay on Arran, waiting for some operation which in the end never came off. Morale was pretty low until Sir Roger Keyes came on board and made a rousing speech.

'We were eventually told we were going overseas and embarked on the three ships at Gourock. I became detached from No. 7 and found myself on the *Glenroy* with a group of officers which included Evelyn Waugh and Randolph Churchill. They seemed to spend most of their time gambling. We stayed some weeks at Girvan and at one point Lieutenant Colonel Lister, our CO, said I couldn't go as I was under twenty – in fact he was the one to stay behind and the command of No. 7 went to an officer of the Essex Yeomanry. We sailed at the end of January, spent a day or two in Freetown, sailed on to Capetown, where we were received with incredible kindness and hospitality by the South Africans, and then up the East Coast through the Suez Canal to our camp at Genifa, on the Bitter Lakes.'

This small brigade arrived in Egypt on 7 March and was then joined by two locally raised Commando units, Nos.

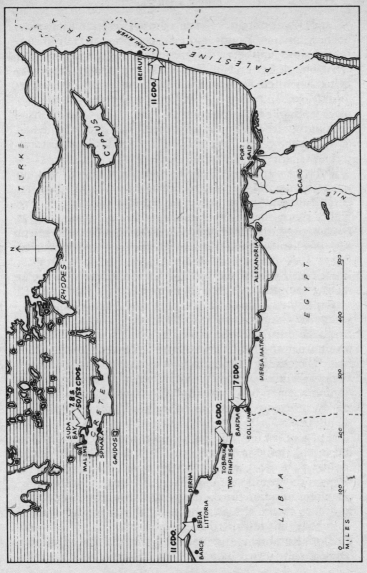

The Eastern Mediterranean

50 and 52 Commandos, the composite formation then being known as Layforce. Layforce promptly fell victim to the Staff and was designated a Brigade in the 6th Division of General Wavell's Desert Army, the units being re-named as battalions. No. 7 became the A Battalion, No. 8 the B, No. 11 the C, and the now-amalgamated Middle East Commando, the D Battalion. These battalions, like the brigade itself, lacked the usual accoutrements of heavy infantry units — engineers, transport, artillery, signals.

Worst of all, though, the Middle East theatre was on the defensive and we were teetering on the brink of defeat. After a long string of successes against the Italians, the Eighth Army met a much more redoubtable opponent at the end of March 1941, when the German General Erwin Rommel landed in Cyrenaica at the head of the Afrika Korps. This mobile, well-trained force, equipped with the latest tanks, struck hard at the Eighth Army and sent it reeling back towards Egypt. As part of this twin-pronged strategic thrust, another German force invaded Greece, where the Greeks had previously given an Italian Army a rough handling, but this time the Greeks too were forced into retreat and the Eighth Army's slender reserves were rushed across the Mediterranean to support them, leaving Layforce behind in Egypt. Staff Officers, harassed to find reinforcements for frontline units, were soon casting greedy eyes at Laycock's brigade of well-trained infantrymen.

This was bad enough, but events were already conspiring to blight the prospects for Commando troops in the Middle East. To begin with, this was an active theatre where other units were already fighting, so the Commandos could not fill the aggressive role they had come to occupy in the UK. Out here there was enough war for everybody. In addition, the Desert Army was now retreating from Rommel's first offensive, and the three Layforce landing ships were taken away to ferry Allied troops across the Mediterranean to Greece. Finally, the Allies lacked air superiority, which made raids west along the coast a hazardous affair for the landing ships.

Clearly, a full brigade of trained soldiers could not be kept in idleness at such a time and Colonel Laycock was soon ordered to mount a raid on the enemy-held port of Bardia, 300 miles west of Alexandria. After one false start, this raid took place on the night of 19/20 April 1941, and was made by 7 Commando carried in HMS *Glengyle*, covered by a powerful escort, including the anti-aircraft cruiser HMS *Coventry*, three destroyers from the Royal Australian Navy and – to carry craft of Captain Courtney's Folboat Troop to act as a navigation beacon and guide the main force into the port – the submarine HMS *Triumph*.

This raid met with an all-too-familiar series of problems. HMS *Triumph* was detected and attacked en route by Allied aircraft, and was therefore late at the off-loading port. The Folboat was damaged, and therefore unable to land and erect the homing beacon; the leading LCA was damaged and landed late; other LCA compasses were faulty and put the men ashore at the wrong place; and a Commando officer, moving about the beach after the landing, was shot and killed by one of his own men. The force stayed ashore for a short while and managed to destroy four guns before withdrawing, leaving about seventy men behind to be captured. It was not a successful début. One bright spot in an otherwise gloomy picture was the arrival in the 7 Commando ranks of a seventy-one-year-old retired Admiral, Sir Walter Cowan Bt., KCB, DSO, MVO. Admiral Cowan was a spritely gentleman, bored with life on the retired list who, as an old friend of Admiral Keyes, had wangled his way into the Commandos.

Lieutenant Milton takes up the story: 'The first plan for Bardia involved 8 Commando as well as 7, with all three landing ships, but this was called off by bad weather and the raid was replanned for 7 Commando alone, in the

Glengyle. As I remember, we were divided into two groups – a smaller group to enter the harbour, land and attack the town's water supply, while the major part landed west of the town to attack a defence battery and do other odd jobs, blow up road bridges and so on. My job was to take my section into the harbour in the leading LCA, land, ascend a cliff path, then march inland to find and demolish a valve that pumped the town's water supply. This, I was assured, would cut off the water for some time. Incidentally, we were accompanied on this raid by Admiral Sir Walter Cowan, a real fire-eater, about five feet three inches tall. He was a friend of Sir Roger Keyes and, with Evelyn Waugh, was embarked for the landing in my LCA.

'When we arrived off the port and went to boat stations at about 22.00 hrs, it was quite rough and choppy. In those days the first wave climbed into the assault craft in the davits at deck level and were then lowered into the water. For some reason our bow davit lowered quicker than the stern one, and we hit the water bows first, smashed into the side of *Glengyle* and damaged our starboard engine. Therefore, though the supposedly lead craft, we limped ashore slowly on one engine. I could see the shore and worked out where we were, but when we were about a hundred yards from the beach we touched bottom on a sandbar and Admiral Cowan ordered our coxswain, Sub-Lieutenant England, to "lower the door". He complied and Admiral Cowan and Evelyn Waugh dashed out and disappeared under the water. I held my men back until we scraped over the bar and arrived at the real beach.

'We went up the cliff path and towards our objective in complete silence, until I saw figures ahead. These turned out to be a troop commanded by the unit's Second-in-Command, Kenneth Wylie, who were going to blow up a bridge. He told me it was too late to go on to the water-pipe and valves, and to recce some buildings nearby. One

of these was found to be full of gelignite in a very critical
state, sweating and most unhealthy. I had no means of
setting it off, having only short fuses for our pipeline
charges, and besides, if that lot had gone off it would have
removed 7 Commando and most of Bardia to the middle
of the Mediterranean. Lance Corporal Isaacs, who was
with me, was very disappointed when we had to leave it
alone.

'I was detailed by Wylie to act as rearguard and so we
embarked late in our damaged craft and went slowly out
to sea, having an awful struggle to get our LCA off the
beach. Then we met Wylie's boat again. He had seen
signalling onshore, investigated and found two more
LCAs stranded. He had taken many on board but even so,
some fifty or sixty soldiers from the western party had
been left on the beach. Anyway, off they went to the
Glengyle and we slowly followed, limping behind. When
we got to the RV, the *Glengyle* had gone.

'Sub-Lieutenant England and I then had a conference
and we decided that the best thing we could do was to
sail to Tobruk, sixty miles or so to the west, which was
then surrounded by the enemy but held by the 9th
Australian Division. So off we went. On one engine we
made very slow progress and I can't remember much
about the night except that it got very rough, and sleeping
with my head on my haversack, which contained 808
explosive, gave me a peach of a headache.

'At dawn we were not far off the shore and it was still
rough. Sergeant Major Murdoch was very sick and I
offered him some whisky, which reduced him to an abject
state. The morning wore on and then a vessel appeared
on the horizon, flying no flag and guns turned upon us as
she came closer. I asked England what we should do if
she turned out to be Italian, expecting him to say we
would have to surrender, but not a bit of it. He was
signalling with his lamp and said he would carry on
signalling until we got alongside. Then we would board

her, capture her and sail her back to Alexandria – the Nelson spirit!

'Fortunately, she turned out to be British, a boom defence vessel. We eventually sailed into Tobruk harbour, the men went off to be fed and I was told to report to General Morshead commanding the 9th Australian Division. On the dockside I found a truck, driven by a very scruffy Australian soldier, who looked me up and down and said, "I suppose you went to Sandhurst?" I looked him up and down and said, "As a matter of fact, I did. Do you want to make anything of it?" He gave me a half grin, so that was obviously the right reply, which was a good thing as he was much bigger than I was, and we drove up to Div. HQ, getting thoroughly shelled on the way. The HQ was hidden away deep in some tombs, and there I met the General, who also looked me up and down and said, "What you need is a drink." One of his ADCs or Staff Officers went off and returned with half a tumbler of whisky and stood there while I drained it. As I swallowed the last mouthful, he sighed and I said, "What's the matter?" He said, "You have just drunk the last mouthful of whisky in Tobruk."'

Jock Davidson gives another view of the Bardia raid: 'My troop in one LCA went into the harbour to blow up anything of use and a bridge on the coast road from Sollum to Sidi Barrani. We did a good job on the bridge and a fuel store – a good big bang and a lovely blaze. I think the other troops blew up an ammo dump and caught a few German motorcyclists on the hop. On the way out to the ship we saw lights and had to go back in to pick up some chaps who were stranded. The *Glengyle* was already moving off as we came alongside.'

F. E. Freeman, a private in 7 Commando, was in the same LCA. 'We had to leave a number behind as some of the ALCs would not start, so they were unable to get back to the ship. The ship had orders to sail by 02.00 hrs whether the troops were back or not. She was quite large

and the Germans would certainly have caught and
bombed her if she was in range at daybreak. Coming out
from Bardia we had about a hundred men on board, some
hanging on the sides. When we found *Glengyle* she was
already moving, but we were winched up and made it
back to Egypt, where we had a church service for the men
left behind. Some of them made their way to Tobruk and
rejoined us later.'

Back in Egypt, Layforce continued to train while awaiting fresh tasks. 'It may be worth recording,' writes
Lieutenant Ted Galbraith of 8 Commando, 'that during
the time we were based at Mersa Matruh, a number of
officers and guardsmen – including Randolph Churchill –
volunteered for the pioneering of the "aperture" parachute drop. All ranks were most unsuitably attired for
parachute jumping. Strong winds carried many of them
off the drop-zone onto rocky ground, ending up with badly
grazed knees and elbows.' Among the more seriously
injured was Lieutenant David Stirling of 8 Commando,
founder of the SAS.

As the only body of trained troops not fully committed
to one or other of the now-embattled fronts, Layforce was
both denied replacements and steadily bled of trained
men. This practice was encouraged by the fact that here,
as in the UK, the Staff had no real interest in Commando
soldiering and felt, not unreasonably in the circumstances, that such trained soldiers would be more useful
serving in the regiments of the line. So at the end of May
1941 Layforce began to disintegrate. No. 11 (Scottish)
Commando (the C Battalion), was sent to Cyprus, while
the other units were absorbed into the general reserve.
Then on 20 May, having driven the British from the
mainland of Greece, German airborne forces invaded the
island of Crete. The situation soon became serious and
the garrison began to withdraw from their positions
around Heraklion and retreat across the central mountains to Suda Bay, where Nos. 7, 8 and the Middle East

Commando were landed as reinforcements on the night of 26/27 April.

The battle for Crete is a story of great courage against ever-increasing odds. German parachute troops began landing on the north coast on 20 May, and were initially contained, suffering heavy casualties, but they gradually won ground around the airport at Maleme. With this secured, Junkers transport aircraft began to arrive, bringing in reinforcements and artillery, while the defenders were kept under constant air attack, which pounded their positions and the ships bringing reinforcements to their aid. The many naval losses included the destroyer HMS *Kelly*, then commanded by the future Chief of Combined Operations, Lord Louis Mountbatten. Within three days the Germans had landed over 20,000 men at Maleme and the only way to stop more arriving was to recapture the airfield. This was considered a suitable task for Layforce, but the plan was abandoned on 26 May when the British front began to crumble and the Layforce units arrived only to hold the beach-head while the main forces withdrew into it. Being without heavy weapons, this was a task for which the Layforce Commandos were badly equipped.

Private Freeman: 'About the end of May, we sailed for Crete on HMS *Abdiel*, a mine-laying cruiser, and landed at Suda Bay. When we landed the port had already been bombed and was full of sunken ships. Wounded men were being taken off – they said it was hell. We moved out of the port area and dug slit trenches while the Germans dive-bombed and machine-gunned us constantly. They had taken Maleme, though the New Zealand and Australian troops fought very bravely. We had no air support, no planes. We fought a rearguard action while the New Zealanders and Australians withdrew. After a day or so we withdrew, marching for half a day through olive groves. There were burned-out lorries with bodies aboard, and the enemy were around, even behind us. They got on a ridge, probably waiting for us. Nobody seemed to know what was happening, and my mate got a machine-gun burst in the stomach. The officer said, "Make him comfortable," so I gave him a cigarette and put his small pack behind his head.

'We marched across the island to Sphakia, where the evacuation had taken place, and hid in caves, but after a Sunderland flying boat came in and took off some officers, a German patrol found the caves and took me prisoner of war. Their front-line troops were not too bad, but I thought I was the only prisoner taken and felt bad. After walking for about an hour with the Germans, we went over a ridge and there were *thousands* of British, New Zealand and Australian POWs. I tried to escape in Greece but was recaptured and sent in a cattle truck to Germany – sixteen days – and a lot of men died on the journey.

'The man who was shot in the stomach recognized me at the Commando reunion a few years ago. After a lot of beer and saying how I saved his life, he said the Germans were going to shoot him when an English-speaking officer came up and told them to put him with their own wounded.'

Layforce moved inland under heavy air attack and began to dig in while the retreating garrison streamed past towards the beaches. German ground attacks on the Layforce perimeter began soon after dawn on the 28th, with mortar concentrations and dive-bombing, a bombardment followed by infantry attacks, which 7 Commando, assisted by New Zealand infantry and two Matilda tanks, were able to drive off before withdrawing towards the positions of the Middle East Commando.

Then began a leap-frog retreat back across the mountains towards Sphakia. 'An exhausting march, of which the chief features were heat, thirst, hunger and Stukas,' records Major F. C. C. Graham, the Brigade Major. Having taken up a new defensive position, the Brigade IO Captain

Evelyn Waugh (8 Commando) was sent to find the garrison Commander, General Freyberg, who ordered that Layforce, now reduced to around 400 men, should take up defensive positions around the embarkation beaches and cover the garrison withdrawal which was completed, in spite of continual German air and ground attack, on the night of 30/31 May. The Royal Navy had already lost too many ships in the waters around Crete and stated that any troops not brought off that night must be abandoned. Permission was given for Colonel Laycock and some of his staff to embark for Egypt, but most of D Battalion (50 Commando) and much of what was left of the A Battalion (7 Commando) passed into captivity, only about half of those who landed returning to Egypt, although some men got away in an abandoned landing craft. Among these was Jock Davidson.

'On Crete we were supposed to raid Maleme and get in among the German aircraft, but that didn't come off. We dodged the Stukas for about a week, then went back to Sphakia. When we got there, some of us in A Troop and two other troops were unable to get on the *Glengyle*, as it and other boats had to leave long before daylight to avoid the bombers. Captain Savage of 7 Troop told us we were technically prisoners of war, as the senior officers had already gone to meet the Germans and formally surrendered. Our choice was to take to the hills, but as dawn broke Ron Rogers and I saw an LCM and a ship's longboat lying out about 200–300 yards, left by the *Glengyle*. We stripped off and swam out and found we could get one engine going. Just then, Lieutenant Day (Welsh Regiment) swam alongside and came aboard with one of his chaps. We went in to the beach to pick up Bill Smith and about eight or ten of Lieutenant Day's men, and our boys of course. We left quickly as we could hear aircraft becoming active. We landed on a small island, Gaudos, waiting for darkness to avoid detection by German planes. We found a number of political exiles, living a very basic existence, but they killed two of their goats and cooked them for us, for which we paid well, Greek money being of no further use. We also got water from their well. At dusk we set off, towing the rowing boat behind, heading for, hopefully, Tobruk, or if possible, Sollum. Next afternoon the diesel fuel gave out. We rigged a square sail with a tarpaulin and blanket on a long pole, but the LCM was very unwieldy and obviously would take many days to make the landfall of North Africa, even with the then favourable strong wind. It was agreed that Tom Rogers, Bill Smith and I, with Lieutenant Day and two of his men would go in the long rowing boat to make land as soon as possible and get relief help for the LCM. We rigged a rough sail out of groundsheets and set off. The sea had quite a heavy swell and a number were sick. Fortunately, I am one of those very lucky people who have never been sea or airsick. We had one or perhaps two tins of bully and two or three biscuits each, among six or seven of us, and our water bottles. As far as I can recall, we were three days and three nights, with strong wind and heavy sea at night, and then becalmed during the day, when we took turns rowing. During the day it was scorching, with clear blue sky. About 10.00 hrs on the third day we saw on the horizon what appeared to be a long streak. Was this land or just the horizon? We thought we saw flashes and wondered if this was Tobruk or the firing line at Sollum. When on Crete there were several rumours that Tobruk had been relieved; or the Tobruk garrison had broken out and joined up with the main line; or a new front line push had started to relieve Tobruk, etc. Anyway, our main concern was to get help for the chaps left on the LCM with very little food and water.

'Eventually we got ashore, pulled the boat up in case we would have to go back and move along the coast, this being scrubby desert country. After walking for 15 or 20 minutes inland, we saw some dust clouds from vehicles in the distance. A couple of personnel threw caution to the winds and moved up to the area, and there was an Italian lorry group with machine guns mounted on the back. So we really were POWs this time! The LCM made it to North Africa and the men in it returned to the British lines.'

Until well into the Second World War, the French nation was roughly divided into three parts. First, there were the Free French, based in England and commanded by General de Gaulle. Across the Channel the French nation lived reluctantly under German occupation north of the Loire, and in the Unoccupied Zone, or Vichy France, to the south, under Marshal Pétain. Vichy France, a mildly pro-German – or at least anti-British – regime, was at best neutral in the early years of the war. Vichy France also ruled in the overseas territories of France, most notably in Algeria and Syria. Relations between Vichy France and the British had been particularly soured in 1940 when the British Fleet invited the French warships, based at Mers-el-Kebir, to scuttle or surrender before they could be taken over by the Germans. When the French fleet refused to surrender, the British opened fire, sinking many French ships with great loss of life. In 1941, problems again arose in Vichy French Syria when, fearing that the Germans would land there and open a third front or at least obtain the use of the Syrian airfields, the British, urged on by General de Gaulle, invaded from Palestine and Iraq.

On 6 June, the 7th Australian Division, the main force, struck north from Palestine, heading for Damascus and Beirut, while other forces drove west into Syria from Iraq. The advancing Australians soon met with increasing French opposition and were slowed to a halt before the Litani river south of Beirut where the French troops were known to be well dug in. It was decided to dislodge the French from this position by landing No. 11 (Scottish) Commando on three beaches north of the river behind the French lines to seize and hold a crossing over the

Litani until the Australian 25th Infantry Brigade could join them. The Commando landed from HMS *Glengyle* at dawn on 9 June, getting ashore without undue difficulty, but soon running into opposition.

Lieutenant Gerald Bryan of No. 1 Troop tells his story of the Litani operation: 'I raced madly up the beach and threw myself into the cover formed by a sand dune. The men behind me were still scrambling out of the landing craft and dashing across the twenty yards of open beach. Away on the right we could hear the rattle of a machine gun and overhead the whine of the bullets, but they seemed fairly high. I was just beside a dry stream bed and so started to walk along it, at the same time trying to untie the lifebelt attached to my rifle. Colonel Pedder was shouting to us to push on as quickly as possible. Soon the ditch that I was in became too narrow and there was nothing for it but to climb out into the open. The ground was flat with no cover. The machine guns were now firing fairly continuously but were not very worrying.

'When I got out into the open – rather like moorland – I started shouting, "A Section No. 1 Troop," which represented my command. Before long we were in pretty good formation, with myself, batman and tommy gunner in the centre. We came to the main road and saw on the other side a trench showing clearly in the white chalk. It was empty, but behind it were two caves in a little cliff. I fired a rifle shot into the left-hand cave. There were sounds of commotion inside. We stood ready with grenades and tommy guns and shouted to them to come out. Seven sleepy French emerged in pyjamas and vests. We had certainly caught them sleeping. My batman remained with them to hand them over to the Colonel who was coming up behind. It was now quite light, the time being about 04.45 hrs. The rest of the section had pushed on, so I followed, and came on a wire running along the ground. This I cut with a pair of wire cutters.

'I found the section held up and under fire from snipers.

Also, which was more to the point, they had found a 75mm gun. It was about thirty yards away and firing fairly rapidly. We flung some grenades and it stopped. However, we had three casualties, which wasn't so good. A corporal was shot through the wrist and was cursing every Frenchman ever born. As he couldn't use a rifle I gave him my Colt automatic pistol and he carried on. We crawled through some scrub to get closer to the gun. Here we met B Section officer Alastair Coade, and a few men also attacking the gun position, so we joined forces. The gun itself was deserted, the crew being in a slit-trench. We bunged in a few more grenades and then went in ourselves. It was rather bloody. My section was comprised mostly of RA blokes who knew how to handle the gun, and in a few minutes the sergeant had discovered which fuses to use from one of the original gun crew. This gun was the right hand gun of a battery of four, the others being anything from about 100 yards to 300 yards away. They were still firing. Our gun was pointing away from the battery, so we grabbed the tail piece and heaved it right round so that it was pointing towards the nearest gun. The sergeant took over command of the gun, shoved a shell in and sighted over open sights, then fired. The result was amazing. There was one hell of an explosion in the other gun site and the gun was flung up into the air like a toy. We must have hit their ammo dump. No time to waste. The Sergeant traversed onto the next gun, sighted rapidly and fired. There was a pause. Where the devil had the shell gone? Then there was a flash and puff of smoke in the dome of a chapel about half a mile up the hillside. A thick Scottish voice said, "That'll make the buggers pray!" The Sergeant hurriedly lowered the elevation and fired again, this time a bit low. However, the gun crew started to run away and our Bren opened up and did good work. Just then, a runner turned up with orders from the Colonel to report to him with as many men as possible when we had finished off the battery. It did not take long to get a good hit on each of the two remaining guns. The Sergeant then broke off the firing pin of our gun with the butt of a rifle. We had to cross about 300 yards of open ground to reach the Colonel, so we just ran like hell, and although there were a few bullets flying around, I don't think we had a single casualty.

'I arrived at Commando HQ and reported to the Colonel. He explained that he was pushing in some men and wanted our section to support them and pick off snipers. We took up what positions we could but there wasn't much cover. I left the Colonel and went over to a Bren-gun post about fifty yards away but it took me a good ten minutes to get there as I had to crawl the whole way. The French had spotted us and were putting down a lot of small arms fire – very accurate. The whole time bullets spat past my head and sounded very close. It was very unpleasant and hard to think correctly. When I reached the Bren posts, they were stuck. Every time they tried to fire, an MG opened up and they couldn't spot it. Suddenly the B Section officer said he had spotted it and grabbed a rifle, but as he was taking aim he was shot in the chest and went down, coughing blood. Then the Sergeant was shot in the shoulder, from a different direction, which meant that we were being fired on from two fronts. I crawled back to Commando HQ but when I was about ten yards away, I heard someone shout, "The Colonel's hit. Get the medical orderly." I shouted to the Adjutant and he replied that the Colonel was dead and that he was going to withdraw the attack and try his luck elsewhere. So I shouted to my men to make for some scrub about a hundred yards away and started crawling towards it. All the time bullets were fizzing past much too close for comfort and we kept very low. The Sergeant, who had been wounded, decided to run for it, to catch us up, but a machine gun got him and he fell with his face covered with blood.

'As I was crawling I suddenly felt a tremendous bang on the head and knew I had been hit. However, when I opened my eyes I saw that it was in the legs and decided not to die. I dragged myself into a bit of a dip and tried to get fairly comfortable, but every time I moved they opened up on us. I could hear an NCO yelling to me to keep down or I would be killed. I kept down. After a time (when the initial shock had worn off) the pain in my legs became hellish. My right calf was shot off and was bleeding, but I could do nothing about it, and the left leg had gone rigid. By now the sun was well up and it was very hot lying there. I was damned thirsty but could not get a drink as I had to expose myself to get my water bottle, and each time I tried I got about twenty rounds all to myself, so I put up with the thirst and lay there, hoping I would lose consciousness. After about two hours, a lot of fire came down and the next thing was twenty-five French advancing out of the scrub with fixed bayonets. The four men left from my section were captured. I raised my arm and one of the French came over and gave me a nasty look. I was carrying a French automatic pistol that my Sergeant had given me in exchange for my rifle. It had jammed at the first shot but like a fool I had held on to it. Anyway, he just looked at me for a while and away he went and I was left alone. I had one hell of a drink and felt better. About half an hour later my four men were back with a stretcher, under a French guard. Both the Colonel and B Section officer were dead, so they got me onto the stretcher and carried me down to a dressing station, where a British medical orderly gave me a shot of morphia. While we were lying there, a machine gun opened up and the French medical fellows dived into a cave, but the bullets were right above our heads and they were obviously firing over us at something else. Some time later an ambulance turned up, and we were taken to a hospital in Beirut. In the ambulance were two wounded French, two Sergeants from our side, and myself. We remained as prisoners of war in Beirut until the British entered the town six weeks later.' Lieutenant Bryan lost his leg and later left the Commando to work as an explosives expert with the Special Operations Executive (SOE).

The northern, left-flank party, under Captain George More, destroyed transport on the coastal road and occupied high ground around the Kaffa Badr bridge, taking many prisoners before coming under attack from artillery and armoured cars, which pounded the Commando positions until they were first forced back into the hills, and then down to the Litani bank, where they were surrounded by the enemy and forced to surrender.

The central force, commanded by Commanding Officer Lieutenant Colonel Dick Pedder, headed directly for the Kaffa Badr bridge but met increasing resistance from a redoubt guarding the crossing, and was brought to a halt, Lieutenant Colonel Pedder being killed and all his officers wounded. RSM Fraser then took command of the centre force and captured a French barracks. Unfortunately, the southern or right-flank party, commanded by the unit Second-in-Command, Major Geoffrey Keyes, son of the then DCO Admiral Sir Roger Keyes, had landed by mistake on the south side of the river. Keyes soon found a boat and ferried some troops across the river to join the central force, and there, under heavy attack, they managed to hold on while the rest of Keyes' force captured a position on the south side of the river. The French eventually succeeded in blowing up the Kaffa Badr bridge just before the Australians arrived. The Commandos held out north of the river, covering the crossing until a pontoon bridge could be slung across the Litani, and after a night attack by the Australians, the French surrendered, Captain More's captors laying down their arms and surrendering to him. In spite of all the difficulties, No. 11 Commando had done well, but at the cost of a quarter of their strength. Major Keyes took command and had the much depleted unit returned to Cyprus.

Meanwhile 8 Commando, based at Mersa Matruh, was being steadily bled of men needed for the defence of beleaguered Tobruk. Here, in July, much later in the siege, a party of seventy men from 8 Commando carried out a classic little raid on a position called the Two Pimples, a position held by Italians which overlooked the positions of the 18th (Indian) Cavalry. 8 Commando began by patrolling No Man's Land intensely. On the night of 18/19 July, led by Captain Mike Kealy, the Commandos infiltrated through two lines of Italian defences and were in the rear of the enemy when the Indian Cavalry began their diversionary fire from the front. Forming an assault line, the Commandos then swept through the Italian position, firing rifles and tommy guns, grenading trenches. The Italians fought well, refused to surrender, and were mostly killed, the whole fight lasting less than five minutes. The Commandos had just got off Two Pimples when the Italian artillery plastered it with DF tasks. The Commandos returned to their own lines at the cost of one man killed and four wounded.

Layforce now hardly existed as an effective force and in August 1941 it was formally disbanded. Those men, like Lieutenant Milton, who had battalions of their parent units serving in the Middle East, were sent to join them, some from 7 Commando went on to Burma, while many of the rest joined 'L' Detachment of the Special Air Service, a new force established by Lieutenant David Stirling, who had gone out to the Middle East with 8 Commando.

Layforce was unlucky. It had arrived in the Middle East as a complete Commando formation, carried in proper assault ships, but at a time when the military situation was under great stress, and in a constant state of flux. No one at a high level of command had either the time or the inclination to bother with a new-fangled kind of infantry unit, and Layforce found itself caught between two stools, without the orders or craft for a Commando role, and without the transport, artillery or engineer 'tail' necessary for a heavy infantry brigade. It was frittered away on too-little-too-late operations, but when it was given a chance to fight, it fought well.

Winston Churchill was less than pleased when the word reached Whitehall that another Commando force had been wasted. He at once issued a minute to the Chiefs of Staff that the Middle East Commando was to be reformed and commanded not by a committee but by a local Director of Combined Operations – say Laycock – reporting not to the Army Staff but to the Naval Officer commanding in the Mediterranean, Admiral Cunningham. Churchill added one final cutting comment on the fate of Layforce. 'Middle East Command has indeed maltreated and thrown away this valuable force.'

Robert Laycock returned to the Middle East, but in spite of Churchill's orders, the last unit, the 11 (Scottish) Commando, was disbanded on 1 September. The Force was then reconstructed and a 'new' Middle East Commando was formed – probably to keep the Prime Minister quiet – from the following Special Force units: L Detachment SAS, which was designated as 2 Troop; remnants of the Palestinian soldiers who had served in 51 Commando as 4 and 5 Troops; 6 Troop formed from the SBS under Roger Courtney, and 3 Troop formed from all that was left of 11 Commando under Major Geoffrey Keyes. This troop, of sixty men, insisted on calling itself 11 Commando, while the other troops, giving only lip service, if that, to the new 'Middle East Commando', simply went about their own affairs. Then, in November 1941, 11 Commando took on a final and most dramatic task.

During much of 1941 and 1942, the Eighth Army had a propaganda and morale problem. Ever since his arrival in North Africa, the German General Erwin Rommel had exercised a fascination on both the Axis and the Allied armies. It was generally conceded that he was the finest professional general in either, or even any, army; but it went much further than that. In the words of one Australian infantryman, 'We all thought Rommel was a bloody good bloke.'

When Brigadier Desmond Young wrote his biography of Field Marshal Rommel after the war, the British Field Marshal Sir Claude Auchinleck wrote a foreword praising Rommel's 'resilience, resourcefulness and mental agility. I salute him as a soldier and a man, as a brave, able and scrupulous opponent.' This is generous praise, but in 1941 Sir Claude, then Commander-in-Chief, Middle East Forces, found it necessary to issue an order to all his Commanders on the subject of the charismatic Rommel:

TO: ALL COMMANDERS AND CHIEF OF STAFF

FROM: HEADQUARTERS, BTE AND MEF

There exists a real danger that our friend Rommel is becoming a kind of magician or bogey-man to our troops, who are talking far too much about him. He is by no means a superman, although he is undoubtedly very energetic and able. Even if he were a superman, it would still be highly undesirable that our men should credit him with supernatural powers.

I wish you to dispel by all possible means the idea that Rommel represents something more than an ordinary German general. The important thing now is to see to it that we do not always talk of Rommel when we mean the enemy in Libya. We must refer to 'the Germans' or 'the Axis powers' or 'the enemy' and not always keep harping on Rommel.

Please ensure that this order is put into immediate effect, and impress upon all Commanders that, from

a psychological point of view, it is a matter of the
highest importance.

(Signed)   C. J. Auchinleck
GENERAL
COMM-IN-CHIEF, MEF

Trying to impress on the private soldiers of the British
Army that Rommel was after all but a man was one
method of combating his baleful effect. The No. 11
(Scottish) Commando were ordered to try another way.
They were ordered to kill him.

In October 1941, at the outset of General Auchinleck's
counter-offensive – Operation Crusader – against the
Afrika Korps, Rommel was believed to live in a house at
Beda Littoria, near the headquarters of the Italian forces
in Northern Africa, where Rommel also had his headquarters. 11 Commando, now just sixty strong, were
ordered to land from submarines on the coast nearby,
attack the Italian HQ, destroy telephone and telegraph
connections and, above all, kill or capture General
Rommel.

The raid was scheduled for the night of 18/19 November. The force, commanded by Major Keyes and under the
overall direction of the old Layforce Commander, Colonel
Robert Laycock, sailed from Alexandria on 10 November
in the submarines HMS *Torbay* and *Talisman*, arriving
off Beda Littoria on the 14th. That night the force made
contact with an Intelligence Officer, Colonel Haselden.
He had been carried through the enemy lines by the
LRDG to carry out some preliminary reconnaissance, and
gave them details of the HQ at Beda Littoria.

The main Commando force, under Colonel Laycock
and Keyes, came ashore in rubber dinghies. Due to rough
weather only Laycock and seven men got ashore from
HMS *Talisman*, which reduced the size of the raiding
force and necessitated a change of plan. Keyes was ordered

to attack Rommel's house and HQ while the rest, under Haselden and Lieutenant Cook of 11 Commando were to ambush the roads round about, while Laycock remained with a small reserve at the beach, hoping that the balance of his party would come ashore the next night from HMS *Talisman*. Information then arrived from friendly Arabs that Rommel was not at his HQ but living with his staff in a house at Sidi Rafa, near Beda Littoria. So once again the plans were changed. Keyes took seventeen men with him and entered Sidi Rafa just after midnight, slipping past the grain silos and a hotel in torrential rain, up to the two-storey house where Rommel was said to live. All was in darkness.

After deploying his men around the grounds and quietly trying the back door and windows, Keyes, accompanied by Captain Campbell and Sergeant Jack Terry, decided on the direct approach and marched up to the front door, pounding on the panels while Captain Campbell called loudly in German for admission. The door was opened by a sentry whom they tried to overpower but he resisted, shouting warnings until Campbell shot him with his service revolver. This roused the house, the sentries, and the entire vicinity.

Sergeant Terry tommy-gunned two Germans who came rushing down the stairs from the first floor, while the men outside engaged and shot German sentries running towards the house. Meanwhile, Keyes and Campbell began to clear the downstairs rooms with grenades until, flinging open one door, Keyes was hit by a burst of Schmeisser fire from within and fell mortally wounded. His attacker was killed by tommy-gun fire from Sergeant Terry and a grenade from Captain Campbell. They then started to carry Keyes from the house but a bullet hit Campbell in the calf and broke his leg. With firing now coming at the raiders from both inside and outside the house, Captain Campbell ordered Sergeant Terry to round up the party and withdraw, though not before lobbing all their spare grenades into the house. Geoffrey Keyes died shortly after this and Campbell ordered Sergeant Terry to leave him and withdraw. Sergeant Terry and seventeen of the raiders managed to rejoin Laycock at the beach, and on the evening of the 18th, HMS *Torbay* surfaced offshore and closed the beach, but the weather was still too rough to permit a withdrawal. HMS *Torbay* withdrew and dived, returning again on the following night, but yet again heavy surf prevented the force withdrawing. The party was finally located by the Germans on the afternoon of the following day and soon came under fire. Later in the day, Laycock ordered the survivors to break out in small parties. Laycock, accompanied by Sergeant Terry, finally got back to the British lines on Christmas Eve after walking for forty-one days across the desert. The rest of the raiding force were either captured, or murdered by the Arabs.

Later Sergeant Terry, DCM, recalled: 'I'd joined up in the Royal Artillery in 1938, and went to the Middle East in No. 1 Troop of 11 Commando, with Lieutenant Bryan and Lieutenant Coade, who was killed as soon as we got ashore at the Litani river. On the Rommel raid, I was on HMS *Torbay*. It was only about twenty miles as the crow flies from the beach to Beda Littoria, but as it walks, up and down the jebel, over the escarpment, it took until the third night.

'Rommel was just one of the jobs we had to do. We had an Italian HQ to attack and a radio post by a crossroads as well. We went in after midnight, very dark. Keyes posted men about the place, and we went in through the back. I wouldn't have known Rommel from anyone else, but the idea was that we would kidnap him. But if someone fires at you, you kill them, don't you.

'Captain Campbell was taken prisoner and lost his leg. We took about a day to march back to the rendezvous. I nearly fell over the escarpment and lost my tommy-gun. At the beach, the sea was still very rough, although the sub floated in a dinghy with food, but we couldn't get off, and then the Italians found us. They'd been tracking us. We could see Germans up on the escarpment and had two choices, to head for the alternative beach or go inland to find an LRDG patrol. Lieutenant Pryor tried a recce and got wounded, so we left the wounded in a cave and broke out in small parties. I went with Colonel Laycock and we tried the alternative beach, but we heard German voices, so they must have found maps or been told of our intentions. Then we tried the LRDG patrol position, but in the end we walked back. It took forty-one days and I went down to nine stone. We lived on berries and some-times a goat. We had Italian money and could tap-up any lone Arabs for assistance, but not groups; they didn't trust each other. When we got back to our lines the Town Mayor at Cyrene gave us some rations and passed us on to General Ritchie's HQ, and we were flown back to Cairo. No one else got away, they were all killed or taken prisoner.'

Sergeant Terry joined David Stirling's SAS and served with them in the desert and Italy, before returning to the UK for D-Day, after which he fought in France with the Maquis near Dijon.

And Rommel? Rommel was not at Sidi Rafa, nor at Beda Littoria. Rommel's HQ was actually much deeper in the desert, close to the front line, but when the raiders splashed ashore on the 15th, Rommel was not even in Africa. He was in Rome with his wife, celebrating his birthday (which fell on 16 November) and consulting with his Italian allies on future strategy.

Like so many of their best-laid plans, this last Layforce operation was unsuccessful. It was still a classic and gallant little raid, and for his part in leading it, Lieutenant Colonel Geoffrey Keyes was awarded a posthumous Vic-toria Cross, the first VC awarded to a Commando soldier.

The Great Raids, 1942

'Follow . . . Follow . . .
Leave your England, as dead midnight still
Guarded by grandsires, babes and old women,
Either past or not arrived at pith and puissance.
For who is he, whose chin is but enrich'd
With one appearing hair, that will not follow
These culled and choice drawn cavaliers to France?'

HENRY V: ACT III

The Second World War began to swing in favour of the
Allies in 1942, and this year ushered in many changes for
the Commando forces. The first indication of a major
change came when the first of the Royal Marines Commandos, the 'A' Commando, was formed in February
1942. This unit, which later became No. 40 (Royal
Marine) Commando, an all-volunteer unit, formed at Deal
under Lieutenant Colonel Picton-Phillips, formerly of the
Inter-Service Training and Development Centre.

In the same month, it was decided to centralize all
basic Commando training at the Commando Basic Training Centre which was opened at Achnacarry House, the
home of the Cameron of Lochiel, seven miles from Spean
Bridge in the Highlands of Scotland. Up to this time each
Commando had recruited and trained its own men, but
with the rapid expansion of Combined Operations under
Mountbatten, the age of 'private armies' was clearly
coming to an end. Brigadier Charles Haydon appointed
Major Charles Vaughan of The Buffs, and 4 Commando,

as Commandant of Achnacarry, and from then on all potential recruits, and even entire units, would have to pass the Achnacarry Commando course before receiving the green beret. They would then pass on to the Holding Operational Commando at Wrexham for further specialist training before being posted to their units. Achnacarry training made such an impression on those who endured it, that one very experienced Commando soldier told me he was not a real Commando because he had not been to Achnacarry. The only exceptions to this Achnacarry training were volunteers for the Commando units in the Middle East and Italy, who were often forced to recruit and train their own men, as before, although they too received periodic drafts from the Holding Operational Commando.

Achnacarry training was tough, physically and mentally. It was not sufficient simply to finish an assault course or a training exercise. It was necessary to complete the task smiling and ready for more. All exercises used live ammunition and recruits were told that provided no more than ten per cent of the recruits were injured on any course, no questions were asked. These lessons were driven home by a series of (empty) graves by the main gate, each one marked with a notice giving the cause of demise. 'He forgot to wet his toggle-rope'. 'He ran in front of the Bren', and so on. The Commando course consisted of plenty of PT, rock climbing, cross-country runs and exercises, landing rehearsals from boats on the loch, night schemes, cliff climbing and abseiling – this last down the walls of the castle – unarmed combat, knife-fighting, weapon training, and forced marches. All ex-Achnacarry Commandos remember the relentless pace and pressure of the training, the drenching Highland weather, and the hard slog of the speed marches. These required the troops to march and run long distances carrying full equipment with platoon weapons, covering a mile in ten minutes, whatever the terrain. The pass-out speed march covered fifteen miles, down to Spean Bridge and back, and the final event of the course was 'milling', an all-in boxing contest supervised by the CO, where the troops, paired into roughly equal sizes, set about each other with bare fists for a full minute. Then a gong was struck and another pair leaped into action. Much of the training was on a 'me-and-my-pal' basis, where two men teamed up to work together, digging trenches, building a bivvy, soldiering together. Whatever one man did, his pal did as well.

Ted Kelly of 2 Commando recalls his experiences at Achnacarry. 'I was 18 years old when the word "Commando" came to the public notice. I recall seeing a news item at the cinema about a raid on Norway and, in the style of those days, the narrator greatly dramatized the situation. To me this was very exciting. In the cinema we were used to identifying with the hero. When Colonel Newman visited our unit on a recruiting drive, I could hardly believe my good fortune. Volunteers were interviewed much like job applicants. My then job as a regimental physical training instructor was a suitable qualification. It was a condition of acceptance that any non-commissioned rank held must be surrendered. Everyone started equal. The surrender of one stripe seemed a small price to pay for the opportunity to join this venture.

'Before long I was on my way by train to Scotland. It was winter and the temperature fell dramatically as the train moved northwards. I had never been to Scotland before and the stark beauty of the scenery kept my mind off the implications of what I had done. Arrival at Achnacarry Castle suggested that this was going to be a more comfortable billet than I had thought, until I was directed to one of the Nissen huts which was to be the only refuge for the next six weeks. I have forgotten the name of the Sergeant-Instructor who was to take charge of our intake, but I can see him now. A veteran soldier, he was a tough, wiry Scot, as hard as nails but totally lacking any suggestion of brutality or malice. We were to be his lads for the duration of the course and we were not expected to fail.

'The course was hard, unremitting toil. We learned a great deal – weapons, mountain climbing, unarmed combat, using boats, fieldcraft, demolitions. We sweated over assault courses designed to break the spirit, with leaps off twenty-feet-high structures, precarious rope bridges and death-slides. We learned to speed march. This fiendish activity was to become a permanent feature of our lives. Marching in fighting kit, with rifle, no breaking into a double permitted. It was heel-first marching all the way at a pace which covered seven miles in the hour. As an erstwhile body-building enthusiast, I knew the name of the muscle which suffered most from this maltreat-ment – the *tibialis anticus*, the muscle at the front of the shin bone. It began to hurt within the first mile and got progressively worse. By the fifth mile it was the teeth and jaw which vied for attention from prolonged clenching to hold on.

'The learned skills and powers of endurance were periodically tested on night exercises, which included wallowing in mud, crossing rivers and scaling heights in mock battles in which the "enemy" used live ammu-nition to keep our heads down. I can remember returning to the hut, muddy, soaking wet, and taking off my boots to find my socks soaked with blood where blisters had burst and the skin had rubbed raw. No one had any difficulty in sleeping when given the opportunity – we were stretched to the limit.

'The important thing was never to give in. The disgrace of being sent back to your regiment as unsuitable was not to be contemplated. And so somehow, from somewhere within yourself, you found another breath, another ounce of effort and will. Only later did you come to understand that that was what it was all about anyway. As far as I can remember, I was at Achnacarry when the St Nazaire raid took place. I can certainly remember the pride I felt to learn that I was to join No. 2 – Charlie Newman's own Commando.'

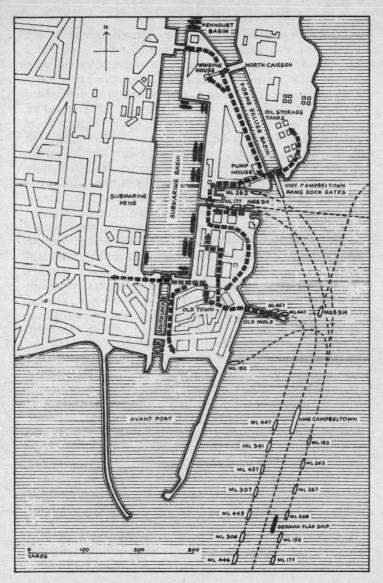

St Nazaire

Achnacarry training aimed to do more than simply toughen up the men for action. It aimed to prove that a fit, trained Commando soldier could always do more if he had the right attitude. 'It's all in the heart and the mind' is one famous Commando saying. Vaughan also expected a high standard of drill and turnout, and however exhausted, squads returning to camp had to tighten their rifle slings and march into barracks at the slope, perhaps for a little arms drill or a practice shoot on the range. Those who passed through Achnacarry felt that they could do anything. Those who fell by the wayside were RTU'd. That was, and remained, the only Commando punishment. If you weren't good enough, you had to go.

In early 1942, the Commando organization was roughly as follows: Under Combined Operations HQ came the Special Service Brigade HQ, which had under command the Army Commando units 1–12, plus the Royal Marines Commando units, as they were raised successively from 1942 until 1944. In addition, there was the Basic Training Centre at Achnacarry and the Holding Operational Commando at Wrexham. Meanwhile, the raiding went on, beginning on the night of 27/28 March 1942, with the greatest raid of all on St Nazaire.

The port of St Nazaire lies in Brittany, six miles upstream from the mouth of the River Loire. The great feature of St Nazaire was a huge dry dock, the Forme Ecluse (or Forme Louis Joubert), then the largest dry dock in Europe and the only one capable of receiving and repairing large capital ships of up to 85,000 tons.

This fact was of particular interest to the Royal Navy, for since 1939 they had been obliged to keep valuable units of the fleet based at Scapa Flow to check any foray into the North Atlantic by German battleships, and in particular the mighty *Tirpitz*. In 1941, the *Bismarck*, sister ship of the *Tirpitz*, had broken out into the Atlantic, ravaged merchant convoys and sunk HMS *Hood* before she was finally sunk by the Royal Navy while heading for St Nazaire. Without the security of St Nazaire and the possibility of repairs there, the likelihood that *Tirpitz* could repeat the voyage of *Bismarck* was considerably smaller. Bombing this vast dock into ruin was not considered possible, not least because any attempt to do so would certainly cause heavy casualties among the French population. It was therefore decided to mount a raid to destroy the dock and the harbour installations, and the task was entrusted to Lieutenant Colonel A. C. Newman of No. 2 Commando.

The plan was to destroy the Forme Ecluse and its pumping station, and do as much damage as possible to the nearby U-boat pens. The main force for this task would consist of 100 men from No. 2 Commando, who would attack gun positions and provide the covering parties for demolition patrols drawn from other Commando units, 1, 3, 4, 5, 9 and 12. Since they would certainly resist large amounts of explosives, the gates of the Forme Ecluse would first be rammed by a destroyer, the bows of which had been packed with explosives. This destroyer would carry part of the landing force, while the rest would be conveyed to the attack in motor launches. Lieutenant Colonel Newman would command the landing parties, while the naval contingent would be led by Commander R. E. D. (Red) Ryder.

St Nazaire is a large town. In 1942 it had a population of some 50,000 people, plus a large German garrison, naval and military who, apart from manning the ships and submarines, manned searchlights and coastal batteries and maintained tight security in and around the port. Attacking St Nazaire would stir up a hornet's nest and it was conceded that while, with surprise and luck, Newman's force might get in and do the job, their chances of getting out again were slim. 'There's certainly a VC in it,' said one senior officer. In the end there were five.

Newman and Ryder's plan called for a bold approach,

straight up the river with no firing at all unless detected, at least until the destroyer rammed the gates of the Forme Ecluse. Then the landing parties would swarm ashore from the destroyer and the motor launches to carry out their tasks, and with luck withdraw to the Old Mole, which lay slightly downstream from the Forme Ecluse, re-embark and head out to sea. The plan was approved by the Chiefs of Staff on 3 March, and the raid, codenamed Chariot, took place twenty-three days later.

While the demolition teams and Newman's protection parties began to train – though without knowing for what – the search began for a suitable and expendable destroyer. The ship finally selected was one of the fifty old American destroyers sent to Britain in exchange for bases in Bermuda, the four-stacker USS *Buchanan*, re-named HMS *Campbeltown*. HMS *Campbeltown*, under the command of Lieutenant Commander S. H. Beattie, RN, was first stripped of as much equipment as possible to reduce her draught for the shallows and the sandbars of the Loire, which must be crossed before she could ram the gates. In addition, the four funnels were reduced to two, both of them cut and altered to resemble those of the German *Möwe*-class frigates which were known to be based at St Nazaire. This weight loss was balanced by the tons of explosives packed into her forecastle, and by special steel bulwarks welded along the decks to give some protection to the Commandos lying there as HMS *Campbeltown* surged in to ram the dock gates.

Corporal Arthur Woodiwiss from No. 2 Commando was detailed to sail in *Campbeltown*: 'Every man chosen for Operation Chariot was given a general briefing and then each man was briefed on his particular task. Each man had to produce his own plan to achieve that objective, and then all the plans, from the privates' to the colonels' were discussed and criticized. We had plans of the dock area which we had to draw and re-draw and a wonderful scale model, which we could study in different light to help us identify our targets. As an assault group commander I rehearsed street fighting to the gun positions I had to demolish. Our full dress rehearsal at Devonport was an absolute disaster and the Home Guard were delighted.'

These models were drawn from air photographs and from detailed plans of the Forme Ecluse which the British happened to possess. Demolition teams also visited the King George V Dock at Southampton, which had gates similar to those at St Nazaire. Some idea of the task may be drawn from the gates' dimensions 167 feet long, 54 feet high, 35 feet thick. The destruction of the gates depended on *Campbeltown* ramming them fair and square. The port facilities were the task of the Commandos.

The demolition teams were training hard for this, preparing charges to destroy pumping machines, visiting docks and learning how to run about at night while carrying rucksacks filled with 90lbs of high explosive, while the protection parties from 2 Commando were busy rehearsing their street-fighting role. The entire force assembled at Falmouth on an ominous date, Friday 13 March 1942.

The first task facing the naval forces and the Commando units was a formidable one. The ships had to sail up six miles of heavily defended shallow estuary before even reaching the dock gates. The tides had to be just right, timings were crucial. Though the rehearsal, Exercise Vivid, went disastrously wrong, for some reason everyone regarded this as most encouraging. Then air photographs revealed a new snag. In addition to a flak-ship moored permanently near the dock, four German *Möwe*-class frigates had recently berthed at St Nazaire, close to the landing area, and showed no signs of leaving, while the bombing programme, designed to distract the enemy's attention while the landing force sailed up the river, was suffering from contradictory orders even at the planning stage. On the one hand the RAF were asked to rain bombs on St Nazaire and keep defenders looking skywards during the approach up-river, while on the other hand they were told to avoid civilian casualties at all costs. Colonel Newman rightly predicted that the bombing plan would not work and would indeed alert the Germans to the fact that something else was in progress.

Escorted by two Hunt-class destroyers, the force, totalling 630 soldiers and sailors, sailed on the afternoon of 26 March, embarked on HMS *Campbeltown* and sixteen Fairmile 'B'-class launches supplied by Coastal Forces. These were wooden launches with a maximum speed of sixteen knots, armed with machine guns and newly-fitted Oerlikon cannon, and in addition to their normal fuel-tanks, carried long-range 500-gallon petrol tanks strapped on the upper deck. These launches were therefore very vulnerable to enemy fire. The last two craft in this little fleet were MGB 314 and MTB 74. This last craft carried delayed action torpedoes which would be fired at the dock gates if HMS *Campbeltown* was sunk on the way in.

Sailing in three columns, the force first headed west into the Atlantic in the hope that any German aircraft or submarine which saw them would report them as an anti-submarine force on a sweep. A German submarine was sighted on the second day and promptly engaged by the destroyer HMS *Tynedale*, and hove-to at 20.00 hrs that night (Friday 27th) while Lieutenant Colonel Newman transferred onto MGB 314. At 22.00 hrs the convoy sighted the beacon of the submarine HMS *Sturgeon*, which was marking the entrance to the Loire, and with *Campbeltown* in the van, the force entered the river. The Commando soldiers now preparing to land numbered 277 men.

The RAF bombing raid began about 23.30 hrs, but the strange behaviour of the aircraft soon alerted the defenders. This was no rain of incendiaries and high explosives, for the bombers simply cruised about over the estuary, dropping one bomb at a time. After half an hour, Captain Mecke, commanding the anti-aircraft defences around St Nazaire, sent a warning order round his area command posts: 'Conduct of enemy aircraft inexplicable . . . suspicion of parachute landing.'

On receipt of this signal, one of his subordinates turned his attention to the estuary and saw a force of small ships forging upstream. This was reported back to the Harbour Commander, who confirmed that no convoys were expected, and at 01.20 hrs on Saturday 28 March, Captain Mecke sent another signal. 'Beware landing.' When that signal reached the defending batteries, HMS *Campbeltown* was within two miles of the dock gates and working up to full speed.

The first sign of enemy action came when a big searchlight snapped on, combing the river to illuminate HMS *Campbeltown* and her supporting craft. Two German signal stations at once challenged, and one or two gun positions fired warning shots. On Ryder's instructions *Campbeltown* signalled back, slowly, in German, using codes discovered on the Vaagso raid: 'Proceeding up harbour in accordance with orders.' The firing stopped and the searchlight snapped out. The force had gained a precious few minutes.

There was another brief exchange of signals, Ryder firing a red recognition flare, which was unfortunately not the German shade. Then, at 01.27 hrs, with the dock gates now in plain sight, HMS *Campbeltown* hauled down the German colours, hoisted her battle ensigns and every gun in the force opened up on the defending batteries. 'For about five minutes the sight was staggering,' wrote Ryder, 'both sides loosing off with everything they had. The air was full of tracer, flying horizontally and at close range.'

HMS *Campbeltown* struck the dock gates at 01.34 hrs ramming her bow deep into the *caisson*. The troops swarmed ashore, joining the five assault and demolition parties now landing at various points around the harbour.

Corporal Woodiwiss, MM, remembers the run-in: 'When the German searchlight picked up HMS *Campbeltown* it first shone on the German flag at the masthead, which confused them. When the Germans finally engaged us, the Swastika was pulled down and quickly cut into pieces for souvenirs. Captain Roy had a piece sewn on his beret for the rest of the war. When we hit, the *Campbeltown* rode much higher up the *caisson* than we expected and my assault ladder did not reach the dock, so I had to jump down to attack the nearest gun position which was raking us with enfilade fire. Pausing to get my bearings, I saw a potato-masher grenade flying towards me. I fly-kicked this, luckily hitting the handle. It went back where it had come from and sorted out the group who had hurled it. After bitter hand-to-hand fighting, I eliminated the sentries, forced my way into the gun position and sprayed the crew with my tommy gun. I then wrapped my prepared explosive charge around the breech and destroyed the gun. I returned to my assault group and we attacked all the remaining gun positions, then placed our incendiary charges into the oil storage tanks. Lieutenant Roderick ordered our withdrawal. I covered this so that our survivors could re-cross to the ship and regroup. I then climbed the lashed ladder up to the bows and pulled this up to prevent pursuit. A burst of fire indicated a counter-attack. A large group of Germans were forming to cross the open area we had just left. Lying abandoned on deck behind the shrapnel shields were Brens with 100-round magazines which had been fired as we sailed up the Loire. I set up three of these behind the shields and began firing each in turn to prevent their advance and forced them to withdraw.

'The fuses in the six tons of Ammonal below had already been activated, the fire below decks still smouldered and I was lying feet above the charge. I thought discretion was the better part of valour, so decided to leave. I dropped all the spare weapons I could find into the Loire, collected all the tommy magazines I could carry, rejoined my section and shared out the ammo. We assaulted across the dock bridge and advanced into the town. Lieutenant Hopwood joined me and we formed a rearguard, breaking down back doors and climbing over garden walls, when things went very quiet. "Hoppy", hanging by his fingers, first whispered to me to be quiet, then he dropped several feet onto a huge sheet of corrugated iron, covered with broken glass; then all hell broke loose. When we ran out of ammunition and had gathered a large number of seriously wounded, we were forced to surrender. After my capture, the surname "Woodiwiss" aroused suspicions, for their first question was, "Are you a Bolshevik?" I replied, "No, I am an evangelical atheist." The German then asked why the English were so very optimistic about winning the war when they had already lost. I told him no one back home was optimistic but all were confident. The interrogation was terminated when a tremendous explosion heralded *Campbeltown*'s completion of our task, taking about one hundred and fifty Germans with it.'

Fighting in small groups scattered across the dockyard, the Commandos soon took it over, but just two tales must serve to illustrate the many actions of that wild night. Lieutenant Stuart Chant of 5 Commando had the task of destroying the impeller pumps which filled and emptied the Forme Ecluse basin. Wounded on the way in, Chant and his demolition team of four sergeants came ashore from HMS *Campbeltown* following the soldiers of Roy's 5 Troop across the dock, only to find the entrance to the pumping room barred by a steel door. This they blew open, and with Chant leading, they slipped inside. The pump house closely resembled the one they had already inspected at the King George V Docks at Southampton. Leaving Sergeant Chamberlain, who had also been wounded, to guard the door, Chant led the others down the steel stairs to the pumping station forty feet below. Here they quickly placed their charges, amounting to one hundred and fifty pounds of explosive, pulled the igniters and ran back up the stairs to the open dock, the wounded Chant now limping heavily. Out in the dockyard bullets and tracer fire were lancing in every direction, the scene lit up by gun flashes and the many blazing launches out on the river. Chant's party ran for cover behind a wall and two minutes later their charges exploded. Chant then made his way to Lieutenant Colonel Newman's command post at the Old Mole and reported his task complete. One after another the commanders of the other teams came in, having destroyed the winding houses and other dock installations. The time was now about 02.30 hrs and right for the force to withdraw, but out on the river another battle was raging between the motor launches and the shore defences, the crews using tommy-guns and Brens as well as their 20mm Oerlikon cannon against German artillery, cannon and heavy machine guns. The river battle at St Nazaire has been compared to the Charge of the Light Brigade, for the MLs swept in to land their troops with every man at his post and every gun firing, while the short defences on both sides of the river and from rooftop positions in the docks poured in their fire at close range, the whole scene lit by tracer, searchlights and blazing craft. The losses among the landing craft were terrible.

ML 192 was hit by shellfire off the Old Mole, and caught fire, running in well ablaze in an attempt to put her troops ashore, though only five men made it. ML 262 forged up the river, pinned by searchlights and under heavy fire from 20mm cannon. It slid past ML 177 and tied up to *Campbeltown*, to put her survivors ashore, while Stoker Ball provided covering fire with his Lewis gun. ML 268 was set ablaze by tracer and blew up, with only one man surviving. MLs were now drifting all across the river in pools of blazing petrol, being steadily shot to pieces, but those which could manoeuvre still came in to land, taking it in turns to pour fire into a German flakship which was raking the dockside with her cannon. The five German frigates were at sea that night. In all, seven MLs with many of their Commandos and crew were lost on the way in, while others were destroyed during the landing or withdrawal. The story of one of these, ML 306, must stand here for all the rest.

ML 306, commanded by Lieutenant I. B. Henderson, RNVR, withdrew from St Nazaire about 02.30 hrs with twenty-eight men on board, fourteen of them troops from No. 1 and No. 2 Commandos. One of these was Sergeant Tom Durrant of No. 1 Commando. At 05.30 hrs, when they were well out to sea and looking forward to the return to England, ML 306 ran into the five ships of the German 5th Flotilla, now returning to port. Two of the German ships passed them by in the dark, but the third, the *Jaguar*, detected the darkened ML, illuminated it with a searchlight and then opened fire. The ML crew replied with Lewis and tommy-guns, the two ships engaging each other at close range, circling about with the German ship trying to ram, and bringing her heavy machine guns to bear until twenty of the British were dead or wounded. The *Jaguar* then stood off and asked Lieutenant Henderson to surrender. Henderson declined. Sergeant Durrant, who was manning a twin Lewis gun, had already been wounded three times, but called for more ammunition as the German ship moved back in, the Captain still calling on the British to surrender. Durrant, now hanging in the harness of the Lewis guns, immediately opened fire, putting one burst right across the chart table in the German wheel-house. The *Jaguar* withdrew until her main guns could bear and open fire again, killing Lieutenant Henderson and riddling Durrant with bullets. It was now broad daylight and when the *Jaguar* once again came alongside the sinking launch, Lieutenant Swayne of No. 1 Commando, the only unwounded man on board, stood up among the dead and called out apologetically, 'I'm afraid we can't go on.'

ML 306 had fought the *Jaguar* for nearly an hour. The ML sank as the surviving British were helped on board the *Jaguar*, where they were well looked after. 'You had no chance,' said Kapitan Paul of the *Jaguar* to Lieutenant Swayne. 'But I must compliment you on a brave fight.' Paul also asked for the name of the Army Sergeant who had manned the twin Lewis.

Some weeks later, an officer from *Jaguar* called on Colonel Newman in the prison camp at Rennes, told him about the battle with ML 306, and in particular about the fight put up by Sergeant Durrant, describing it in some detail, 'as you may wish to recommend this man for a high decoration'. Sergeant Durrant was later awarded a posthumous VC, the first ever awarded to a soldier for a naval action, and on the recommendation of an enemy officer. Four other VCs were awarded, to Lieutenant Commander Beattie of HMS *Campbeltown*; to Lieutenant Colonel Newman of 2 Commando; to Lieutenant Commander Ryder; and posthumously to Able Seaman Savage of the RNVR. Only 270 of the 630 soldiers and sailors who took part returned to England. Twenty-five per cent of the participants were killed. Of the 19 ships which entered the river, only 4 returned to England, but the Forme Ecluse was not repaired until some years after the end of the war.

Five months later, Combined Operations mounted yet another major raid on the coast of France, when the 2nd Canadian Division, supported by three Commandos, Nos. 3, 4 and the recently formed Royal Marines 'A' Commando (later to become 40 [Royal Marine] Commando) assaulted the port of Dieppe.

The Dieppe Raid has been a centre of controversy ever since. Opinions still vary on whether it was a total disaster or a necessary prelude to D-Day. It was certainly

a chapter of accidents, and the main objective, to seize
Dieppe, then land tanks and proceed inland for a number
of miles before withdrawing, was never achieved. The
Canadians were checked on the beaches and suffered
terrible casualties, and although this book is concerned
only with Army Commando operations, the fate of the
Canadians and the Royal Marines must be briefly
described. The Royal Regiment of Canada, landing at
Puits, was machine-gunned on the beach and cut to pieces
in five minutes, losing all its officers and 496 of the 528
men who got ashore. On the other flank, at Pourville, the
South Saskatchewan Regiment got ashore and crossed the
river, where their CO won the VC for gallantry under fire.
The battalion was then forced to withdraw, linking with
the follow-up battalion from the Queen's Own Cameron
Highlanders of Canada. These two battalions then fought
on until they ran out of ammunition, the South Saskatch-
ewans losing 19 officers and 498 men, the Queen's Own
Highlanders 24 officers and 322 men. The main assault,
across the esplanade at Dieppe, never got off the beaches,
and the Essex Scottish, the Royal Hamilton Light Infantry
and the Fusiliers Mount Royal, three fine battalions, plus
the tanks of the Calgary Regiment were decimated in the
attempt. The Royal Marine Commando was sent in at
around 08.30 hrs and met a murderous fire as soon as they
emerged from the smoke, 200 yards offshore. Colonel
Picton-Phillips was killed standing up in his LCM to
wave the follow-up craft away, and so saved his Commando from total destruction, but their casualties were
severe.

The original plan for the Dieppe Raid, Operation Rutter,
called for parachute landings on the coast east and west
of Dieppe to knock out heavy coastal defence batteries
that would otherwise deal severely with the ships and
landing craft. This plan was dropped and when the second
plan, Operation Jubilee, was drawn up, parachute troops
were replaced by Commandos. No. 3 Commando were to

land at Petit Berneval and attack the battery at Belleville, while No. 4 would land west of Dieppe at Varengeville and deal with a six-gun battery in the woods behind the cliffs. Matters began to go wrong when No. 3 Commando, sailing to the attack in Eurekas and escorted by steam gunboat SGB 5, ran into a German coastal convoy at 04.00 hrs on 19 August 1942. Charles Hustwick of SS Brigade Signals was attached to 3 Commando for the Dieppe operation, and takes up the story.

'The night before the raid we were shown a model of the area to be attacked. It all looked rather grim with high cliffs and minefields to negotiate before getting to the objective. Everything was to be done at speed with a great deal of running involved. We boarded Eureka landing craft with fast engines and additional fuel drums strapped to their top-sides. I don't think there were more than twelve chaps in our boat. The passage through the minefield, which had been cleared by the Navy, was uneventful until nearing the French coast, when a star-shell went up and we were bathed in glorious light. My number two, Signalman H. H. Lewis, MM, and I were having a pee over the side when this happened. Then all hell let loose. We had been caught by armed trawlers belonging to the enemy who were escorting a convoy into Dieppe. We had not been told of our destination until we had been an hour at sea. Before setting sail we had been told that we had to get ashore at all costs. However, our flotilla was now dispersed over a wide area, smoke and the smell of cordite was everywhere, dawn was breaking and a heavy curtain of fire was coming from the shore where the enemy had been alerted. We were sitting ducks. After some argument between the Adjutant who was in our boat and the coxswain, we made our way back to the steam gunboat which was supposed to be protecting us. What a grim spectacle she was, full of holes, like a colander. The bridge had been destroyed, the steering gone and only one gun was still firing. We were hoisted

Cross-Channel Raids

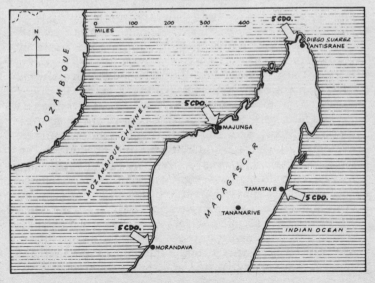

Madagascar

aboard and the Adjutant and the CO of 3 Commando, Lieutenant Colonel Durnford Slater, got into our landing craft to try and find the HQ ship, HMS *Calpe*, with the overall Commander aboard.

'We had no means of letting the powers-that-be know what a disaster our effort had been. There was no wireless communication as the radio on board the gunboat had been destroyed, and with no steering the gunboat was now going round in circles. We were eventually taken on board an RAF rescue launch and after picking up a fighter pilot from the water, arrived back at Newhaven around 13.30 hrs. I don't really know what the survival figures of 3 Commando were, but at breakfast the following morning there were treble helpings for all. One man's name that comes to mind was the RSM of 3 Commando, Beasley, who was taken prisoner and later killed in a railway accident while on his way home after he had been released at the end of the war – a really first-class chap. I can see him now, inspecting us prior to moving off for Dieppe. He had a kit-bag beside him with all kinds of army gear inside, inspecting everyone to ensure they had clean underwear, ID discs, new uniform, and boots in good order.'

Six of the surviving No. 3 Commando landing craft put their men ashore on Yellow Beach 1 near Berneval, where they were promptly engaged by the enemy. Pressing on, they headed for the enemy batteries until they could go no further. Only one man of those who landed returned to England. Over one hundred were killed, wounded or taken prisoner. The final 3 Commando craft, carrying Major Peter Young and eighteen men from 6 Troop, landed without opposition on Yellow Beach 2 near Belleville, and climbed the cliff up a gully choked with wire. At the top they set off to attack the battery, which they could now hear firing on the offshore shipping. They managed to keep the battery under fire until all their ammunition was exhausted and they had to withdraw,

rejoining their patiently waiting craft just after 08.00 hrs,
Peter Young being dragged behind the Eureka on a lifeline
until they were out of rifle range. Peter Young, who won
three MCs and the DSO during the Second World War,
still regards Dieppe as one of his best exploits. 'I took
eighteen men ashore, did the job we had to do, and
brought eighteen men back.'

No. 4 Commando, under Lieutenant Colonel The Lord
Lovat, MC, landed from LCAs having been carried to
within ten miles of France in the landing ship HMS
Prince Albert. Lovat split his force into two parts, of
which the first, under Major Derek Mills-Roberts, would
land on Orange 1 beach below the Pointe d'Ailly light-
house, climb a narrow gully and advance to the edge of
Varengeville to give covering fire, while the second,
Group 2, commanded by Lovat himself, landing a little
further south on Orange 2, would assault the battery
which lay about one kilometre inland from the beach.
This battery, codenamed Hess, consisted of six 15-cm
guns, protected by infantry machine guns and barbed
wire. Mills-Roberts' party landed exactly on time, just
before dawn, only to be startled by the tremendous noise
as the battery opened fire on the offshore shipping, long
before Lovat's assault party could be in position. Mills-
Roberts received a report from the beach that the Dieppe
convoys were already in sight of the shore and apparently
within range of the battery. Mills-Roberts decided to
attack the battery at once and, forcing their way up a
wire-choked gully, his party made their way to a point
overlooking the battery and began to engage the enemy
with rifle, Brens and mortar fire. Half an hour later Lovat's
Group 2 began to mount their attack from the right flank.
The garrison, now alert and aggressive, opened a heavy
fire on the assault wave, killing two officers and wounding several men. The fighting on the battery perimeter
now became hand to hand, Captain Pat Porteous killing
one German with his pistol before leading a bayonet

charge through the wire to the guns. Porteous stayed at the head of his men as they shot and bayoneted their way through the position, finally falling into one of the gun-pits, shot through the thighs. For his gallantry that day, Captain Porteous received the Victoria Cross. 4 Commando captured and destroyed the Varengeville battery at the cost of twelve men killed, twenty wounded and thirteen missing. 4 Commando then withdrew to the beaches without further loss and returned to England.

The Dieppe Raid was a success for the Commando element in the landing force, and apart from No. 3 and No. 4, introduced other units to the war – the American Rangers, who supplied fifty men, and others from a curious Commando unit, No. 10 (Inter-Allied) Commando, which had been formed in June 1942 under Lieutenant Colonel Dudley Lister, once of No. 7 Commando. 10 (I-A) was made up of troops from many nations, French, Dutch, Yugoslav, Polish, Norwegian, even Germans, these last after enlisting under assumed British names. The Commando never fought as a complete unit, but sent the troops to serve with other Commando units in theatres where their linguistic skills would prove as useful as their fighting abilities.

Dr Anthony Hodges served with No. 10 (I-A) from the early days. 'I had already spent a year and a half at Lochailort, and was promoted to Lieutenant Colonel to train Army Medical Officers in living off the land under very hard conditions. I gave them hell. However, I couldn't see myself as a Lieutenant Colonel sitting at a desk, so I asked for demotion to Captain and transfer to a Commando; everyone thought I was a complete idiot. I was then sent to Harlech, North Wales, to No. 10 Commando, which was then being formed – an amazing unit. My first friend there was a Jewish Hungarian Count, very good looking, very well built, who had escaped to England from the Gestapo. Other nationalities then began to arrive in small batches to be thoroughly interrogated by our IO, and medically examined by me. Some of the German Jews who arrived to join X Troop were in very bad condition, many having endured some time in concentration camps. They confided very little to me and all took British surnames. Among the French was Philippe Keiffer, who led the French troops of 4 Commando later. The Norwegians were a magnificent lot and I often went up to Shetland where they frequently arrived after sailing or rowing from Norway – many were fishermen. The Dutch were also remarkably good Commandos.'

Between the great cross-Channel operations at St Nazaire and Dieppe, No. 5 Commando sailed to the Indian Ocean with a large expeditionary force, charged with occupying yet another Vichy French outpost, the island of Madagascar. Early in 1942 Japanese submarines started to operate in the Indian Ocean, and this led directly to the British invasion. Brigadier Eric Holt, then a Major in 5 Commando, carries on the story: 'It was considered by the Chiefs of Staff in London that the French Vichy Government might well offer the Japanese the excellent facilities of the magnificent harbour at Diego Suarez at the North East tip of the island of Madagascar. From such a base these submarines would seriously imperil the Allied convoys sailing up from the Cape to East Africa and more particularly to India, so it was decided that the British would mount the first ever amphibious operation, sailing from the UK to seize the harbour 9,000 miles away, and thus deny it to the Japanese. The principal assault formation was 29 Infantry Brigade with 5 Commando under command for the operation. The Commander was Brigadier Festing, who was later to become Chief of the General Staff in the rank of Field Marshal.

'The Force Commander, Admiral Syfret, flew his flag in the ageing battleship HMS *Ramilles*, and the air support for the land force was provided by naval aircraft in the fleet carriers *Illustrious* and *Indomitable*. There were also

119

two cruisers, nine destroyers and six minesweepers in the naval force. The assault force was embarked in the civilian transports, the SS *Winchester Castle*, *Keren* and *Karanja*, with assault landing craft replacing the lifeboats in the davits. The plan was that 29 Brigade would land on 5 May on two selected beaches on the north-west coast of the island and then move across country to seize Diego Suarez from the south-west.

'Overlooking and dominating these beaches were two French artillery batteries and their neutralization was the task of 5 Commando, who made a silent landing before dawn, before the Brigade hit the beaches a few miles south. This landing went according to plan; complete surprise was achieved and the two batteries surrendered after a brief fight during which the Commando suffered only light casualties but took over 300 prisoners of war.'

Geoff Riley recalls his part in the Madagascar campaign. 'On 23 March No. 5 Commando sailed from Glasgow in the *Winchester Castle* in one of the largest military convoys to leave Britain by that stage of the war. We totalled 365 men, part of a force which included the 29th Independent Brigade and the 13th Brigade. The convoy consisted of more than fifty Royal Navy ships and on reaching the Indian Ocean, the total force by then included three battleships, three aircraft carriers, frigates, destroyers and corvettes. We carried French Intelligence Officers on board and guessed our destination was a Vichy-administered colony. Our briefing eventually explained the absolute necessity of stopping the Japanese from taking the island of Madagascar, as it was known they had their eyes on Diego Suarez, the third largest natural harbour in the world. Had they taken it, there would have been no El Alamein as we could not have supported the Eighth Army in North Africa or the 14th Army in Burma, and South Africa would have been under threat.

'At dawn on 5 May, we landed at Courrier Bay on the

north-west coast of Madagascar, some eleven miles from Diego Suarez. In ALCs, we were mine-swept down a channel by corvettes. There was no opposition. We caught them completely unawares because of a triumph of seamanship by the Royal Navy and Merchant Navy who penetrated coral reefs believed impassable to a force this size. Above us on cliffs fifty feet high was a battery of six-inch guns. We climbed the cliffs and caught the Vichy gunners by surprise. They were asleep! There were French Officers, NCOs and Malagasy and Senegalese troops, who were herded together and guarded. At first light the Vichy counter-attack began. On our flank, forty colonial troops with two NCOs charged up the hill towards us. We carried out a bayonet charge and the NCOs were killed. They gave up and threw down their weapons, our casualties being light.

'Captain "Chips" Heron went forward to take the surrender of a separate party of battery observers on the hill nearby. As they came forward to surrender, some grenades were lobbed over from their rear, wounding Captain Heron and others. They did not get the chance to surrender again. In sweltering heat, loaded like pack mules, we marched against a hot wind across the eighteen-mile isthmus to Cap Diego, loaded heavily with ammo and grenades. There was a fracas with a troop of Foreign Legionnaires. We shot them before they surrendered. There were fifty wounded. We carried out mopping up operations against colonial troops, while the two Brigades took the capital of Antisrane with heavy casualties. Actually it was a manoeuvre by fifty Royal Marines which saved the day. They came off HMS *Ramilles* in Courrier Bay and boarded the destroyer HMS *Anthony*, which then entered the harbour at 22.00 hrs in pitch darkness under fire from every gun which could be brought to bear on her. She ran alongside the wharf with the Royal Marines tumbling over the side and rushing ashore. Their orders were to attack everything except the barracks and magazine, which were strongly held, but in half an hour they were in possession of both of them. They had accomplished everything with one casualty. They prevented much street fighting and damage to the town. The official report quotes: "These fifty Royal Marines created a disturbance in the town out of all proportion to their numbers."

'We then sailed to Mombasa to rehearse the next show, which was leaping off destroyers as they came in at thirty knots along the quayside. We then set out to take Majunga, the largest port on the west coast of Madagascar. The plan was to land right in the docks, but the operation went wrong. The landing craft broke down and instead of landing before dawn, we had to go in during broad daylight. They opened up on us on a small frontage with four machine guns. We had good cover from the Royal Navy, keeping our casualties down. We didn't need scaling ladders – we went up that quayside like scuttling rats! I could see our chaps going down like ninepins out of the corner of my eye. We had street fighting, dealing with snipers from windows, and our first objective was the PO, to cut communications with Tananarive, the capital. The second objective was the Residency, the capture of the Governor and raising of the Union Jack.

'We took both targets and it was here that I had my first close-hand bloody encounter. We had swept into the courtyard and I took up a position at the bottom of the balustrade; my chum Matt Bolton was opposite, against the other wall. A few yards to my left was the rusting hulk of a car. I chatted to Matt and turned my head to spot a rifle barrel coming into view, followed by a fez from behind the car. As the man stood straight up, dodging to the right, I fired from the hip, killing him. Our Captain, Geoff Rees-Jones, ran in seconds afterwards, took a quick look, and said, "Dead as a doornail – well done, Riley," but at the time I felt quite horrible.

'French casualties were heavy. We re-embarked back to

Diego Suarez, and transferred to destroyers, HMS *Arrow*, *Active* and *Blackmore*. Escorted by HMS *Warspite*, the carrier *Illustrious*, three cruisers and fourteen destroyers, we sailed for Tamatave, the largest port on the east coast. The plan was to arrive at dawn, the Navy would form a semi-circle half a mile from the port docks, and *Warspite* and *Illustrious* would be ten miles out. We sent in an envoy under a white flag to demand unconditional surrender. If he was refused or fired on, there was to be a fifty five-minute bombardment by the destroyers and *Warspite's* 15 inch guns. *Illustrious* would send in Seafires and Swordfishes. After this, our destroyers would ram the boom at thirty knots, pull hard against the quay, and we would leap off.

'The envoy went in, then signalled he was being fired on. Immediately there was a salvo from HMS *Birmingham*, the signal for the bombardment. This lasted three minutes, during which time 2,000 shells made contact. White flags went up everywhere. Our destroyers steamed in with the boom opened for us by the subdued French. We started the advance on Tananarive while the KARs advanced from Majunga. The Rifles got there first. We then chased the remnants of the French southwards, which is another story. In October an armistice was signed. The whole island surrendered with the French troops signing up for de Gaulle. We embarked for home, arriving in December.

'Other memories? Well, during the first week of the Madagascar campaign we had to move on and capture one of two forts guarding part of the peninsula. These were situated fairly high up the slopes, which led down to the sea. Way down, just lying offshore, was our covering destroyer, 1942 Hunt-class HMS *Blackmore*. Suddenly we came under fire and ended up pinned down amid a clump of rocks. The CO came crashing down among us to find out what was happening, sized up the situation, looked around and saw me with semaphore flags sticking out of my small pack. "Right, Riley," he said, "run off to the end of this concrete runway and send this message to the *Blackmore*: DAVI (our codename) MOVING ON FORT, PLEASE WATCH." I duly departed with one of the chaps to cover me as we were under fire all the way. Then, perched at the end of the runway, making a lovely target, I duly sent off the message, receiving the usual recognition light from the destroyer. I was quite certain I was going to be knocked off. The ship was so far down, it looked about two inches in length. When it was all over and we had reached the Fort, Captain Geoff Rees-Jones, our Troop OC, got me to use the telephone there to try and make the French Commander of Diego Suarez surrender. The voice which answered was one of our chaps, who had beaten us to it! This was only one of dozens of actions during the six-month campaign, and as I spoke French, I was involved in commandeering vehicles, which included a train, when I had to go up front on the tender and atually drive it.'

Major Holt continues his story: 'The Commando was then ordered to march at speed to seize the northern side of Diego Suarez harbour, while 29 Brigade, supported by an independent squadron of tanks, advanced towards the town of Antisrane at the southern side of the harbour. The Brigade was held up during the afternoon of 5 May and the morning of 6 May, largely by a substantial anti-tank ditch, which was not evident from the air photographs. The French resistance at this point was subsequently overcome and the advance to Antisrane continued. Meanwhile the Force Commander ordered the destroyer HMS *Anthony*, with a Royal Marine detachment of fifty aboard to sail north, sneak into the main harbour from the east under cover of darkness and land the Marines on the quayside at Antisrane. This bold action was planned to coincide with the final and successful assault of the Brigade from the west. By this time 5

Commando was widely deployed along the north side of the harbour.'

Fred Musson was there: 'That evening all hell was let loose. A Japanese two-man submarine had entered the harbour, fired a torpedo into the stern of a tanker, which went down but the bows were still above water. The HMS *Ramilles* was hit in the bows, but remained afloat. Destroyers using depth charges damaged the submarine which was then beached on the north side of the harbour. The two Japanese crew took flight, making for the northern tip of the island. A party of 2 Troop, 5 Commando, under the command of Captain Fox, gave chase and caught up with them. The two Japanese were fired on and were both killed. Captain Fox had one trophy, a shot-up Japanese pistol.'

Corporal Wall remembers this incident. 'I was part of a section guarding a battery of nineteenth-century naval guns, located on the west side of the harbour to protect the narrow harbour mouth. That evening there were some terrific explosions from the direction of the anchored shipping in the harbour. The next morning I was out taking pot-shots with a French Army rifle, when I saw two natives running towards me. It was pure Saunders-of-the-River stuff, as one of the natives carried in his outstretched arm a long cleft stick, at the top of which was a large envelope addressed to the "Honorable Capitaine d'Artillerie". None of us could read the French writing of the enclosed letter, but with the few words we did know and the miming of the two natives, we gathered that two Nippon were in their village dressed in aviator clothing. Our small Section was all for abandoning the useless cannon and joining after these two Japanese. However, wiser counsel prevailed and a radio message was sent to Commando HQ telling them of the event. We were told to stay put. All that day and the next wreckage was being washed up on the beach just below the battery. On 1 June, a Commando patrol walked into our camp

THE RAIDERS

carrying the clothing from the two Japanese who had been
shot after refusing to surrender. They had apparently put
up a fierce defence, using their hand-guns. We learned
from the patrol that a Japanese midget submarine had
penetrated the harbour and sunk the tanker *British Loyalty* and holed the HMS *Ramilles*. Later we learned that
two midget submarines had been launched from the I-16
and I-20, sea-going submarines. The midget submarine,
from which the dead submariners had escaped, was
beached near the harbour mouth and it was assumed that
the crew were making for a rendezvous prior to being
picked up. I never knew what happened to the second
submarine.'

Major Holt again: 'Several days later the Commando
alone took part in the assault of the ports of Majunga on
the west coast and Tamatave on the east side. The street
fighting at Majunga lasted all morning, until the French
capitulated. For the assault on Tamatave the Commando
was embarked in four destroyers, and on arrival the
French were invited to surrender but declined to do so.
The destroyers bombarded the town for fifteen minutes
or so, and then each destroyer in turn steamed quickly to
an isolated quay where the Commando troops stormed
ashore.'

Fred Musson continues: 'Majunga, on the Mozambique
Channel side of the island, was our first objective. 2
Troop were taken by Eurekas ("R" boats) up the River
Ikopa to cut off any Vichy forces retreating from Majunga.
As we travelled up the river the tide began to go out and
we began to run aground on sandbanks. The river was full
of crocodiles, so before we could get into the water to
lighten the craft and push them off the sandbanks, hand-
grenades were thrown into the river to keep the crocodiles
at bay. Eventually we reached our destination, but there
were no retreating French. We learned later the main
force of the Commando had overcome all opposition with
some fierce machine gun fire.'

Major Holt: 'After spasmodic street fighting the garrison of Majunga surrendered. The formal surrender of the Government at the capital city of Tananarive took place a few days later. However, this operation was not completed until several determined groups of French soldiers in the area of Antisrane, to the south of the capital, had been overcome. The second-in-command of the Commando, with some sixty officers and soldiers, many of whom were mounted on locally procured horses, moved south, and after a series of dawn ambushes and fighting patrols, this detachment rounded up the French soldiers. There was no further resistance to the British occupation, and shortly afterwards, No. 5 re-embarked and sailed back to the UK.'

Although St Nazaire, Dieppe and Madagascar were the three major Commando operations before the Anglo-Americans invaded North Africa in November in Operation Torch, raiding activity on a smaller scale continued all the time. Although the Small Scale Raiding Force falls somewhat outside the limits of this book, some of their exploits can hardly, in fairness, be omitted. Lord Mountbatten proposed the formation of the SSRF to the Chiefs of Staff in February 1942, in the form of a fifty-man force, based on two large motor launches. This force came into being a month later, partly under the command of SOE, although Mountbatten had operational control. Also known as 62 Commando or STS 62, the SSRF had a strong contingent from No. 12 Commando. The Small Scale Raiding Force mounted many operations across the Channel, using a fast and famous motor torpedo boat, MTB 344, known to her admirers as *The Little Pisser*.

Corporal Percy Cotter remembers several operations with No. 12 Commando and the Small Scale Raiding Force. 'We spent some time in the Shetlands operating small scale raids in motor torpedo boats handled by the Norwegian Navy. The main purpose of these raids appeared to be to land and observe movement of German vessels in such places as Flora, and during our observation period the MTBs would hunt out enemy shipping and lay mines. Many years later, in 1985, when visiting Amsterdam, I met some Norwegians in the bar of the Kraznapolski Hotel. It turned out that one of the party had been a skipper on these same MTBs and remembered his trips with the Commandos. We had a long and interesting evening.

'At this time I also had the good fortune to be with a small party from No. 12 who were on detachment to STS 62 at Anderson Manor in Dorset. This was the Small Scale Raiding Force, and while with them I took part in a raid on the French-occupied territory, near Cherbourg. Our target was a radar station, and the object was to uplift defending enemy troops to establish the quality of the men on coastal defence, and also destroy the station. Captain Rooney was in charge, but we were also fortunate in having the assistance of the highly experienced Major Appleyard. The force moved to Churston Hall in South Devon and we sailed in a very small Motor Torpedo Boat No. 344 from Dartmouth. Nine of us including Sammy Brodison, Ellis Howells (killed later in an operation in Italy), Sergeant Bruce Ogden Smith (an Instructor at the STS), Lance Corporal Joe Barry and Jim Connor, were shoehorned, for want of a better description, into a small equipment store in the bow of the vessel, with Major Gus Appleyard and Captain Rooney sharing the comfort of the bridge with the skipper and others of the crew. There was no lighting in our accommodation, and we had one bucket to use in case of seasickness or as a toilet. Around midnight the hatch entrance was partly opened and a shaft of torchlight lit the interior of our habitat. From behind the glare Major Appleyard informed of difficulty in locating the island of Alderney, a vital navigation checkpoint, without which we would be unable to make the correct landing for the target area. As always, the

Navy rose to the occasion and about twenty minutes later we were called out on deck to help lower a small dory for our final progress to the shore. The view as we moved into our position on deck was really beautiful. We were in a wide bay with the shore some 400 yards on our beam, and we could then see the high ground rising some 100 feet from the shore to the target. In silence we climbed down into the dory with eight of us paddling, Captain Rooney navigating and one man standing by to drop a kedge anchor when we were about 100 yards from our point of landing. The purpose of the anchor was to give us the means, after disembarkation, to leave one man in the craft, who then pulled the craft some 80–100 yards offshore and so avoided possible detection by a prowling shore patrol. On this occasion, our boat guard was to spend a lonely four hours awaiting our return.

'Once on the shore, we scrambled up the cliff as quietly as possible, although there were some grunts and curses, the latter aimed at the needles of some undergrowth. As I was carrying a Bren gun with a considerable number of loaded magazines, I was more than pleased to receive from Ellis Howells, a few timely thumps around the rear to assist me in the climb. On the top of the cliff our first job, having orientated ourselves with the target, was for one person to shin up nearby telephone poles and cut the communication between the radar station and a nearby village. We had been informed by intelligence that our target was undefended but patrolled regularly by troops stationed in the village. In addition to our normal arms, i.e., rifle and bayonet, we had fighting knives, also a Sten gun with an odd attachment which was supposed to act as a silencer (we had little faith in this weapon). Captain Rooney had armed himself with a bow and arrow in case our information on the target was not correct. The force, myself excepted, now made a cautious approach towards the target and I settled down to cover them in the event of a cycle patrol coming round from the village.

'After about half an hour I heard a slight noise from behind me and as I whipped round, a hoarse whisper, which in the silence of the early morning sounded like a roar, said "Cotter, it's me. Don't shoot." I recognized the voice and by now the bulky figure of Captain Rooney. The skipper explained that the target, far from being undefended, was surrounded by the usual German triple Dannert wire fence, behind which two enemy guards kept a watch, and at intervals one remained in a position opposite where our men lay under cover, while the other man made a patrol round the camp. An undisclosed entry was not on.

'Having reminded me to keep a sharp lookout for any activity from the village, Captain Rooney then made his way slowly back to the rest of the force. After some time, the silence was suddenly shattered by a tremendous explosion. As we had noticed a German sign at the top of the cliff reading "Achtung Minen" I thought one of the boys had trodden on a mine. Almost immediately, however, I heard the sound of automatics firing and voices, in German saying, "nicht schiessen", followed by more firing. Apparently, on the return of Captain Rooney, our party first thought of trying to eliminate one sentry with either the silent Sten gun or an arrow while the second man was on his patrol round the station grounds. But this was dismissed because of the difficulty in trying to line up the target. In addition to the weapons carried, Captain Rooney had taken along a two-pound plastic explosive grenade which was activated like a Mills grenade, by the removal of a cap. As the grenade was thrown a tape unwound and withdrew the safety pin, thereby allowing the grenade to explode on contact. Captain Rooney decided to use the grenade when the two sentries were together having their periodic discussion. The grenade was thrown over the defensive wire and fell between the sentries, who were blasted before they realized what had happened.

'At this point Ellis Howells threw himself over the triple Dannert wire fence to make a platform for the rest of our force to enter the area of the radar station. German soldiers then appeared from what seemed to be a guardhouse and were engaged by our force. After a short period it became obvious that the radar station had sufficient men to defeat the object of the exercise, and with the prospect of reinforcements coming to hand very quickly from the village, it was decided to withdraw. As the firing continued, I heard men approaching and was relieved to hear the Irish brogue of Sammy Brodison, identifying the party now coming into sight. After a quick check, a speedy descent was made to the shoreline, where we were all more than pleased to find the dory ready and waiting. Firing was still continuing from the direction of the radar station as we paddled with great zeal towards the approaching MTB, home and safety, but alas, empty-handed.

'Later, in June 1943, I was attached to a Small Scale Force, again under Captain Rooney, No. 4 Parachute Troop, who were made up in the main of men from B Troop No. 12 Commando. Shortly after I arrived they took part in a small operation, taking off from Stoney Cross and parachuting on to the cliff top near Abbeville. The only others I can recall by name who took part in this raid were Jim Connor and Private Sims. The purpose of the operation was again to take prisoners for the object of identifying the type of troops manning that section of the German defences, and the force would consist of a ten-man stick. Pre-planning envisaged the force splitting on arrival, with Captain Rooney and seven men looking for the prisoners, while Jim Connor and another man would look after the escape arrangements from the cliff to the shore line, where they would be uplifted by a small boat and conveyed to an MTB for return to the UK. The idea was for Connor to lower the other man down the cliff, as it was the task of the latter to contact the MTB and, by a blue light, signify the position of the proposed uplift via the small boat to be dispatched by the MTB for this part of the operation. Simple in practice. In the event the stick landed safely and the split-up duly took place.

'Connor's partner had agreed that when he reached the cliff bottom he would signal to Connor, who would then throw down the remainder of the rope for his partner to collect and subsequently return to the UK. The reason for this action was to leave no trace of their visit and so deny the enemy knowledge of how the removal of some of their defenders had been accomplished. Incidentally, the same rule applied to the parachutes. But because these were made of silk, and the men preferred their ladies in silk, they decided to bring back these valuable pieces of equipment themselves. Connor had a further task, namely to prepare a rope he had taken on this operation for use by the rest of the force as well as himself in their escape to the cliff base. This necessitated using a mallet to knock a piton (both items taken with him) into the ground a safe distance from the cliff edge. A clever system had been devised, whereby the main rope and a thin secondary line could be attached to the piton in such a manner that the last man down could release both ropes from the piton, pull them down, and both could then be brought back, leaving nothing for the enemy to connect with a raid.

'Now back to the raid, the cliff top part in particular. Connor, with his back to the sea, paid out the rope attached to the other man, who proceeded on his way down. The arrangement was that two tugs on the rope would serve as a signal that he was safely on the ground. All went well for about two-thirds of the way, when the rope became entangled in some growth on the cliff face. The man on the rope gave a couple of tugs to free himself and Connor, reading this to be the signal that the man was on the ground, threw the balance of the rope down the cliff, thereby expediting the descent of his colleague with sufficient force to render him unconscious. At the appointed time the MTB arrived offshore, but of course received no acknowledgement of its signal. Fortunately the vessel remained on watch and subsequently the main force arrived back at the cliff top and the men commenced the abseil to the cliff base.

'A search was made for the contact, amid some apprehension concerning possible shore patrols, when one of the party stumbled over the inert figure of the man they were looking for. The MTB was successfully contacted and immediately released the small craft to uplift the force. Due to tidal conditions this craft was driven well away from the position of the men, who had to trail along the sand for about a mile as dawn approached, only to find the craft upside down with a tired sailor trying to make it seaworthy. The ladies had to go without their silk as the men had to dump the chutes and bury them in the sand. All duly returned safely and the injured man recovered. When the Commando forces were organizing for D-Day, No. 4 Parachute Troop was disbanded and we were posted to 6 Commando which had recently returned from North Africa.'

Other Commando units also mounted raids during 1942, some successful, others total failures. On the night of 21/22 April Lord Lovat took troops from No. 4 Commando and some Canadian troops ashore at Hardelot in the Pas de Calais, but ran out of time before engaging the enemy. In the same month a force drawn from No. 1 and No. 6 Commandos attempted to land at the mouth of the River Adour, close to the Basque city of Bayonne. Charles Hustwick, still with Brigade Signals, was on this operation.

'After fourteen days at sea in ships disguised as Spanish merchantmen, the operation was called off when we were actually in the landing craft, with the shore in sight. Apparently, there was a sand bar across the mouth of the river and the surf was too rough for comfort. We in the

Army were keen to get ashore, but when afloat the Navy were in charge. I was in a support landing craft (LCS) fitted with two heavy machine guns, our destination a bridge two miles upstream to stop enemy troops – there were said to be ten thousand in the area – from crossing during the action. This was the stuff the Commandos were raised for, but it was not to be.'

During 1942, the major losses at St Nazaire, Dieppe and elsewhere meant that the Commando units needed a steady stream of replacements. All of these passed through Achnacarry and then on to the Holding Operational Commando at Wrexham for draft to units. In August 1942 the Commandos received a remarkable infusion of strength when policemen were allowed to volunteer for military duty, a fact recorded in many of the unit histories, which recall the policemen as outstanding recruits.

Frederick Palmer, late of 5 Commando, was one of the first volunteers. 'I was a policeman serving with the Durham County Constabulary. It was not until August 1942 that I was relieved after making the usual request to the Chief Constable. I was one of ninety policemen from all over the country who reported to Achnacarry, and I reported a day early! That one day gave me the chance to watch the others arrive on 15 October; policemen from Glasgow, Bristol, Surrey, Sussex, all over. They turned out to be the finest bunch of pals it was possible to meet, and we still keep in touch.

'After a few weeks' basic training, we started our Commando training – speed marches, PT, assault courses, death slides. The total course lasted seventeen weeks under the cream of Drill Sergeant-Majors from the Irish Guards, Paddy Rooney. I think we had one day without rain in the seventeen weeks we were there. Having gained our green berets, we were posted to various Commandos. I, along with about a dozen others, went to No. 5, which had just returned from Madagascar, and eventually embarked with them for the Far East, where I was wounded twice – but that was okay.'

Dudley Cooper, later of 2 Commando, was then in the Manchester City Police: 'At the end of July 1942 I found myself getting off a train at a God-forsaken place in the Scottish Highlands known as Spean Bridge. We went in trucks to Achnacarry, which was the last time I travelled in transport until after we passed out on our Commando course; during that interval fifty per cent of our travel was at the run. We were taught to keep going under the hardest conditions. You relied on your mates, they relied on you, and the reliance was total. There was danger even in everyday training, with two per cent deaths and ten per cent injuries allowed without enquiries. One of my squad was drowned crossing a river in full kit; one man was accidentally shot dead, and two injured by bullets from a Bren during a landing practice. I had to put my fingers in the bullet holes in our canvas boat. The training was hard, but never boring, and a lot of it on the me-and-my-pal principle. After the course, I went with several others to join No. 2 Commando at Ayr, and sailed with them for Sicily and Italy.'

The ever-mounting number of Commando raids was clearly causing considerable vexation to the enemy, and these continued into the autumn, notably when No. 2 Commando attacked a Norwegian power station in November. A month earlier, on the night of 3/4 October, a more effective raid, Operation Basalt, by the Small Scale Raiding Force and some men of 12 Commando on the island of Sark, had some far-reaching effects. A number of distinguished Commando officers took part in this raid: Captain Ogden-Smith, later to recce the Normandy invasion beaches with the Combined Operations Pilotage Party (COPP); Captains Pinkney, Appleyard and Dudgeon; and the fighting Dane, Anders Lassen, who was to win a posthumous VC at Lake Comacchio in 1944. This small force broke into the Dixcart Hotel, then a German command post, and took five prisoners, tying their hands and leading them to the beach. On the way the five attempted to escape, and four were shot down. The discovery of their bodies, hands tied, gave Hitler the excuse to issue the infamous 'Commando Order'.

When this order was distributed throughout the Wehrmacht, General Jodl, the overall commander, added a note: 'This order is intended for senior commanders only and is *on no account* to fall into the hands of the enemy.' Even so, news of the 'Commando Order' soon became known to the Commandos, although it made no difference to their operations, which continued with mounting ferocity.

The 'Commando Order' was invoked to shoot the Royal Marines taken prisoner after Operation Frankton, the canoe raid on Bordeaux, and from October 1942 until the end of the war, many Commando and SAS soldiers were executed under its provisions. Captain Graham Hayes of the SSRF, captured on an SSRF raid in September 1942, managed to escape to Spain, only to be arrested there, handed back to the Germans and shot in July 1943. Two other soldiers captured on this operation, Sergeant Williams and Private Leonard, were shot the day after they surrendered. The SSRF suffered heavy casualties, almost all the founder officers, Captain Peter Pinkney, Gus March Phillips, Anders Lassen and others, failing to survive the war.

The Fuhrer.   TOP SECRET
No. 003830/42

Fuhrer HQ. 18.10.42
12 Copies
12th Copy

1. For some time now our enemies are using methods in their prosecution of the war which are outside the agreements of the Geneva Convention. Especially brutal and vicious are the members of the so-called Commandos, which have been recruited, as has been ascertained to a certain extent, even from released criminals in enemy countries. Captured orders show that they have not only been instructed to tie up prisoners, but also to kill them should they become a burden to them. At last orders have been found in which the killing of prisoners is demanded.

2. For this reason it was announced in an appendix to the Wehrmacht report from the 1.10.42 that Germany will in future use the same methods against these sabotage groups of the British, i.e., they will be ruthlessly exterminated wherever German troops may find them.

3. I therefore order: That from now on all enemy troops which are met by German troops while on so-called Commando raids, even if they are soldiers in uniform, to be destroyed to the last man, either in battle or while fleeing. It doesn't matter whether they are landed by ship, plane or parachute. Even if they want to surrender no pardon is to be given on principle. A detailed report of any such surrender is to be made at the AKW for publication in the Wehrmacht report.

4. Should single members of such Commandos either as agents or saboteurs reach the Wehrmacht, e.g., through the police of the occupied countries, they are to be handed over to the SD without delay.

5. They are not to be kept even temporarily in military custody or POW camps.

This order does not affect the treatment of enemy soldiers taken prisoner during normal battle actions (major attack, major seaborne or airborne landings). It also does not affect prisoners taken at sea or flyers who saved themselves by parachute and were taken prisoner.

I shall have all Commanders and officers who do not comply with this order court-martialled.

(Signed): A. Hitler

6

Torch and Tunisia, 1942

'Tell the Constable,
"We are but warriors for the working day,
Our gayness and our gilt are all besmirch'd
With rainy marching in the painful field,
But, by the Mass, our hearts are in the trim!"'

HENRY V: ACT IV

Operation Torch, the Allied landing on the west and north coasts of Africa in November 1942 designed to sandwich the German forces between the British Eighth and First Armies, was originally envisaged as a purely American affair. The Vichy Government were still hostile to the British but it was hoped that if an American force came ashore on their territory, the Vichy French resistance to the landings would be, at worst, slight. Therefore two of the landings, at Casablanca and Oran, were made by American forces only, convoyed directly from the USA. The third landing, at Algiers, was made by a mixed force of British and American troops. Apart from British Commandos, the force included American Rangers, the US equivalent of the Commandos, some of whom had participated in the Dieppe Raid. Many Ranger units had trained at Achnacarry. The British Algiers force was composed of two British Commando units, No. 1, commanded by Lieutenant Colonel Tom Trevor, and No. 6, commanded by Lieutenant Colonel I. F. McAlpine, who embarked for this operation from Belfast. They began to go ashore at Algiers early on the morning of 8 November.

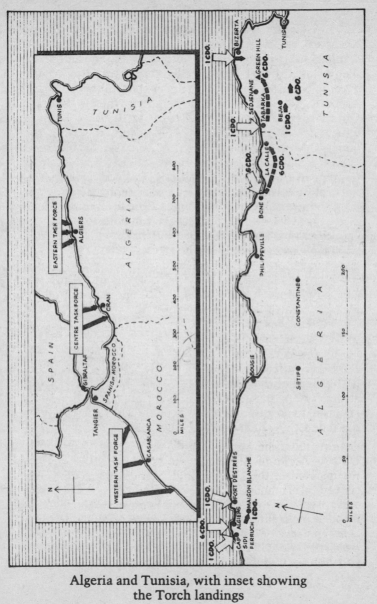

Algeria and Tunisia, with inset showing
the Torch landings

No. 6 Commando sailed as a complete unit on the transport vessel *Awatea* but No. 1 Commando was divided into two parts for Operation Torch; one half under Lieutenant Colonel Trevor sailed on the SS *Otranto*, the other in the USS *Leedstown*, under the Colonel's cousin, Major K. R. S. Trevor. Henry Brown, then a Warrant Officer, remembers the *Leedstown* well. 'As a Warrant Officer I was allowed, with RSM Cann, to eat in the Officers' Mess. On our first entrance, we took our seats opposite a number of American officers, ranked from Captain to Colonel. Although a fairly good sailor, I was not feeling all that brilliant at the time as the ship was rolling quite a bit, but I thought I could manage bacon and eggs. However, I hadn't got far before a Colonel opposite asked me to pass him the molasses. I wondered what he wanted it for, since he too was having bacon and eggs, but he promptly spooned out the syrup and poured it over his bacon. Need I say more! I was up on my feet and moving much quicker than I had entered, to find the most convenient spot on the deck-rail.'

CSM Edmans of No. 1 Commando also recalls the move. 'We arrived at Larne in pouring rain and were given tea by the WVS before embarking. I went on the *Leedstown*. We sailed after some days and when we got to our destination we boarded our LCAs and went ashore, with shells coming over our heads. Later on, when they were shelling the fort, we were too near and got hit by our own naval gunfire, which caused casualties.'

This rough reception was preceded by a comfortable voyage, at least for the *Leedstown* contingent, who revelled in rich American rations. To maintain the fiction that this was a purely American affair, the British troops wore American helmets, carried Garand rifles and were brigaded with the US 168th Regimental Combat Team.

No. 1's plan for the Algiers landing called for the CO, Lieutenant Colonel Tom Trevor, to take half the unit and land on the right flank at Cap Sidi Ferruch, ten miles west of Algiers, and capture a fort. This they achieved without a shot being fired, capturing, among other notables, the German Ambassador to the Vichy Government and his family. With that achieved, Tom Trevor took his half-Commando off to capture the airfield at Blida. The other half of No. 1, under the unit's second-in-command, Major Ken Trevor, were not so lucky. Their task was to capture Fort d'Estrées on the left flank of the landing area, and a coastal defence battery, the Batterie de Lazerete. They landed in a heavy onshore swell and in the wrong place, and the French forces defending the fort and the battery put up a stiff fight. At 11.00 hrs Ken Trevor called for naval gunfire support which came swiftly from a destroyer, but the fire salvos fell by error on the Commando positions, causing many casualties. The fort was finally dive-bombed by the Fleet Air Arm in the early afternoon and surrendered.

Landing on the wrong beach was an all-too-common problem, and one that Commando units were to endure for much of the war. As we have noted, this was not always the Navy's fault. Visibility from an LCA is very restricted, most landings were made at night, compasses could be faulty and the crews were not always well trained. In an attempt to reduce the number of errors, navigation beacons were often provided, sometimes by submarine, sometimes, as here, by canoe parties, who went in ahead of the main assault to mark the beaches. Stan Weatherall of 101 Troop, 6 Commando, was carrying out just such a task here for the American Rangers landing at Oran and describes his part in the operation.

'The convoy left Greenock on 4 September and took thirteen days to reach Gibraltar, having gone well out into the Atlantic on the way. On Sunday 1 November, Sub-Lieutenant Peter Harris of COPP (Combined Operations Pilotage Party) and myself slung two canoes on board the submarine HMS *Ursula*, one in the forward mess desk, one in place of a torpedo. We sailed that night, submerging by day, surfacing at night to charge the batteries. On Wednesday 4 November we reached the bay of Arzew near Oran and began a periscope recce, surfacing on Saturday 7 November, six miles offshore. The sea was very choppy as we launched the canoe over the starboard ballast tanks and we shipped a lot of water, which I baled out with my green beret. The dolphins were a nuisance, stirring up phosphorescence, but we made good time and reached Z Beach, dropped our kedge anchors and sat there, wet and cold, about 200 yards offshore.

'At 00.15 hrs we began flashing "Z" seaward by morse RG, an infra-red lamp, and the US Rangers' first landing craft came in about 01.15 hrs and landed on our starboard side about ten minutes later. More craft then came in, veering off to right and left to discharge their troops, and all was very quiet for about an hour when the first shots were heard. We guided the last craft – a tank and jeep carrier – in just before daylight, paddled off to "Green" and "Red" Beaches, and finally boarded the *Reina del Pacifico*. She was under fire from a French artillery post, which hit her twice before the gun was silenced. One shell which hit the ship knocked out a rivet, which landed in the Captain's wash-basin.' Stan Weatherall and his mate had an adventurous time canoeing around North Africa and Italy and we shall return to him again.

6 Commando were to land on the west side of Algiers, but poor handling of their landing craft, even during the lowering from *Awatea*, disrupted their assault. They too were put ashore on the wrong beach and several hours late. Some of their craft had to beach under fire and in broad daylight, but once ashore the Commando moved on to attack the coastal battery at Fort Duperre, three miles west of Algiers, which was still firing on the landing craft offshore. One party, under the Second-in-Command, Major Ronald, landed in front of the Algiers defences, and all were killed or captured. The rest of the Commando lacked the heavy weapons necessary to subdue the fort,

but another dive-bombing attack by Fleet Air Arm Alba-
cores did the trick and the fort finally surrendered at
about 14.00 hrs.

Frank Barton took part in this operation. 'I landed with
6 Troop 6 Commando on 8 November from the troopship
Awatea. Our landing craft were American R boats. Our
object was to take Fort Duperre. The landing was a
shambles as the boats kept breaking down and were
letting in water. We did get ashore eventually and took
the fort with American Ranger Troops in support. An
unfortunate incident happened in the fort. Some French
Marines had locked themselves in a building and would
not come out, although they did not want to fight. Then
a trigger-happy Commando emptied a tommy-gun magazine through the doorway . . . I walked away in disgust.'

6 Commando barely had time to celebrate the successful conclusion of a rather mixed day when they were
called back to the beach and, together with a force of US
Rangers, embarked on two British destroyers and were
sent to seize airfields near the port of Bone, 250 miles east
of Algiers, in an attempt to forestall German intervention
from Tunisia. 6 Commando reached Bone on 11 November and marched onto the airfield just as the first troops
of 3 Para, from the British 1st Airborne Brigade, landed on
the airfield. The Allied build-up around Bone continued,
with 1 Commando arriving on 18 November. Four days
later, Stuka dive-bombers arrived over Bone and the
expected German counter-attack began, so 6 Commando
advanced to meet the approaching enemy near Tabarka,
sixty miles east in Tunisia. They went to Tabarka by
train, being twice strafed by enemy fighters on the way,
suffering nearly fifty casualties, before detraining and
moving into the hills near Sedjenane.

C. L. G. Bryen remembers this journey and noted the
event in his diary. '22 November, Sunday: Making good
headway. Stopped at MORRIS, where we made tea and
picked oranges from the groves beside the track. Spitfire

escort from Bone with us, but forced to return to refuel every half hour. At 10.15 hrs two FW 190s flew very low down the length of the train firing MGs and cannon. The result was chaos. The train pulled up and men jumped out while it was still in motion, many being dragged beneath the wheels and mangled. Grenades which were packed on open wagons were detonated by the cannon shells. Result: eleven men killed and twenty-five badly injured, twenty-two less seriously hurt.

'T. S. M. Barlow, like several other men, had been cut to ribbons on falling beneath the wheels. The Arab driver took to the hills and did not return. Troops lay up at El Tarf until dusk, when two troops went on to La Calle by train, one of our lance-corporals driving, to attack an enemy tank harbour, holding up the advance of First Army. The rest of the Commando marched eighteen miles to La Calle, which we reached in a pretty tired condition and slept in a school. A day to be remembered.'

It was now the end of November and the North African weather was atrocious, with very cold nights and continuous torrential rain. During this period the First Army, led by the 78th Division, was moving forward towards Tunis, and the leading Battalion, the 8th Argyll & Sutherland Highlanders, clashed with the German defenders ten miles east of Sedjenane, where the enemy were entrenched astride the road on two features, Bald Hill and Green Hill, and the Argylls suffered heavy casualties when attempting to force a passage.

On 30 November, 6 Commando were ordered up to attack the German positions on Green Hill, while an infantry battalion went for Bald Hill. Four troops attacked the hill at 04.00 hrs on the 30th, and met with fierce resistance from an enemy well-equipped with heavy and medium machine guns. After repeated attempts to consolidate their small advances, both the infantry battalion and the Commando withdrew, with the loss of another eighty men, which forced the Commando to reorganize into four troops.

C. L. G. Bryen's diary again: '29 November, Sunday: Warned in the afternoon that MG nests were holding up the 36th Brigade at Green Hill, JAFFNA. Four troops of Commando ordered to attack and capture the hill. Made a hurriedly formed plan, without good recce. Did not take American steel helmets owing to their resemblance to German. Moved forward by MT in the evening. Debussed a mile from Green Hill and crept into position at 20.00 hrs. Plan was for 5 Troop to put in a feint attack at 04.00 hrs, while 3, 4 and 6 Troops came up over the top of the hill, and dealt with the MG nests. Dead Argylls lying everywhere, with British equipment and rifles etc. Going pretty hard, across several ploughed fields and Arab villages. Troop in position by 22.00 hrs and waited for zero hour.

'30 November, Monday: Zero hour 04.00 hrs and no sign of any enemy, so opened up with LMG and rifle and mortar fire according to plan. This, we learnt later, only had the effect of waking up the enemy, who then opened fire with the machine guns on their fixed lines. 3 and 4 Troops came over the hill, but were unable to penetrate the deadly fire of the machine guns, and lost several men in the attempt. When day came, several more attempts were made to capture the hill, but we were forced back every time, the enemy changing his position constantly. The Buffs, who were attacking Bald Hill at the same time, were meeting with better success, and the Royal West Kents were pushing on. 11.00 hrs. My section were sent to the North side of the hill to attempt to cut off any enemy who might try and withdraw during the attacks. Royal Artillery came up and gave us supporting barrage, but enemy so well dug in that the shells had no effect on them. Captain Mayne, OC action, recalled all Commando to top of hill at 13.00 hrs in an attempt to capture the hill by following a creeping barrage, but the section were ambushed by Afrika Korps soldiers disguised as Arabs, and we split up, only five men reaching the top of Green Hill. Attack was pushed in, with five men of 5 Troop in reserve, sixty-seven men in all making the attack. Artillery ammunition ran very low, and Captain Mayne forced to withdraw his men to foot of Hill. Captain Scott shot through the head while taking a machine gun. Heavy rain came on, and force withdrew to Brigade HQ to reform, carrying several wounded, but leaving dead and badly wounded. Could not contact 2 Section, 5 Troop, so were forced to leave them out. Hot meal at Brigade HQ and back to Sedjenane by MT. Troops very exhausted, having no rest.'

Frank Barton continues his story. 'After Algiers we boarded the destroyers *Whealand* and *Lammerton*, bound for Bone. As we came ashore, the 3rd Battalion Parachute Regiment were dropping on the so-called airfield. After Bone we travelled in open rail trucks bound for Tabarka. Our escort plane left us to refuel and we were attacked by two FW 190s, and we had eleven men killed in this attack. We continued on to Sedjenane and to the attack on Green Hill, where we suffered more heavy casualties. We made the assault on 30 November at night. The Germans seemed to be using numerous Spandaus against us, and were firing just above our heads on what appeared to be fixed lines, using tracer bullets. We couldn't get anywhere near them without being mowed down. In the end we had to withdraw. I noticed that I had skinned my wrists trying to get near the guns. We made another assault in the afternoon, but again with no success. In the two attacks we lost eighty men and were reduced to four troops. Then Lieutenant Colonel McAlpine was taken ill and replaced by Lieutenant Colonel D. Mills-Roberts. After this came the battle at Steamroller Farm, where I was taken prisoner.'

Sergeant Blackburn of 6 Commando saw the attack on Green Hill. 'For the last attempt on Green Hill (which never fell in spite of several attempts by our Commando and the main force) our troop was given the task of occupying a neighbouring feature – I think it was called Sugar Loaf – from where we could see and hear the main attack on Green Hill. That attempt also failed and we were ordered to withdraw under cover of darkness. Unfortunately, we had wounded men who could not make the journey out, so our section stretcher bearer volunteered to remain with them and be taken prisoner, a very noble and brave act.' This stretcher bearer was to return to 6 Commando later, under curious circumstances.

In early January, the unit attacked Green Hill yet again, losing their CO, Lieutenant Colonel McAlpine, who had a heart attack. 6 Commando, much reduced, was reformed into four depleted troops under a new CO, Major McLeod, who led the unit until Lieutenant Colonel Derek Mills-Roberts, late of 4 Commando, arrived from the UK after an eventful six-day journey from England, scrounging lifts on various planes through Gibraltar and Algiers, hitching lifts on trucks and finally reaching his Commando HQ, which was established in a railway tunnel.

While 6 Commando were tussling for Green Hill, 1 Commando, with four American infantry companies under command, had been brought forward, re-embarking at Tabarka for a raid behind the enemy lines, with the task of cutting the enemy communications and feeding men forward to the German lines around Green Hill.

Charles Hustwick, the signaller who seems to appear in every Commando operation, was now serving as a corporal with the HQ of No. 1 Commando. 'After the capture of the aerodrome at Maison Blanche, we thought it was home for us, but it was back on a train – cattle trucks or horse boxes – for a nightmare journey to Bone, the most easterly port of Algeria, and then, after being constantly bombed and strafed there, we went onto landing craft for Tabarka. The town had been knocked about quite a bit. First Army had now ground to a halt but were

anxious to capture the port at Bizerta, so it was decided
to send 1 Commando in along the coast, to cut inland, sit
on the main road and cut the supply line to the enemy
forward troops. This we did after a really wet landing. We
had donkeys on this operation to carry the 3-inch mortars,
but they were last seen swimming out to sea; not one
made it to the beach, anyway. We waited all day for the
Army to come up, but no joy, and wireless communication was impossible. The enemy had by now discovered
our existence and some right tussles took place, causing a
lot of casualties for the Commando but on the other hand
we took a lot of prisoners. We eventually withdrew
through our own lines, spending two days and nights on
the march with almost no food. We lived off the land,
with slaughtered stray sheep to keep us going . . . and so
back to Tabarka.'

The No. 1 Commando force landed at 03.00 hrs on the
morning of 1 December, and divided into two halves, as
at Algiers, under the CO and Second-in-Command Ken
and Tom Trevor. They advanced five miles inland behind
the enemy lines without encountering any opposition. By
first light they were astride the main inland road from
Bizerta to Tabarka, and a secondary road along the coast,
which they held shut for the next three days. Here 1
Commando stayed, shooting up any enemy transport that
came along, beating off attacks by local forces, dominating over one hundred square miles of enemy-held territory
with fighting patrols, but at a price; No. 1 lost sixty men,
the Americans seventy-four killed, wounded or missing,
before withdrawing to their own lines.

While the two Commando units were fighting their
hard war in Tunisia, Stan Weatherall of 101 Troop was
conducting a private war from a submarine. We can rejoin
him on the SS *Reina del Pacifico* in the Bay of Arzeu,
Algeria. 'At 23.00 hrs on Friday 13 November, the *Reina*
was attacked by a U-boat, and a near miss was recorded
in that a torpedo had passed twelve feet in front of the

ship's bows. I discovered that the pongos to whom the CPO had referred were members of my own SBS, who were all in the survivor's rig (civilian clothes) and had been operating in Oran Harbour, some fifty miles west of Arzeu. They told me that our Sergeant Major J. Embelin had been killed on a British ship by two Vichy French vessels firing at it from either side, while he was preparing explosives. The *Etric* arrived and berthed at Gibraltar at 13.30 hrs.

'On 14 November, having had to call there for water and provisions, I went ashore and reported to the 1st officer on HMS *Maidstone*, who told me I was not to travel on the *Etric* as another job was in the offing. I went back onto the *Etric* and re-joined our other SBS members, who sympathized with me. The next morning at 08.45 hrs I left the *Etric* with my canoe and gear and on 15 November I boarded the *Maidstone*. On 17 November the *Etric* left Gibraltar for England. The following day, the seven members of the SBS who had sailed on the *Etric* were brought back to the *Maidstone*, as the *Etric* had been torpedoed and sunk 160 miles from Gibraltar. They and others had been picked up by a destroyer.

'Captain Livingstone told me he had obtained permission from General Mark Clark for the two of us to fly back home in a Fortress the next morning at 09.00 hrs, as the Fortress was returning home for repairs. At 06.00 hrs I was sent for by the officer of the watch, who gave me a written message which said I was to fly back at 05.00 hrs instead! At 09.00 hrs Captain Livingstone and Captain Courtney sent for me and said that I wasn't to fly back after all, as the job I had been told about on the 14th was now on. Captain Courtney, Lieutenant Foot and the other SBS personnel were to fly on the Fortress.

'On 20 November, Captain Livingstone and I boarded the submarine at 11.15 hrs and at 11.30 hrs left the harbour. As soon as we were clear, the klaxons sounded for diving stations, and we submerged to periscope depth.

21 and 25 November were spent sailing up the coast of Spain into the Gulf of Lyons, where the sea became extremely rough. The sub rolled to 55 degrees on the night of the 26th, scooping up water with the conning tower, which went down the hatch and flooded the control room. One of the diesel engine's big-end bearings went, then the Asdic, Sperry and wireless transmitter gave up. The klaxons sounded and the sub went down to 125 feet; the waters were somewhat rough at this depth and the vessel rocked. The engine room artificers got to work on the engine, and with continuous effort, made and fitted new bearings. Other things which had gone wrong were also put right.

'On the night of the 27th, the sub surfaced, the sea was not as rough as before but one or two members of the sub's crew were sick, so I volunteered to do lookout on the bridge, using night-glasses for scanning the sea, focused on infinity. While travelling on the surface the sub changed course every five minutes, by five or ten degrees to port and then starboard, but at the same time keeping on a straight course. We reached the edge of the Gulf of Genoa, north of the Lugurian Sea, and while submerged on the 28th we did periscope reconnaissance of the beach where we were to land. The sub surfaced on the night of the 29th, and with the aid of Asdic depth soundings the skipper took us into a small bay to within about 1,200 yards of the beach edge. We slipped the canoe at 10.00 hrs and paddled to the beach, picked up the canoe and carried it up the sand to a four-foot dirt sea wall, right onto the "V" of a "Y"-shaped road junction. One road followed the coast, the other went through the village, which was not far from Ventimiglia. In the "V" of the "Y" stood a large house with lots of bushes and shrubbery in the garden. Two large iron gates to the house directly opposite us were fastened with wire. A courting couple came down the road, and we were held up for over half an hour because they stood necking at the iron gates. After

they left and were well up the road, Captain Livingstone
nipped across, cut the wire and opened one of the gates.
We carried the canoe across the road into the garden,
where we hid it among the bushes. Then, leaving the
garden, we crossed the other road into an orchard on a
sloping hill. We then located the railway track on a
twenty-foot embankment and walked along the bottom
of this for some distance before we crawled up the
embankment onto the track and proceeded towards the
tunnel. We came to a building with a verandah and were
in position on the verandah, listening to voices inside,
when suddenly the door opened and a man came out. He
was talking over his shoulder to his comrades as he made
water, not knowing that two knives were at the ready no
more than a yard away. However, we knew that as he had
only just come from a well-lit room, his eyes would not
be adjusted to the darkness outside and therefore he
would not detect us. This was a guardhouse for the
soldiers guarding the mouth of the tunnel, for we discovered that one sentry was at the top and one on the side
of the track, and they called to each other occasionally.
We backed off the verandah to the bottom of the track
and crawled along a hedgerow, through which we heard
something moving about and thought we had been
detected, so lay low for some time, but what we heard
must have been animals.

'Skirting the edge of the track at the bottom for quite
some distance, we got up onto the track just as a very
long train of wagons rumbled by, going westwards. We
then walked further down the track and found that it
curved ideally. We placed charges on the rail, positioned
to blow a six-foot gap. We also placed charges on two iron
posts which carried cables supplying the villages with
electricity and also carrying the feed cables for the railway
engines; all charges to go off simultaneously with a
pressure switch under the rail. It was now past 23.00 hrs
and we had no time to lose in making our way back to

the sub by 23.30 hrs, when the moon would rise. If we didn't get back by then the sub would have to leave and come back for us the next night. We cut our way through some wire netting and got back onto the main village road, down which we moved at a brisk pace, passing several soldiers talking together in a group.

'Captain Livingstone was whistling some tune from an Italian classic, when twenty yards further on we passed another group of people talking under some trees on our right, then a lone figure came towards us, a drunken soldier, who looked at us as we passed him. We retrieved our canoe, and ran down the beach with it to the water's edge, launched it and paddled back to the sub with no time to spare. We hurriedly got the canoe aboard, and the sub left the bay, moving away from the area. At about midnight the lookouts on the bridge saw a brilliant flash and heard the explosion from the charges we had laid. It was published in the *Gibraltar Chronicle* that the Blue Express line was blocked for some days. It would have been blocked for very much longer if we could have derailed it in the tunnel, but our orders were "to let the enemy know we had been, only after we had gone!"

'The sub then began the return journey, keeping fairly close inshore. The next night the sub cruised on the surface and by day submerged, following the coastline, when the periscope was used a great deal. At 01.45 hrs on Monday 30 November, a vessel was sighted and the sub's gun-crew went into action and fired a few shots across its bows. It stopped and turned out to be an Italian Asdic schooner, looking for enemy submarines. We sidled up to it and found no one aboard; the Italian crew must have beat a hasty withdrawal in their dinghy after the first shot was fired. Captain Livingstone and I boarded the vessel with some plastic HE, which we placed in depth charges on the stern, while members of the sub's crew took off two Breda guns, with ammunition, two machine guns, and several ·25 rifles, also the latest sea charts, very

152

valuable to the navy. We set the "L" delays going and got back aboard the sub, which hung about for around an hour while the "L" delays did their job, setting off the high explosive charge which in turn blew up the depth charges. It was an enormous explosion, causing a huge black column of smoke which rose about 300 feet into the air. A little further down the coast we were spotted by the enemy who fired Very lights, so the skipper ordered diving stations and we crept away submerged.

'We were waiting for a train to come along the coast to gun it. On Tuesday 1 December at 22.30 hrs a train was sighted. The gun-crew went into action, first firing a star-shell which lit up the area, then shells were fired which hit the train amidships. The rear half caught fire while the other half was hauled by the train's driver into a tunnel and stayed there, no doubt until he thought it safe to emerge.

'In peacetime Lieutenant Laken, RN, had been on holiday in this area and knew the whereabouts of an olive oil factory, and so at 01.00 hrs on 2 December the skipper brought the sub under the lea of a sea wall, and trimmed the craft so that the sub's gun was pointing just over the top of it. The gun took to action stations, first firing a star-shell. The following shells hit the olive oil tanks, which caught fire, the factory chimney was hit and collapsed, and a pillbox was demolished. The sub was creeping away from the wall when the enemy opened fire on us. The nearest shell fell fifty yards away, so we crash-dived to safety. The next night at 18.30 hrs, soon after surfacing, a vessel was sighted heading east. The gun-crew went into action. I was below in the control room, assisting in handing the shells up through the conning tower hatch to the gun-crew. Several shots were fired, the vessel stopped and one Very light was fired from it, which was the only armament on board. A torpedo was released which passed harmlessly under the ship as, having no cargo, it was too high out of the water. The ship, the *St*

Margueritte II, was manned by twenty-three Germans, most of whom had either never been to sea in their lives before, or were merchant seamen. They launched two lifeboats, but one was smashed and so they all had to cram into one boat, which was hauled alongside the sub. The Captain and Chief Engineer were taken aboard as prisoners, but the rest were given a direction and told to row away. One man in the lifeboat stood up and, in English, asked for food and water, but the skipper told him we were not in a position to provide any, and they were only eleven miles from land, so they rowed away.

'A rope-cum-wooden-ladder was made fast to the ship and sub and several of the sub's crew boarded her to take anything valuable to the Navy in the way of radio and charts. Captain Livingstone and I boarded the ship with a 25lb charge, which we could not place until the crew had taken off anything of value and were ready to re-board the sub. While they were doing this I went into one or two of the ship's cabins situated on deck, and put my loot into a leather satchel – lipstick, face powder, perfume, cigarettes, German and French currency. The crew got aboard the sub and we laid the charge in the forward hold below the water-line, and set a ten-minute "L" delay fuse, which gave us ample time to get back on the sub. The charge went off, creating a big hole in the vessel's plating. The ship, of some 5,000 tons, was built in Dublin and was being taken by the motley crew from Marseilles to Naples. My loot had been intended by the crew as presents to their wives when they got home and had been purchased in Marseilles. This incident took place off the Isles d'Hyères, where the vessel, as far as I know, still rests on the sea bed.

'The Captain of the vessel was an arrogant pro-Nazi, while the Chief Engineer was a dear old soul, whose job in peacetime was fishing on the Dogger Bank. He had been a prisoner of war in British hands during World War One. He had a son who was a prisoner of war in Canada, and another son on the Russian front at Voronesh. At the end of the patrol he asked to stay on the sub as one of the crew, which he preferred to a POW camp. The leather satchel, he said, belonged to him, so I gave it back to him.

'On 6 December we were off the coast of Spain when a vessel was sighted by periscope. The submarine surfaced and ordered the ship to stop. The skipper hoisted a Nazi flag and as we drew near the vessel, the ship's crew gave us the Nazi salute, which we returned. They lowered a rowing boat and came alongside the sub, and the Navigating Officer and a CPO got into it and were taken aboard the ship, which they found was laden with salt. They presented us with two loaves of bread and a bottle of wine, again giving us the Nazi salute, which we returned as we drew away. They must have thought we were a German U-boat.

'Up to then the sub was making her way back along the coast of Spain to Gibraltar, but a radio message was then received, telling the skipper to alter course for Algiers, and we arrived there some time during the morning of 9 December. I went ashore with two CPOs and we made our way into Algiers and proceeded up the hill into the Casbah, which unknown to us, was out of bounds for all troops; we were escorted back to the safety of the town by the Red Caps. The following day HMS *Maidstone* arrived, which I boarded and berthed in the PO's mess. During the patrol I had saved my issue of neat rum in a water bottle, which was now about full. I stayed aboard the *Maidstone* until 16 December, and one night I took out my water bottle of rum and made many friends by offering it round the mess; the POs couldn't understand why anyone should want to give away his rum – unheard of in the Navy.

'On 16 December, Captain Livingstone and I left the *Maidstone* and by truck went to Maison Blanche airport, where we boarded a USA Douglas transport plane named "Old Crow" and took off. It was a good name to give it, for its wing tips went up and down about three feet. We landed at Oran airport, a veritable quagmire of red mud. At 11.00 hrs we picked up some more passengers, took off again and landed at Gibraltar at 15.30 hrs after a very bumpy flight. I stayed in the Almeda RAF camp until 22 December, when Captain Livingstone and I boarded the mine-laying cruiser HMS *Adventurer*. The vessel carried numerous people who had fled from the Germans, a good many coming over the Pyrenees, escorted by guides who charged them a vast amount of money, and by devious routes and methods reached the sanctuary of the British in Gibraltar, and were now being taken to England.

'HMS *Adventurer* was a very fast ship, capable of doing forty knots. Christmas Day was just the same as any other day, as the ship was not provisioned for Christmas fare. We arrived at Plymouth at 16.00 hrs on 26 December. I found the family with whom I had stayed in 1940 and they made me welcome. The Axis bombers had literally flattened the whole of the shopping centre and some distance around. On 28 December, Captain Livingstone and I left Plymouth for Fareham, and on 29 December I went to our HQ at Hillhead, obtained my furlough form and went on leave to see my wife and baby son, who had been born on 7 October.'

During December No. 1 Commando, previously organized in ten troops, with their American allies on the unit strength, reorganized into six troops and spent time serving in the line, a role for which lightly-equipped Commando units are not well suited. Charles Hustwick again: 'We were then used as infantry of the line, both 1 and 6 being fully extended. Our numbers were getting less and less and our American friends had finally been withdrawn. We spent Christmas in the line and the weather was terrible – very cold and raining all the time, not a bit like the Africa you read about at school.'

CSM Edmans, with 6 Troop of No. 1 Commando, recalls one sharp little fight during this period in the line.

'We were deployed facing down a track with 2 Troop on our left, but too far to shoot. After a while we saw Afrika Korps troops jumping across the track right to left, too far to shoot, so we waited patiently – Felmingham and Freddie Witton, the Bren-gun team, Fusilier Wales with a Garand rifle, myself with a tommy-gun. Suddenly someone shouted "Enemy left" and there, coming through the bushes, was a German. He fired a burst, hitting Freddie in the stomach, Sergeant Smith in the back, and Lance-Sergeant Sims in the knee, before Felmingham turned and killed him. We reckoned they had got behind us, so Sergeant Smith said, "Get out, more are coming." So we got out, running back through the smoke with enemy bullets helping us on our way. Freddie was in great pain, but we reached HQ and gave our report. Then, leaving a rearguard, we walked seven miles to a hospital. Freddie walked those seven miles with a stomach wound, sucking a wet handkerchief and gripping hard on his Colt ·45. You could see he was in great pain but we could not let him sit down.'

No. 1 Commando were joined in their endeavours here by a reinforcement of sixty-five American soldiers who had all been with the Commando on Operation Bizerta and volunteered to stay with No. 1 during the campaign. No. 1 and No. 6 Commandos stayed in North Africa until the end of April 1941, returning to the line again and again, and becoming notably skilled at fighting patrols.

Lieutenant Colonel Derek Mills-Roberts' No. 6 Commando were now attached to the 78th Division and in mid-January 1943 decided to dominate their part of the line by aggressive patrolling, having first established the unit – now reduced to about 250 men – in strongpoints. Aggressive action was necessary since the Afrika Korps had inflicted a telling repulse on the American forces further south at the Kasserine Pass, and were now attempting a similar blow against the British near the coast. On one occasion, a 6 Commando patrol bumped into a large German force of mountain troops from the crack Hermann Goering Jaeger Parachute Regiment. The patrol battle built up, with Mills-Roberts reinforcing the patrol with the rest of his Commando and No. 6 fought the German regiment to a standstill, although the Germans brought up tanks and infantry reinforcements.

Ray Pudner was in this action: 'I was armed with a Garand rifle and fifty rounds, on sentry-go from 04.00 to 06.00 hrs. It was a very cold morning. First a huge lorry nearly ran me down and then a lorry patrol – two vehicles – of 6 Commando ran into a battalion of the Hermann Goering Division. The battle lasted five hours and we inflicted very heavy casualties on the enemy; I was very nearly a casualty myself. A bullet struck the butt-plate of my rifle, another struck the stone I had placed in front of my head. They got behind us at one point and I ended up next to a German machine-gunner, who I thought was my prisoner. He put up his hands and I dismantled his MG and threw away the parts.'

Frank Barton was also in this battle with 6 Troop of 6 Commando. 'On 26 February 1943 I was captured when we engaged the Germans at Steamroller Farm – there was a steamroller in the farmyard – near Mejas-el-Bab in Tunisia. Steamroller Farm is one of the Commando battle honours. We were getting the better of this Hermann Goering Jaeger Regiment when they brought up Mark IV tanks. We were ordered to withdraw when Sergeant Bob Harris was killed at my side and Lieutenant Bonnin was badly wounded. I was captured while tending him. I was taken to Italy, to Camp 66 near Capua, and then to Camp 54 near Rome, where I met my brother, Sergeant Fred Barton of the South Notts Hussars, who had been captured at Tobruk in 1942. In September 1943 we managed to escape from the camp near Rome. On 8 September we woke up to find there were no guards on the camp and we broke out. Most of the chaps were content to stay put, but my brother and I took to the hills to try and make the

Allied lines, walking mostly by night in a southerly
direction, but also slightly east to get inland a little. I got
a rough direction by the stars, finding the Plough and
then the North Star. The Italians helped us as much as
they could with food and we found plenty of mushrooms,
which we roasted. In November we knew we were getting
somewhere near the front line with the amount of Germans we had to hide from. We had one narrow escape
when a German came looking along the hedge bottom
where we were hiding. After about two-and-a-half
months' walking, we reached the British lines, and eventually we were repatriated back to England where, after
leave and a lot of persuasion, I managed to rejoin 6
Commando who were then at Brighton. I had first landed
with them in North Africa and then I landed with them
on D-Day and served right through to the end of the war
in 1945, so really I did not miss many of 6 Commando's
actions.'

6 Commando lost forty per cent of its men in the
Steamroller Farm engagement, but severely mauled two
battalions of the enemy and forced them to a halt, until
the enemy were driven back to their own lines by battalions from the Coldstream Guards and the Royal
Sussex. For this action Mills-Roberts was awarded the
DSO.

Here in North Africa, as previously in Crete, the Commandos were used as line infantry, a role for which they
lacked both the manpower and the necessary equipment.
Their problems were compounded by the fact that they
received no reinforcements and were steadily reduced in
numbers until, in early April 1943, they were taken out
of the line, and after a few days' rest in Algiers, finally
embarked for the United Kingdom, though not before
Lieutenant Colonel Trevor and Derek Mills-Roberts had
received and circulated a warm letter of thanks from
General Eisenhower.

Dear Colonel Trevor,
You, and the men you have commanded, have been
identified with the Tunisian campaign since the day
on which the initial landings were made. Since then
you have been engaged on the most difficult, mountainous terrain of the entire front. As the time draws
near for your departure, it is a real pleasure for me to
express to you and your gallant men, a commen-
dation for a job well done. You have exemplified
those rugged self-reliant properties which the world
associates with the very name Commando.

Please transmit my appreciation to the officers and
men of your command.

Sincerely yours,
(Signed): Dwight D. Eisenhower

Corporal Hustwick sums up the end of the campaign.
'After many skirmishes and battles in the area of Sedjenane, rumours were about that we were to go home, which
we did not believe until it happened. From the railhead at
Souk-el-Arba we went in horse trucks back to Algiers –
both No. 6 and No. 1 Commandos. On arrival there, we
camped in a wood about eight miles south, and had some
lively nights out in Algiers before embarking in a ship. I
can't recall the name, but it had just disembarked 2,000
troops and our 150 or so had it all to themselves. We
came home to Liverpool in six days, unescorted, getting
bombed by Focke-Wulf Condors off the south coast of
Ireland. Incidentally, before leaving Algiers we scoured all
the hospitals for our men and made sure that all our
wounded who could move discharged themselves and
came home with us . . . then fourteen days' leave.'

Ray Pudner of 1 Troop 6 Commando remembers one of
his wounded comrades. 'On our way home to the UK, I
went to visit my wounded mate, Hendy Henderson, in
Algiers Hospital, where he was desperately ill and unable

to leave. It was forty-two years before I saw him again, at the London Commando Reunion. He told me he had evaded capture for five days. In hospital he was so ill that he heard the doctor tell the nurse to put him in the corner and let him die peacefully. He then said, "I appealed to someone else," and indeed he made a good recovery, although he was discharged from the Army medically unfit. We in 1 Troop know he was a believer, because he had a Bible and would read it at every opportunity. A year after the reunion I heard he had died suddenly. I never saw Hendy Henderson again, but I shall always remember his words, "I appealed to someone else."'

No. 12 Commando had been disbanded about this time and a number of these men came to add their numbers to the now depleted ranks of Nos. 1 and 6 Commandos. Among other recruits was Jim Coker, one of the police volunteers. 'I was posted to No. 1 Commando, which was a thrill. I thought there must be something special about No. 1, with their motto *Primus inter Pares* – First Among Equals. The unit was then at Winchester, having just returned from North Africa, where they had served with distinction, and they told us replacements some tales of their escapades. At the time I thought we weren't all that welcome, but later on in Burma I realized how it felt to have had so many mates killed and wounded and how hard it is to take to new blokes. Anyway, here I was in the best of all Commandos, and into civvy billets outside Winchester, with a lovely couple who let me keep all my billet money – 30p a day – as they had two sons in the Army. This was the life, on parade at 9-ish, mess about till 4, then back to the digs ... smashing! The trouble was that it didn't last long.'

7

Sicily and Italy, 1943

'Soldiers, I cannot offer you honour or wages.
I can offer you hunger, thirst, forced marches,
battles and death . . . anyone who loves his country
can follow me'

GIUSEPPE GARIBALDI, 1882

With the opening of the Italian campaign, which began with landings in Sicily, the Commandos were to take on two roles which were to occupy them for the rest of the war: landing in the van of major invasions and serving in the line alongside other larger infantry units. Nos. 1 and 6 Commandos had performed just these tasks in the Torch operations, and the pattern they had set was to continue. In Italy the Army Commandos found themselves brigaded for the first time with the Royal Marine Commando units, for the Commando units now assembling in the UK and North Africa for the campaigns in Sicily and Italy consisted of Nos. 2, 3 and (later) 9 Army Commandos, and Nos. 40, 41 and (later) 43 (Royal Marine) Commandos.

This book is concerned with the Army Commandos and a number of contributors have stressed the fact that while all Army Commandos were composed of volunteers, the Royal Marine Commando units were not, most being simply Marine battalions made over into Commando units from regular service. This is only partly

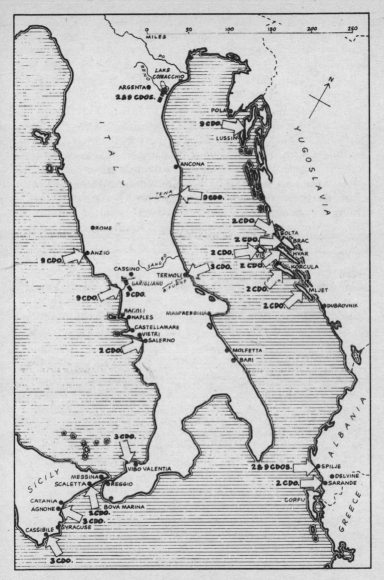

Sicily, Italy and Yugoslavia

accurate. No. 40 Commando was an all-volunteer unit and no Army Commando has a bad word to say about those Marine units with which his unit was brigaded in the field, while the Marines I have spoken to have nothing but praise for their Army Commando comrades and the Army units. Nos. 41 and 43 (Royal Marine) Commandos fought alongside Army Commando units in Italy, notably at Salerno and in the Adriatic, and both were largely volunteer units. The Royal Marine Commando units which formed later, when the Royal Marines Division was broken up, were indeed made-over battalions, but the men in them still had to undergo Commando training at Achnacarry and the RTU was swiftly applied to those who failed to meet the exacting Commando standard. The Corps of Royal Marines expanded to a strength of 80,000 men during World War Two, and therefore had plenty of vacant posts for men who had no taste for Commando soldiering. Having said that, every Royal Marine would freely admit that one volunteer is worth three pressed men, and few Marine Commando units possessed the dash and flair of the best Army Commando units.

No. 2 Commando had reformed after St Nazaire and had a new CO in Jack Churchill. One of his officers was Captain R. J. Bavister, who volunteered for Commando service in 1942. 'I received instructions to report for interview by 2 Commando, reporting first of all to the RTO, St Enoch, who would give me directions for finding them. Their location at Ayr was apparently secret! I was interviewed by the CO, Second-in-Command and Adjutant, was accepted subject to dropping to my substantive rank, given a set of black and white 2 Commando shoulder flashes and sent on leave. The Commando had black and white flashes until the Combined Operations' red and blue replaced them, except on officers' service dress uniform.

'The order of the day was weapon training and physical

fitness, with plenty of route marching. Unlike many
others, I was never at Achnacarry. The Commando had a
distinctly Lancashire flavour about it when I joined, a
hangover from the old Independent Company days, they
being recruited from specific divisions. We had a number
of exercises in the Highlands in the vicinity of Loch Fyne,
acting as enemy to American troops training for the North
African landing. There was also a mock attack on ships
in dock and a mid-winter coastal landing. I missed these
by being sent on a three-inch mortar course and being in
hospital. I believe I got a "distinguished" rating on the
course and was invited to become an instructor but, more
to the point, I got friendly with a Royal Marines officer and
the next time I met him was as the officer in charge of the
assault craft taking my section into Scaletta. That was the
first time I fired or directed a mortar. My fellow Section
Leader in 4 Troop was Allan Walker, older than most in
his middle-to-late thirties, a farmer and TA officer in the
Beds and Herts Regiment. I mention him because he had
been in Malta on coastal operations from submarines.
The CO was, of course, Jack Churchill – "Mad Jack" – a
striking-looking man of thirty-five or so, with very fair
hair, moustache and eyebrows. He was unusual in many
respects and made the Commando quite distinctive with
white blancoed webbing, the unique fighting knife badge
and Scottish headgear (caps TOS for the other ranks and
Balmorals for the officers). The officers, in battledress
walking-out order, wore a fighting knife on their left hip,
with a silvery finish rather than the blue of the active
service knife. I still have mine, made by the Wilkinson
Sword Company, though the sheath with its nickel-plated
tip has gone. My Scottish father-in-law-to-be christened
me "a Galloway coo" in consequence of the white belt. It
was noticeable that, when the Commando was issued
with the green beret in the winter of 1943, they wore it
like a Scottish cap, pulled forward rather than back as
prescribed by the War Office instructions for berets. The

top of a cigarette tin behind the badge helped in this respect.'

We can now follow these units to the battlefields of Italy, beginning with the veteran No. 3 Commando, which left the UK in July 1943 and sailed via Gibraltar and Algiers to Port Said, where they came under the command of General Dempsey's 13th Corps. No. 9 Commando later served in Gibraltar during the period of the Torch operations and were replaced by 2 Commando, after which 9 Commando returned to the UK. No. 2 remained in Gibraltar, while Nos. 40 and 41 sailed to the Sicily landings directly from the UK, embarking with the 1st Canadian Division. Nos. 3, 41 and 40 Commandos were then briefed for the invasion of Italy, and with No. 2 were brigaded into No. 2 SS Brigade, commanded by Brigadier Robert Laycock, but we can consider their exploits separately, beginning with No. 3 Commando, in Sicily.

No. 3 Commando's task during the invasion of Sicily was to land from HMS *Prince Albert* south of Syracuse and capture a battery of coastal artillery at Avola, three miles inland near the town of Cassibile. The assault began at midnight on 10 July, after just managing to avoid landing on the wrong beach. 'I am more than ever certain,' wrote Laycock afterwards, 'that we can never expect to land where we wish.' Although there was some machine-gun fire, No. 3 got ashore dry and without loss. Making their way inland, they captured the battery without further ado. The two Royal Marine Commando units also carried out their tasks successfully, killing some fifty Italians and taking many prisoners. No. 3's next operation was a raid, mounted at short notice three days later on 13 July. This did not go so smoothly, for the Commando soon encountered fierce opposition from elite German forces.

No. 3's task was to land at Agnone, several miles behind the enemy lines, and then push inland to the Punta dei Melati bridge over the Leonardo river, seven

miles from the sea. At around the same time a parachute
force would drop and seize another bridge at Primasole. If
both these bridges could be held and not destroyed by the
Germans, then the advancing Allied army would be
greatly aided in their attempt to make a rapid advance
towards Catania. Durnford Slater was given just three
hours to plan this operation.

At a brief meeting on the quayside at Syracuse, Durnford Slater had been informed that the landing beaches
and the bridge were held – if at all – by easily discouraged
Italian troops. Durnford Slater was not so sure. He felt
that if the bridge was worth taking, it was worth guarding.
His plan called for a landing in two flights, the first of 1,
2, 3 and 4 Troops, the second of 5 and 6 Troops. The bulk
of the unit was then to advance and seize the bridge while
one troop went north to contact the paratroopers at
Primasole and another went south to contact 50th Division. They were in the van of the Eighth Army and
would, it was hoped, get to the bridge by first light next
day, 14 July. In the event, the Punta dei Melati area was
held not only by Germans but by troops of the 1st German
Parachute Division. This time 3 Commando were up
against an opponent worthy of their steel.

The Commando sailed that evening, being attacked by
an E-boat on the way, and began to land at 22.00 hrs,
meeting opposition from machine gun posts before No. 3
even got ashore. Abandoning all hope of surprise, No. 3's
Brens and the landing craft guns engaged the shore
defences with all arms and the troops went ashore under
fire. Some confusion on the beach was rapidly sorted out
by Major Peter Young and the recently-commissioned
Lieutenant George Herbert, and the unit began a rather
straggling advance to the bridge, following the coastal
railway line to Agnone station and reaching the bridge at
about 03.00 hrs, bumping on the way into a section from
the paratroops, dropped well wide of their mark at Primasole. Durnford Slater invited the paratroop corporal to

bring his section along with the Commando, but the corporal declined and marched his men away towards his own regiment. Meanwhile No. 3 were taking casualties, including Walter Skrine, shot in the leg, and Captain Leese of 1 Troop, shot in the eye.

The pillboxes at either end of the bridge were manned by Italians, all too busy talking to hear the stealthy approach of the Commandos, and quickly disposed of by grenades slipped in through the loopholes. 3 Commando were then deployed about the bridge, either in the pill-boxes or in the surrounding orange groves and ravines, where they constructed small defensive 'sangars' with rocks, as the ground was too rocky to permit digging in. Then, with the bridge secured, they sat down, ten miles behind the enemy lines, to await events. There were perhaps 350 men in all, armed only with platoon weapons.

Until dawn 3 Commando had a marvellous time, shoot-ing up everything which came along, until the road approaches to the bridge were littered with overturned or burning vehicles, but their arrival had been detected and the Germans began to mortar their positions heavily and, never slow to react, soon brought up a Tiger tank, which began to flay the Commando positions with its 88mm gun, while staying sensibly beyond the range of their only anti-tank weapon, the infantry PIAT. A party sent to stalk the tank could not get close enough over the open ground, and German paratroopers were moving up to box in the troops, causing a steady stream of casualties.

By 04.30 hrs, with no sign of 50th Division, the Com-mando position was becoming untenable. They had many wounded, their positions in the open valley could be overlooked and enfiladed, enemy infantry were arriving in ever-increasing numbers and the tank kept rumbling about behind the ridges, appearing at regular intervals to put down more fire. The only thing missing was 50th

Division, held up by the enemy at Lentini some miles away.

Around 05.00 hrs, Durnford Slater gave the order to withdraw from the bridge in small parties, either to lie up in the hills until the Eighth Army finally arrived or, if possible, infiltrate back to their own lines. Widely deployed and still under tank fire, the Commando withdrew. They were forced to leave the wounded behind, to be captured by parachute troops from the 4th Brigade of the Hermann Goering 1st Parachute Division, who looked after them well – a kindness No. 3 Commando were able to repay a few weeks later at Termoli.

Though suffering severe losses in killed, wounded and prisoners, No. 3 Commando slowly reformed over the next few days, many of those wounded and taken prisoner managing to escape back to the British lines. Peter Young's party met up with a patrol of the Northumberland Hussars; some wounded were left behind by the Germans and recovered later by 50 Division, and the beach party finally linked up with an infantry patrol from the Yorks and Lancs. Even so, 3 Commando had been severely mauled at the bridge, losing many old stalwarts. A total of five officers and twenty-three men were killed, four officers and sixty-two men were wounded and eight officers and fifty-one men missing. This represented some forty-five per cent of the Commando's strength, but they had held the bridge and removed the demolition charges, so it was still intact when 50th Division reached it. After Catania fell, Montgomery ordered Durnford Slater to have a slab of stone, carved with the unit name, cemented into the Punta dei Malati Bridge, now No. 3 Commando Bridge, where it remains to this day. After this battle, Durnford Slater received a bar to his DSO, and Peter Young received his second MC, among many other well-deserved decorations to the unit's officers and other ranks.

On 22 July, having relieved 9 Commando in Gibraltar, No. 2 Commando, commanded by Lieutenant Colonel

J. M. T. F. (Jack) Churchill, MC, arrived in Sicily, and while Brigadier Laycock went to North Africa, Durnford Slater took command of No. 2 SS Brigade, which now consisted of 2, 3, 40 (Royal Marine) and 41 (Royal Marine) Commandos, and the Special Raiding Squadron under Major Paddy Mayne. 2 Commando's first operation in Italy was a landing at Scaletta in Sicily. Ted Kelly recalls this landing. 'For many of us this was our baptism of fire. I wish I could record that it was a successful demonstration of a combined operation. What it cost I shudder to think, but the fact is we landed on the wrong beach and far too late to catch the forces we were supposed to contain. What we encountered were two truckloads of German Army personnel, the tail-enders. These luckless few had us all to themselves, including what must have been the nightmarish sight of Colonel "Mad Jack" Churchill's claymore waved in their faces with suitable vocal accompaniment. At daybreak we assembled for the task of chasing the Germans. After a quiet start we met German mortar fire and we knew that our war had now really started.'

Bob Bavister was also on this operation. 'Because we had been issued with oblique aerial photographs of the coast, I could tell that we were going into the wrong place, because the hills behind had the wrong outline, but we were being guided in by a minesweeper or a similar vessel and the officer in charge of our LCA had no option but to follow it.'

All the units now mustering in Sicily were preparing for their next major operation, the attack on the Italian mainland. For this operation the 2nd SS Brigade was split between the two invasion forces. Nos. 3 and 40 were to cross the Straits of Messina with 13th Corp of the British Eighth Army (Operation Baytown), while No. 2 and No. 41 were to join 10th Corps of the American Fifth Army for the assault on Salerno (Operation Avalanche).

While the invasions were being planned, Major Peter Young, commanding No. 3 Commando while Durnford

Slater commanded the Brigade, sent fighting patrols across the Straits to raid the Italian mainland near Bova Marina, leading the first one himself. Wireless communications broke down at once and Peter Young and his patrol stayed on the mainland, harassing the enemy, and completely out of contact for a full week, before returning to Sicily for Operation Baytown.

The 13th Corps with 3 and 40 Commandos, accompanied by the Special Raiding Squadron, crossed the Straits of Messina on the night of 3 September 1943, and made rapid progress to Vibo Valentia, which they took on 9 September. On the next morning, at 03.30 hrs, the Fifth Army, consisting of the British 10th and the American 7th Corps, began to land at Salerno, where No. 2 Commando and No. 41 found themselves involved in one of the toughest battles of the entire Italian campaign.

The Germans had long anticipated a landing at Salerno and were already dug in on the hills above the beaches when the Fifth Army came ashore. For the Fifth Army to debouch from the landing beaches and capture Naples, they must first take and hold a narrow gap in the encircling hills, called the pass of La Molina. No. 2 came ashore in the first wave to clear the beaches and secure the bridgehead. Then No. 41 and Brigade Headquarters came ashore and this force pushed on to La Molina with the task of taking and holding the pass. No. 2 and Brigade HQ moved into the village of Victri at the seaward end of the pass while No. 41 advanced into the pass itself. Two troops of No. 2 Commando, one commanded by Captain the Duke of Wellington, occupied the northern suburbs of Salerno town, where they soon met enemy tanks and infantry. Meanwhile the rest of the landing was not going at all well. The beaches were under heavy shellfire and the Luftwaffe appeared to bomb and strafe the offshore shipping. Before long the Germans were attacking the beach perimeter with tanks and infantry. As daybreak dawned, German counter-attacks, supported by artillery and tanks, began to develop all around the bridgehead and heavy mortar fire was soon falling on the No. 2 Commando positions at Vietri. German attacks continued throughout the day with a major counter-offensive clearly building around the beach-head.

Ken McAllister of 2 Commando took part in all these operations. 'In June 1943 we were sent to Gibraltar, where we stayed about three months and then landed at Syracuse. From there we did a little raid at Scaletta, up on the coast from Catania, to stop the Germans blowing bridges. This was only partly successful as we were sent in too late to prevent much of the damage. As to Salerno, it would take a book to relate our experiences there. It was sixteen days of pure hell and both 2 Commando and 41 suffered heavily. The name "Commando" and our reputation seemed, to our minds, to convey to the commanders that we were to be used wherever the enemy looked like breaking through. I think it is a wonder any of us lived to tell the tale.'

Dudley Cooper, MM, one of the police draft, saw action in Sicily and at Salerno. 'After landing, the front moved forward and it was decided to mount a raid up the east coast at Scaletta. We boarded the landing craft carrier and everything went well except for hitting the wrong beach. We formed a perimeter and then moved onto the road, with the beach on one side and a wall on the other. Suddenly there was a lorry, right in the middle of the troop, and three Germans on the back firing at everyone. Someone threw a grenade into the lorry, which unfortunately was loaded with ammunition. The grenade set the ammunition ablaze and it exploded in all directions. I moved down the road fast but the lorry followed. Believe it or not, I climbed that smooth nine-foot wall somehow and shot the last moving thing on the lorry, which blew up. It was later found that two of our men had been burnt to cinders. We consolidated the area and went out in pairs, widening it. As we ran up the hill, my companion and I fell into position to cover attack, when suddenly in the foreground we saw two of the Hermann Goering Division soldiers, sitting in full camouflage with their hands up. We took them back to HQ and after interrogation, DUKWs were obtained and we were off back to Messina.

'Every village we came to, Italians in uniform gave themselves up in their hundreds, but we could not spare men and pointed them rearwards. That day I stood on the quay at Messina and guns from across the strait fired at us. We found accommodation and slept the night. Next day we were ordered back to Scaletta. The Americans had had little to celebrate, so they were allowed to attack and take Messina, an empty town. After staying in various places in Sicily, we embarked for Salerno. We landed in the north, moving into the hills. The Guards Brigade hit a very strong point on the flat, a tobacco factory. The Americans were also on the flat and had their own armoured division. They should have moved forward and cut the road before it entered the hills towards Rome. At one time I was on a recce by jeep in their area, and as we moved past their tanks and infantry, we were advised not to go forward as the Germans were up there! The fighting round Vietri was hard, mortars, 88s and Spandaus made things volatile, and part of one troop was behind the German lines. They made their way out and back to reform and hold. During this time, an officer and Piat gunner stopped a tank by firing the Piat from the shoulder, standing up on a balcony. Day and night became as one, and when we had held and settled the battle, we were withdrawn further south and allowed a night's sleep, except for those on guard duty, which I was on. I sat on a balcony and listened to the fighting all round us coming and going all night, but needless to say, most of the men slept through it.

'Next day we were lined up on each side of a valley where the Germans had thrown back and mauled the Ox and Bucks. Moving off from the start line under the hills, we went up the valley until it came out at Pigoletti, where the men on the south side crept into the village and captured the Germans and their Commandant in a short, sharp battle. We dug in at the top of the hill overlooking the road to Naples, listening to traffic below. During the next hour we were shelled with air bursts at the trees and lost two men from our section. It was unanimously decided that things were too hot, so we moved into a position on our right. When night fell we moved back to our own lines and found that the Duke of Wellington's troop were attacking the hill to the north, known as White Cross Hill. They were mauled by machine-gun cross-fire in which the Duke was killed. We were grabbing a little shut-eye on a patio, when the hill around us was shelled. It later turned out to be our own 25lb guns firing on the wrong hill. As there was no sleep to be had, we rounded the patio wall to find six of our lads had been killed by one shell. We watched the attack area of 2 Troop and noted a particular position of two German machine guns. Next morning, while things were quiet, three of us went up to the first floor of a house and with binoculars, pinpointed a position where we believed the machine guns to be. We set up a Bren and fired on the position and could see bullets raking the parapet. We had no trouble from them again.

'Willy Neild was with us, and he saw a German suddenly get up and run across the hill, and at an estimated range of 800 yards he downed him with a rifle shot. To prove it was no fluke, he later hit another on the road below at the same distance. This got him the job of sniper, and he hated being anything other than a rifleman in a troop with his mates. In the afternoon, noise was heard coming up the hill off the road on the German side, and it was not long before a Tiger tank came over, moving in the direction of Pigoletti. Those of us in the house were looking straight down the barrel of the tank's gun, when we heard our mortars fire. The first shot landed right on top of the turret and stopped it dead. A second Tiger rolled up behind it, and to my amazement, a second mortar bomb landed on the turret. A recce to White Cross Hill brought little action from the Germans and we were later taken out of the line. In all, there had been eleven days' constant action, but the beach-head was stable. Things could have been different. The Yanks could have cut the road and trapped half the German Army between us and the Eighth Army. They were the only ones with armour. The 75th Armoured Division should have been landing about three days on, but the weather worsened and it was the tenth or eleventh day before they landed.'

At La Molina, 41 Commando stood off repeated attacks on their positions – infantry assaults interspersed with heavy shelling and mortaring. A direct hit on the Commando HQ wounded the CO, Lieutenant Colonel Bertie Lumsden, and attacks on 41 continued throughout the day, the last being driven off by a counter-attack by Q Troop. 2 Commando also endured infiltration attacks, with machine-gunning, mortaring and heavy shelling, detailing off one troop to help 41 hold on to the south, until at midnight on the 10th both units were relieved by an army battalion from 138 Brigade and withdrew to the shore for a brief rest – eight hours. During the battle of Salerno, Bob Bavister recalls that Captain Randolph Churchill arrived at Brigade HQ, 'and once there, proceeded to tell the Brigadier how to fight his battle. One day, when he was at the Rear HQ with Tom Churchill (our Brigade Major), a runner came back from Brigadier Laycock, saluted and passed the message, "Brigadier's compliments, Sir. Forward HQ is moving to map reference so and so, and on no account is Captain Churchill to know." The following morning Randolph returned to North Africa'.

With the Germans pounding the beach-head, both Commandos returned to their old sangars and trenches at

Vietri and La Molina and held them without rest until
the dawn of 13 September, when the enemy bombarded
No. 2 for an hour and then put in a heavy infantry attack
against both flanks. By now, No. 2 had been fighting for
four days and been reduced to no more than three hundred
very weary men and 41 Commando had already lost
eleven officers, including the CO, and seventy-four men.
The enemy managed to force their way past Vietri and
were in position to take the commanding feature on
Dragone Hill in the Commando's rear, where they were
checked by artillery fire and a counter-attack from the
Brigade reserve, which consisted of one troop each from
No. 2 and 41. The reserve's advance proved sufficient to
stall the enemy and the Germans retreated again into the
La Molina pass while the Commandos were again withdrawn for what little rest could be found back at the
beach. This time they were out of the line for a whole
day.

The two units were called back to the line on the 15th,
and sent to assault the village of Pigoletti, which overlooked the landing beaches. Pigoletti is a hilltop village,
dominated by two other hills, with another high crag to
the east. 41 Commando at once attacked and took this
crag, naming it 41 Commando Hill, while 2 Commando
advanced up the steep valley to Pigoletti itself, led by
Colonel Jack, sword in hand. Colonel Jack eventually got
so far ahead of his Commando, who were clearing enemy
positions as they came, that he entered Pigoletti accompanied by just one other man, Corporal Ruffell. The two
of them overran a German mortar position and taking one
of the prisoners with him as interpreter, Colonel Jack
went on to clear the village by himself, sending forty
prisoners back into the arms of 6 Troop. By that night
No. 2 had captured 136 prisoners and Colonel Jack
received the DSO to add to his Military Cross.

By midnight No. 2 had consolidated below Pigoletti but
they were then asked to advance through Pigoletti again,

and seize the hill behind it, known as the Pimple. This two-troop attack was led by Captain the Duke of Wellington, but they were met with a hail of machine gun fire and grenades just outside the village, which decimated the advancing troops and killed the Duke.

W. G. Bleach remembers the Duke. 'He was OC 2 Troop, 2 Commando at Vietri and later at the Pimple. His batman, Tommy Tombs, Syd Crane the signaller, and I were once pinned down in a cave opposite the viaduct at Vietri, and had been there for two days. Syd got out to try and find some food and returned unsuccessful, so the Duke got out the last tin of "K" rations from his pouch and passed it to Tommy to share out. Tommy cut it into four pieces, but the Duke said, "No, not for me, I'm not hungry." And he said it with such conviction that we all believed him.'

Next morning, No. 2 linked up with No. 41, still clinging to their hill on the flank. Both units were then heavily shelled, firstly by German 88s, then by their own artillery, which accidentally put down a concentration of fire on 41 Commando just as they were about to put in their attack against the Pimple. This barrage cost the life of 41's new CO, Major Edwards, their second commanding officer in three days. 41 did manage to get one troop onto the Pimple and they held it for twenty-four hours, until the last six men still alive were withdrawn. On the 19th, a full infantry brigade attacked and took the Pimple, finding the summit strewn with German and Commando dead. On the same day both units, having lost fifty per cent of their strength in the Salerno battle, were withdrawn to Sicily to rest.

Ted Kelly recalls scenes from Salerno: 'After rehearsals near Palermo we embarked with the vast convoy en route to Salerno. The night before the landing was due we heard of the Italian surrender on the radio. Misguidedly, we thought that this called for a celebration in preparation for the hysterical welcome we would surely receive. So we ate the hard chocolate and sweets which constituted our emergency ration. We were soon to be corrected. Our landing at Vietri sul Mare was on schedule and we were quite hungry when supplies started to come through two days later. Details of this great battle are well documented but just a few personal incidents might be of interest. Early in the landing we were on a hill above Salerno overlooking a valley. German tanks could be seen in the distance far below. One of our men opened up with a Bren gun, which seemed to me to be a noble but fairly useless gesture. It resulted in our position coming under fire from the tanks' 80mm guns. My close comrade, Stan Connor (of Ink Spots' fame) and Tim Burchall were beside me on a forward ledge. A tank shell burst above us not more than fifteen feet away. I saw the actual burst. It was like those artist's impressions of Great War shell bursts which we used to see in the *Illustrated London News*, a fiery centre with shrapnel radiating from it. Both Stan and Tim were hit – Tim to lose an arm, Stan to die. I didn't even get dust in my eyes.

'Elsewhere in the area, after a fierce fight, we advanced through a German position. On the ground was a German soldier who had obviously taken a direct hit from a two-inch mortar bomb. His legs and torso up to the waist were intact. What remained above was the hollowed-out chest cavity so that the body looked like a grocer's scoop. The scoop was full of wasps gorging themselves on his flesh. At the height of the German counter-attack, we were in close combat and under severe pressure. Support was requested from the Navy and was quickly forthcoming. The gunfire was accurate. It landed among us. Nothing the Germans threw at us was ever like this. Naval shells exploding a few feet away lifted me bodily out of my scrape-trench. To paraphrase, I don't know what it did to the Germans, but it scared the hell out of me! On the fourteenth day of the action I succumbed with malaria and was removed to hospital, where I remained when No.

Commando Memorial, Spean Bridge, Scotland.

World War II Landing Craft (Assault) – L.C.A.

Partisan soldiers, Vis, 1944. The one in front is thirteen.

Record of an early raid, Commando Trail, Luc-sur-Mer, Normandy.

Commando bring field artillery ashore on Vis, Yugoslavia, 1944.

2 Troop, 2 Commando. Capt. The Duke of Wellington is seated centre.

Major Leslie Callf and men of 5 Troop, 9 Commando, Anzio, 21–22 July 1944.

Signals H.Q., 2 Commando Brigade, Comacchio, 1945.

Men of 2 Commando landing in Corfu after Battle of Sarande, October, 1944.

Left to right: Mts Turlito, Fuga and Ornito. Faito is beyond Ornito. Taken from the west valley of Ruffiano.

Mt Ornito with monumental cairn at foot. Mike Long playing the pipes.

The Military Governor and Lt. Col. Tod, DSO, passing 5 Troop, 9 Commando, Greece, 1944.

Frank Barton of 6 Commando
(standing far right) at Ranville,
D-Day, 1944.

6 Commando Memorial, Sallenelles,
Normandy.

Grave of Lt. George Herbert, DCM, MM, 3 Commando, Ranville.

Grave of a German-Jewish soldier of 10 (Inter-Allied) Commando, Ranville, Normandy.

Henry Brown (seated centre) with orderly room staff of No. 1 Commando in India, prior to their move to Burma, August 1944.

2 Commando were withdrawn. I fretted to rejoin them and by devious means managed to do so at Molfetta and Bari.'

The Salerno battle was a very close-run thing, and at one point General Mark Clark, the commanding general, was seriously considering an evacuation. No. 2 and 41 played an outstanding part in holding the line while the German positions were pounded by the guns of the fleet. The British Eighth Army finally linked up with the American Fifth on 20 September, and Naples fell ten days later.

Commando operations along the Italian coast had this much in common; it was usually possible to get ashore undetected, or in the face of slight opposition, but then after a short delay of anything from a few hours to a day, the Germans would hit back. 'I've fought a lot of people in my time,' says Brigadier Peter Young, 'but if you haven't fought Germans you don't know what fighting is. However hard they were pressed they usually found something to sling at you.' This fact was borne out in the next two battles in which the Commandos took part, following the departure of Brigadier Laycock, who returned to England in September to take over from Mountbatten as Chief of Combined Operations. John Durnford Slater was promoted to Brigadier and took over command for the landing at Termoli.

Termoli is a small port at the mouth of the Bifurno river on the east coast of Italy. On 19 September 1943 it lay ten miles behind the enemy lines, in front of the advancing Eighth Army units which included No. 3 Commando and No. 40 (Royal Marine) Commando. Eighth Army were now advancing up the east side of Italy at a smart clip, but Italy is a country where the terrain favours the defence, and one of the finest defensive lines available south of the Sangro lay along the Bifurno river, which runs between the steep Appenines, which form the central spine of Italy, and the Adriatic Sea. To prevent the

German Army digging in behind the Bifurno, General Montgomery decided to send Durnford Slater's force, 3 Commando, 40 Commando and the SRS to take Termoli from the sea and hold it until the Eighth Army came up. If they could do this, then any possible German line on the Bifurno would be outflanked. This operation was codenamed Devon, and the assault force sailed from Manfredonia at 11.30 hrs on 2 October. In view of the speed with which the operation had been mounted (two days), intelligence information was scanty, but No. 3 Commando were intrigued to learn that their most likely opponents would be men from the same parachute unit they had met the previous month at the Punta dei Milati. The force went ashore some time after midnight, No. 3 getting a dry landing, No. 40 meeting a deep gulley behind a false beach offshore, drowning all their radio sets as they waded in. Some of the SRS even had to swim. Nevertheless, in the face of light opposition, they soon overran the town and were in their positions by 08.00 hrs, having taken some 500 prisoners, most of them – ominously – from the 4th German Parachute Brigade.

By 09.30 hrs 40 Commando were in position astride a road outside the town, happily shooting up enemy transport; 3 Commando were in the town; and the SRS had already made contact with an advancing battalion of Lancashire Fusiliers from the Eighth Army. Reinforcements from 78 Division crossed the Bifurno and moved into the town and bridgehead throughout the next day and all the next night. Then about noon on 4 October, after a quiet morning, the Germans hit back hard.

Durnford Slater was having lunch when one of his officers, John Pooley, reported 'dozens' of enemy tanks approaching, and he put his men on full alert. The pressure on the Termoli perimeter became intense when the constant rain raised the level of the Bifurno and carried away the only bridge. The Germans were now on the offensive and tanks from a fresh German armoured

formation, the 16th Panzer Division, came up to assault
the town. This assault began at dawn on the 5th and
opened with a bombing and strafing attack by the Luftwaffe. Then artillery concentrations fell in the town,
followed by infantry attacks with tank support. By 14.00
hrs all the flank units defending Termoli had been overrun and the town's defence was reduced to a core of two
infantry battalions and Durnford Slater's small force.
Peter Young, arriving from hospital, and Captain Peter
Hellings of 40 Commando, had at one time to force some
fleeing troops back into position and fire their artillery
pieces at the enemy tanks.

'That was about all I did actually,' says Peter Young,
'because I was in hospital and not at the landing. Arthur
Komrower commanded 3, "Pops" Manners ran 40 Commando, and that huge Irishman, Paddy Mayne, had the
SRS. They took care of things.'

The enemy moved up hard against the Termoli perimeter, raining mortar fire on the town, and by dusk had
moved tanks into position within a hundred yards of No.
3 Commando lines to the west of the town and had more
infantry even closer to 3 Commando HQ. 'We could even
hear them talking,' said Major Komrower. 3 Commando
quietly disengaged and withdrew into Termoli, from
where they prepared to fight it out in the streets. Meanwhile, 40 Commando and the SRS were still holding their
section of the perimeter and the Commandos continued
to hold it until the bridge across the Bifurno was repaired
by Sappers on the 5th, and the 38th Irish Brigade advanced
into the town. 40 Commando beat off another tank and
infantry attack through the town cemetery on the morning of 6 October and the battle of Termoli was over. 'In
the course of numerous actions during the war,' wrote
Durnford Slater, 'this was the only time I really thought
we might be defeated.' General Montgomery of Eighth
Army, delighted with this operation, told Durnford Slater
to take his much-depleted force back to Bari 'where there

is plenty of wine and plenty of girls'. This they did. Even better, at the end of October, Nos. 3 and 41 Commandos and the SRS returned to England. Their places in 2 SS Brigade were taken by Nos. 9 and 43 (Royal Marine) Commandos.

In early November 1943, Brigadier Tom Churchill, brother of Jack Churchill of 2 Commando, took command of 2 Special Service Brigade, which by Christmas consisted of 2 and 9 Army Commando, plus 40 and 43 (Royal Marine) Commando, plus the Belgian and Polish Troops of No. 10 (I-A Commando). The Brigade was based at Castellammare, with the Brigade HQ at Molfetta.

Churchill wanted his new units, No. 9 (Lieutenant Colonel Ronnie Tod) and the IA Commando troops to gain operational experience as soon as possible, so the Belgians and Poles were attached to infantry units along the line of the River Sangro, where they were used by 17 Brigade for night patrols, until heavy snowfalls made foot patrols impossible. While they were still in the line, No. 9 Commando opened their batting with a raid across the Garigliano.

No. 9 Commando were ordered by General McCready to assist in the first assault on the Gustav Line, which marked the opening phase of the Battle of Cassino. The Commando's task was to land and outflank the enemy positions north of the Garigliano river, then march inland and destroy a bridge. In the flat lower reaches of the river, this attack had to be made under cover of night, and the attack went in on the beaches on the north side of the river on the night of 29/30 December 1943. This operation was codenamed Partridge, and the story is well described by those of 9 Commando who took part, beginning with extracts from the Unit History.

'In the previous three years, almost every operation planned for the Commando had been cancelled. In the next three months almost every one planned took place. Fifth Army had now reached the Garigliano, and was held up by a strongly entrenched enemy in the mountains north of the river and further east at Cassino.

'Three weeks were spent training for the operation, and a full-scale rehearsal was carried out from the LSIs *Princess Beatrix* and *Royal Ulsterman*. On Christmas Eve it poured and most troop HQs were a foot deep in mud and water. The day before Partridge, the MO received a Christmas present, a book entitled *Death Tomorrow*.

'The operation started badly as the Commando were landed 1000 yards from the correct beach and an hour and a half late. Once ashore, the Commando split into three parties, X, Y and Z, although X was a boatload short as one craft broke down and failed to arrive at the beachhead. Even so, all the attacks went in, Force X sustaining five casualties overrunning an enemy position at the mouth of the Garigliano. Captain McNeil led Force Y to attack German positions on a hill north of the landing beach where, although suffering casualties from mines on the way, they overran the enemy positions and destroyed a tank. Force Z found that the low country behind the beach was flooded, threaded with wire and sewn with mines, but pushed on to assault the German positions in and around a Roman amphitheatre. After this attack, the troops withdrew to a spot a mile inland from the sea, where a ruined bridge lay across the river, and Captain Mike Long began to guide them across to the British bank.'

Mike Long tells his story of Partridge: 'The whole Commando was to land on the German side of the river, one party going north to attack a defensive position. This was 1 and 2 Troops led by Jack McNeil. They ran into a minefield. The second party, 4 and 6 Troops under Major Cameron, was to attack a position astride the Naples–Rome road at a point where it crossed the Garigliano. The bridge here had been blown up. Commando HQ was by the river mouth on the shore. We landed late, some time between 02.00 and 03.00 hrs. Anyway, Major Cameron's party went inland and we ran into a flooded area. It was only ankle-deep so that was all right. The next thing we came across was a minefield. There was enough light for us to distinguish the "*Achtung Minen*" displayed, I think, for the benefit of the Germans. We crossed this minefield, and luckily no one set off a mine. 4 Troop advanced towards a pillbox by the road and was fired on, with two lance corporals being killed. The rest of the troop went straight in and put grenades into the pillbox and six Germans came out spluttering. The smoke grenades were a godsend. All this took no more than ten minutes.

'The next problem was to get across the river. The total number of 4 and 6 Troops was about ninety plus the POWs. The river was about thirty yards wide, but when the bridge was blown, some of the girders fell into the water and we could use those for eight or nine yards. There was then a gap of, say fifteen yards, where some other girders showed just above the water, but then a gap of eight yards before the British bank. We could make out the girders in the middle of the river, which was fairly fast and very cold.

'We had brought ropes, and I reported to Major Cameron and said I thought that it was possible to swim out to the girders in the middle and that I would attempt this. I got across and attached my rope to the girders. The next man across was a private, with another rope, and he swam his rope from the girder to a tree on the British bank. We had Mae Wests, which were inflated before the men crossed. The next man across was wearing a rucksack. He jumped into the water upstream from the rope, was swept under it and drowned. We never saw him again. This was seen by quite a number of the men.

'The others got in downstream of the rope, and gripped it to pull themselves across. The first light of dawn was about 06.00 hrs, when our artillery opened up with smoke and HE, and the Germans opened fire on our crossing point with mortars and artillery. Fortunately, the ground was very soft and although we were hit by clods of earth, no one was hurt. By 08.00 hrs we were all across. The land was absolutely flat. As we were making our way back, a Messerschmitt came over and strafed us. Our six German prisoners were the first to hit the ground.'

Captain Harry Lucas, OC of the Heavy Weapons Troop, had a bird's-eye view of this 9 Commando operation. 'As was usual in operations of this kind, involving surprise seaborne attacks of short duration and rapid movement while ashore (the classic Commando raid, in fact), there was no role for the Heavy Weapons Troop. It was thought important, however, to arrange liaison with 201 Guards Brigade HQ, whose units were to have a vital role in assisting the withdrawal of the Commando once its tasks had been accomplished. I was therefore attached to 201 Brigade HQ as Liaison Officer for the duration of the operation. I was given a vehicle and a driver, and allowed to take my batman, Ted Healey, but I was not given a wireless set. There seemed at the time to be good reasons for this but, in the event, I was to regret this arrangement.

'I enjoyed my Christmas dinner, when we had quite a ceilidh, and set off with Healey and my driver for Brigade HQ, which was in a fairly large farmhouse about 2,000 yards south of the river. I only remember one thing about this journey – and subsequent ones on the same road. At one point the road ran for perhaps a mile (it seemed more!) in full view of the German gunners in the hills across the river. At the beginning of this stretch stood a military policeman, beside the graves of his two predecessors, controlling traffic movement. He held us up while vehicles came racing down from the north, and I exchanged a few words with him. Then he said, "Right, now's your chance Sir, and good luck" and off we went. I think we covered that bit of road before the German gunners had time to put their cigarettes out.

'We arrived at Brigade as dusk was falling. I reported to the Brigadier, who received me very kindly and soon made me feel at home in the somewhat unfamiliar environment of a Guards Brigade in the front line. "We dine at seven," he said, "but I shall not expect you to change for dinner." He was not joking, nor did he surprise me – I knew, from my experience with a regular Battalion of a Line Regiment in the BEF, that it is the tradition to maintain the highest level of normal, civilized behaviour that conditions will permit. In this case, that included dining at a splendid circular table, on which stood some lovely pieces of regimental silver; the linen was spotless, and all who were not on duty wore service dress. The atmosphere was one of relaxed formality; one soon forgot that this really was the front line, and that the Germans could easily lob a shell into the middle of the table. Why didn't they? In fact, while we were having lunch the following day, there was an almighty "Crump!" outside. "Go and have a look, Charles, would you?" said the Brigadier to one of his subalterns. Charles went and returned. "An 88 in the midden, Brigadier," he said. "Casualties or damage?" "A couple of naked hens and a lot of loose feathers." "Oh, what bad luck," said the Brigadier. I was not quite sure whether he was commiserating with the hens, the farmer or the German gunners.

The next morning, the Brigade Major asked me to discuss with him the arrangements for my part in the operation. The Brigade's task was to secure the south bank of the river so that the Commando would not have to fight its way back after its job was done. Two crossing points were envisaged, one near the mouth of the river by Goatley boat (small folding assault boats), and one in the neighbourhood of the bridge which carried the Appian Way over the river, one span of which had been demolished. The Coldstreams would clear the area round the bridge, and the Scots Guards would secure the south bank near the river mouth. The BM suggested that I should attach myself to the Battalion HQ of the Scots Guards, but that I should have complete freedom of movement,

subject to the final authority of the Scots Guards' Colonel.
I agreed to all this, and indeed it was difficult to see what
better arrangements could be made in the circumstances.
I was also invited to accompany a reconnaissance patrol
which was going out that night to have a look at the river.
This made sense, and at least I would be doing something.

'This patrol was uneventful, but I was pleased to have a
chance of looking at the ground, even in the dark. The
land in the neighbourhood of the Garigliano is flat. It had
been drained during the 1930s as part of Mussolini's great
scheme for the Pontine Marshes which, together with the
punctuality of the railways, is said to be his greatest
contribution to civilization. South of the river, at this
time, it was rather dry and sandy, slashed with drainage
dykes which probably dated from antiquity, not as yet
under intensive cultivation – the few farm buildings
suggested that this land, even in better times, only provided a modest amount of rough pasture. There appeared
to be some enemy occupation of the south bank, and so it
turned out during the raid. But the Guards would deal
with that. As for the going, it would be daylight when the
Commando withdrew – in full view of the enemy, but
that could not be helped; and at least, if things went
wrong, the dykes and other irregularities would facilitate
an ordered withdrawal.

'At about 01.00 hrs on the 29th I was wakened by the
Brigadier's servant, with a message that a patrol had
brought in two prisoners and, if I wished to interrogate
them, I could have first go (tactical squeeze, in the
language of Interrogation Officers). Of course I accepted,
and was taken to the town jail, which was the POW cage
for the time being. These prisoners did not need squeez-
ing; they told me they were Czechs who wished to join
the Allied forces, that they had deserted at the first
opportunity, and that there were many such in the Division facing us. I was not immediately concerned with
this, so I began to question them on the things we needed

187

to know. They then gave me full details of the defences in the area we were to attack, every MG post, the approximate strength of the garrison in each position, and the position of every minefield, and they drew me a sketch. In fact, we already knew much of this, but confirmation was useful, and up to the minute. They also told me that they knew we were coming on the following night, because their Italian girlfriends had told them so, and they were seldom wrong!

'I reported all this to the Brigadier – it was full daylight by now – and got his permission to go immediately back to 9 Commando and give them this information. As they were now on board their Assault Landing Ships, they could not be contacted on the Army wireless net, and security was an important factor. We drove back to Bacoli as fast as we could, against heavy traffic on the Appian Way, and on arrival went straight to the beach, where we could see the ships about a mile offshore. A local fisherman was just putting off in his boat, and I asked him to take me out to the ships. He refused – he had to go fishing. I drew my revolver and said, "Then I'll take the boat." He grumbled, but took me to the nearest ship, which happened to be the one on which the CO had embarked with HQ and half the raiding force. I told the CO (Ronnie Tod) everything I had heard from the POWs. He called all the Troop Officers on that ship, saying to me, "Tell them everything you've told me, Harry, except about the minefields – they've got to go through them, so the less they know about them the better. Then go to the other ship, tell Francis (the second-in-command) all you've told me and ask him to rouse the officers there." I did this and the Officer of the Watch had me put ashore whereupon I returned with all haste to 201 Brigade, only stopping for a quick cup of tea and a sandwich with my cousin Alex in his Battery Mess (all I had consumed during the whole day, and it was to last me all night as well).

'In fact, I did not stop at Brigade, but set off straight
away for the Scots Guards HQ, which had by now (20.00
hrs) moved to its TAC HQ about 600 yards from the river.
At the beginning of the track leading forward, a military
police post had been set up, and Healey was waiting for
me here. "This way for the battle, Sir," said the MP
Sergeant in charge. "You are expected at the Scots Guards'
HQ. Just follow the white tapes." It was like the Aldershot Tattoo – not having seen action with a field army
since Dunkirk, all these trappings of a modern battle were
new to me, and I was duly impressed. The platoon which
was to attack the position at the river mouth had already
left for their starting line, and the Colonel, having offered
me the hospitality of his whisky flask, suggested I should
wait with him at all events until after the preparatory
barrage which the Divisional Artillery had laid on. "Get a
good view from here," he said.

'We did indeed. Neither Healey nor I had ever seen
anything like it. At a few minutes to nine the whole
front, behind us and as far as we could see to our right, lit
up with a tremendous crash, and continued with a shattering din in which it was not possible to distinguish
separate explosions. At intervals coloured tracer from
heavy calibre automatic weapons – Oerlikons, I supposed
– streamed northward, presumably to simulate demar-
kation zones for attacking infantry. We could see shells
bursting in the area which the Commando was to attack
and, especially, along the river line. Clearly the Guards'
assault groups were having a hard time. Eventually they
both signalled that they had taken their objectives, and
were digging in. The Scots Guards had suffered several
casualties, including some killed.

'By this time, the Commando's H-Hour was approaching, and the Colonel whose interest in their progress was
no less than my own, was keeping a sharp radio watch for
news of their movements. By midnight it was clear that
something had happened to delay them, and I began to

ask myself how I would be able to face my kind hosts if
(as had happened only too often in my time with Commandos) the raid was called off, after the sacrifices they
had made. I have no doubt the same notion had occurred
to our own Brigadier, who was at Brigade HQ. Eventually,
however, the Colonel, who must have been aware of my
anxieties, called me and said, "All's well, my boy, they've
landed and are proceeding to their objectives." It now
seemed to me that there was nothing more I could do
here and, although I was loath to cut myself off from my
only link with the Brigade radio net, I decided the time
had come to go down to the river and try to see what was
going on.

'What was going on was a hell of a schemozzle, with a
very great deal of noise. It was not easy at first to
distinguish between enemy and friendly fire, especially as
we were keeping our heads down. Our bank of the river
was getting its share too. What did seem clear was that
Jerry had concluded from the strength and nature of the
artillery preparation that a major Allied advance was
taking place across the river. I did not know where to find
the Scots Guards' platoon HQ, so I had taken as my
guiding mark a small group of farm buildings which I
could see silhouetted against the sky, and lit up by
frequent flashes from bursting shells or mortar bombs.
When we reached it, it was empty and had been hit
several times (incidentally it was the only building I was
able to identify when I visited the area in 1987, still
bearing its wartime scars). It was an unhealthy spot, and
we moved smartly downstream a few yards. Actually the
ground was so soft that a man lying down – as we took
care to do most of the time – was fairly safe from all but
a direct hit. There did not seem to be much falling on the
Commando target area, but quite heavy shellfire could be
seen further north – presumably British batteries trying
to inhibit movement of reserves, and to keep up the
pretence of a general engagement. Later, the stonking

ceased for some while along the river line, and at one point we heard small arms fire and some explosions towards the river mouth. I assumed that this was the attack on the small enemy post in that area, which was one of the Commando's objectives. How I wished I had some means of communicating with the Colonel, to discover whether in fact that crossing point at least was now secure on both banks. However, we moved along the bank almost to the river mouth. It was too dark to see anything. After all the shooting, it seemed to be the darkest part of the whole night. I decided to remain here until it was light enough to size up the situation.

'From time to time we heard quite heavy firing, first in the direction of Mt Argenta, the strongpoint to the north, which I knew to be Captain Jack McNeil's objective. Some time later we heard a piper playing *The Green Hills*. "That's 2 Troop," said Healey. Then, when the sky was beginning to pale, there came the sound of heavy fighting from the direction of the bridge, a mile away to our right, where I believed (rightly) the Coldstream Guards were in control of the near bank. I learned afterwards that these sounds of battle came from 4 Troop's attack on the amphitheatre, and later 4 and 6 Troops fighting their way over the river. Soon, in the growing light, we could see the boats on the mud across the water and figures moving down to the river's edge. As we watched, we saw a tall pencil of smoke and debris shoot up, apparently under the foot of one of the men. "Mine!" said Healey. "Some poor bugger's had it." We learned later that the mine, in that soft mud, had exploded in so narrow a field that the shock wave and debris completely missed the lucky fellow who had touched it off.

'It appeared that some of the small boats had been damaged by shellfire, but some of the wounded were ferried across and began their journey over the rough ground towards Brigade HQ and the Regimental Aid Post.

191

At the same time, we saw at least two DUKWs (amphibious vehicles) approaching from seaward. Again, I was paralysed by the absence of any means of communicating with them, but fortunately they had been fully briefed and made at once for the party on the far bank. This was a great relief, as it solved the problem of transporting the wounded. No such relief was likely to be available to the troops crossing by the broken bridge, and it seemed likely that they might have heavy casualties. I therefore walked back to Brigade, where I was told that evacuation of casualties had been taken care of. However, I found one stretcher party, or rather a stretcher and three bearers, who had already brought in one casualty from the river mouth, and they volunteered to come back and see if we could help at the bridge. On the way we met several members of 4 and 6 Troops, who told me that there were indeed several casualties, among them Corporals Crawford and Balneaves who had been killed. As we approached the bridge area we met 6 Troop, moving in extended order and justifiably very pleased with themselves as 4 Troop had been, despite their sad news. Two men were helping Lieutenant Micky Scott who had been hit in the chest. He refused help, but he was blowing bubbles of bright frothy blood. When we examined him he had a wound in his chest and another in his back, and it was quite clear that a bullet or a fragment had pierced his lung. I therefore insisted that he lie on the stretcher and allow us to carry him back.

'It was a wearisome journey – we had all been busy all night, and I had had no sleep and little to eat or drink for thirty-six hours. To make matters worse, although everything was now quiet in the whole battle area, one German 88 was obviously looking for a target for his ill humour. We were by now the only thing moving on the landscape, and he began to snipe at us. We had to rest from time to time, and while we rested I looked out for the next hole to run for. He had at least half a dozen shots at us, most of them near enough to make us duck, before he eventually decided he had wasted enough ammunition and gave up. We handed Micky over to the Medical Section and went for a late lunch. The next time I saw him he was in hospital in Naples, where he made a complete recovery. Sadly, he was killed a few weeks later at Anzio. It had been a brilliantly successful operation, though rather costly, and the Commando thoroughly deserved the praise bestowed on it by the Higher Command. It was a most heartening start to our share in the Italian campaign. My own part in it was summed up in the phrase I used at the postmortem after our return: "The umpire sees most of the battle." Unfortunately our satisfaction was marred by an event which caused some ill feeling at the time. The Colonel was ordered – despite, I believe, the strenuous protests of our Brigadier, Tom Churchill – to send out a patrol to bring in some dead who had been left on the river bank. The bodies were not found, the area had been re-mined, and a very popular Sergeant had his foot blown off.'

The main body of the unit returned in DUKWs from the mouth of the river. The Commando suffered some thirty casualties on Partridge, including nine killed. They achieved their objectives, killed sixteen of the enemy and brought back twenty-six prisoners.

After Christmas the headquarters of 2 Special Service Brigade was established near Molfetta and then at Castellammare. No. 2 Commando were ordered to prepare for operations with the Yugoslav partisans in the Dalmatian islands, 40 Commando went into the line with the 56th Division, while Nos. 9 and 43 Commandos went north to the Anzio landings.

8

Anzio, Faito and Anzio, 1944

'Our deeds still travel with us from afar,
And what we have been makes us what we are.'
GEORGE ELIOT

The landings at Anzio were an attempt to outflank the Gustav Line and force the German Army to withdraw from the positions around Cassino, where it had stood for months, defeating attack after attack and inflicting great loss on the Allied armies. In the event, Anzio itself became another beleaguered beach-head, and the battle there went on for months until the Gustav Line itself finally collapsed.

The Anzio landing – Operation Shingle – was a repetition of other Italian operations. The Allied troops got ashore almost undetected and were able to make good ground before the Germans hit back and contained them. The difficulty at Anzio was that this containment led to a bloody battle that lasted not just for a few days but from 21 January 1944 until the end of May, during which time the Allied forces suffered severe casualties. At the beginning, however, it all seemed easy.

Captain Lucas of 9 Commando: 'At some time early in January, officers of 9 Commando became aware that the unit was to take part in an operation involving a seaborne landing, followed by a dash to a major city which, or parts of which, they would have to hold until a larger force arrived to relieve them. The Commando would be re-armed with special automatic weapons (MGs with an exceptionally high firing rate, of a type used to arm fighter aircraft). These were issued and training soon began. The whole unit, with all its arms and equipment, was to be landed, and thence conveyed in jeeps to the objective. The mouth of a major river was mentioned, and it did not need much imagination to guess that the city was Rome. "Theirs is not to reason why," but I believe that most of us were not sorry to learn that a somewhat harebrained scheme – even for Commandos – had been abandoned, and that we were not to be the first troops to make a battleground of the Eternal City.

'We were briefed in due course for a seaborne landing by a considerable Allied force on the beaches north of Anzio, with the object of threatening the German lines of communication behind the Gustav Line, and so assisting the main armies now attacking across the Garigliano. The 1st British Infantry Division would land in the first wave, and would form a perimeter on the high ground about a quarter of a mile from the beach. No. 9 and No. 43 (RM) Commandos would land in the second wave, pass through the perimeter (held at that point by the Scots Guards) to seize a hill feature about seven miles away on the main road to Rome, at a point about five miles north of Anzio, and hold it until the beach-head had been extended to include our position. We would then be relieved, and return to our base in Bacoli. Initial resistance was not expected to be heavy, but fairly prompt reaction by the enemy was likely – and hoped for, since this was the object of the operation.

'The Commandos embarked in SS *Derbyshire* on 21 January and landed shortly before dawn the next morning, virtually unopposed. There was a slight hiccup in proceedings when LCAs carrying all except Brigade HQ and 9 Commando's No. 3 (Heavy Weapons) Troop, which I was commanding, grounded on a bank some way offshore. The Brigadier found himself ashore without the greater part of his command for something like an hour.

3 Troop were not complaining – we had the Guards
between us and the enemy, and we also had very heavy
loads to carry, and were glad of the chance to get a start
ahead of the assault troops. There was only one enemy
gun (an 88mm) in action, firing an occasional shell in our
direction. I met the Brigadier just after his servant had
been wounded by this gun, and he agreed that I should
move my troop up to the perimeter and await our friends
there.

'The plan was for 3 Troop, with our three-inch mortars,
our Vickers MMGs and ammunition conveyed in steel-
framed canvas handcarts, to follow a track which ran
north for a few hundred yards, then inland to the top of
the higher ground where the Guards were digging in, to
meet another track running south, parallel to the shore.
From a point opposite where we were standing, a third
track ran inland through the wooded country in the
direction of our objective. I told Lieutenant David Balls,
commanding the Mortar Section, that I, with my batman
Ted Healey, would go directly to the upper track and
identify the track through the forest, while he brought
the troop round by the longer route as planned.

'Healey and I set off up the slope to the perimeter track,
passing on the way (about fifty yards off) a sandbagged
gun emplacement. We soon found the beginning of the
forest track, had a word with one or two Guardsmen, and
sat down to have a cigarette and watch our comrades
coming ashore. As we smoked and chatted away, Healey
said, "No more from that 88mm," and before I could
answer, thirteen German gunners got up, climbed out of
the emplacement we had seen, ostentatiously threw down
their weapons, and surrendered to us, muttering something about their duty. By this time the leading troop of 9
Commando was almost up to us. 3 Troop arrived at about
the same time, so I handed my prisoners over to the
Guards and we all went on our way. I had not had time to

interrogate them, but I am sure this was the gun-crew which had fired on us when we landed.

'The Commando moved through the woodland in an "advance to contact" formation, with flanking parties as well as forward points to avoid being surprised from any direction. 3 Troop found the going very hard as the small-radius wheels sank into the soft, sandy track. After about an hour, however, as we were passing a small farm in the more open country east of the forest area, David spotted, and promptly commandeered a bullock cart, which speeded things up a great deal, and we were able to feel that we were not holding up the more lightly-equipped assault troops.

'No. 43 (RM) Commando meanwhile had branched off to the right to attack the objective frontally, while we were moving round to the north of the feature to take it from the rear. Everything was very quiet until, as the leading section approached a road, we heard a motorcycle and several short bursts of automatic fire as this section intercepted and dealt with an enemy motorcyclist. A brave fellow – after being knocked off his machine by the first burst he had made a very determined attempt to get away, which cost him his life. Eventually we saw and recognized our objective away to the right, and were soon in position to attack. The three-inch mortars were sited and prepared to support an attack with either HE or smoke; the MMGs were sited to cover the left flank of the advance, which was thought to be the more likely threat. My guns were in fact laid, over open sights, on the area round a group of farm buildings on the skyline. I had gone to Commando HQ to say that we were ready, when I was called back to the guns by the MG Sergeant. "Look at that, Sir," he said, pointing to our target, which was about 2,000 yards away. I looked and saw movement, something red and white. With my field-glasses I could see that it was a woman hanging out her washing. I told the Sergeant that I would be with the guns during the advance, and that he must not fire without my order. It was really rather uncanny, or unreal, finding ourselves in a peaceful countryside, whose inhabitants were totally oblivious of our presence, much less our intention to wage war in their midst. I half expected the farmer to come over and ask us what the blazes we were doing on his land! As I turned to look again at the lightly wooded skyline which was our objective, I saw a number of Germans rise up and move down the slope towards us – with their hands up. That battle was over. They all looked very young and rather apprehensive (it seems that they were running away from the Marines, only to find us waiting for them). They were put under guard until arrangements could be made to transfer them to the POW cage.

'Meanwhile, 9 Commando took possession of "our" hill, and set about digging in and preparing to defend it against attack from any direction, together with our Royal Marine comrades, who also, rightly, claimed their share of real estate. During the next forty-eight hours, and for long after that, the rapid build-up of men and equipment went on. Field and medium batteries of artillery, tanks, self-propelled guns, anti-aircraft guns, ammunition, stores, casualty clearing stations and field hospitals – everything an army needs in the field. We had never seen anything like it, as this was 9 Commando's first major invasion.

'We were relieved and transported to Anzio town on the second or third day, and thence by sea to Bacoli. A number of small incidents stick in my mind. On the first evening, Jack McNeil, OC 2 Troop, came over on a friendly visit to 3 Troop and, while we were chatting, a German aircraft flew over quite low firing its cannons. Jack and I dived for the nearest trench. Mine was a foxhole, his was the troop latrine. Fun for all, except poor Jack. A medium battery RA moved in behind my own HQ while I was having an afternoon nap in my foxhole dug in the sand; it fired its first ranging shots and the concussion collapsed my trench, burying me alive, so that Healey had to dig me out. On the first morning we chatted to tank crews returning from a patrol into the outskirts of Rome itself. "Anzio Archie", a very large German gun on a railway mounting, sent his enormous shells screaming over our heads at regular intervals on their way to Anzio town. While we were resting in the town square waiting to re-embark, he gave us one all to ourselves, but no harm done. An awful, inexplicable feeling of doom assailed me, when all was quiet on a bright sunny morning just before we were relieved – as if I had a premonition of all that was to be suffered in that place during the following weeks – a feeling which disappeared as quickly as it came, fortunately. "Anzio One", as 9 Commando came to call it, was a walk in the sun.'

Nos. 9 and 43 Commandos had landed at Anzio at 05.30 hrs on 21 January, advanced almost unopposed towards the foot of the Alban Hills, keeping in contact with the 3rd Battalion of US Rangers, met little opposition, and on the 24th were withdrawn again to their base at Bacoli, north of Naples. 'The Commando never carried more ammunition and fired less,' says the 9 Commando history. Three days later they were called out again, not to Anzio but to support the 46th Division of 10 Corps which had crossed the Garigliano and was now fighting its way slowly through the mountain country north of the river. 46 Division had seized two peaks, Monte Turlito and Monte Fuga, but these were contained to the north by two even steeper and higher mountains, Monte Ornito, which has two peaks, Ornito itself and Point 711. Beyond that, Monte Faito, at more than 3,000 feet, dominated the entire range.

The revised Commando plan for the attack was designed in particular to avoid the valley between Mt Fuga and Mt Ornito. To do this the Brigade Commander decided to move his forces round Mt Fuga and to attack from the north-east. This meant moving through the valley due north of Mt Fuga, in which they might encounter some resistance, but it was considered that this would be less than that offered by the enemy post west of Mt Fuga, which had been reported by the Yorks and Lancs. By going round the right flank, the units would also avoid the heavy defensive fire already encountered by the Yorks and Lancs on the ridge of Mt Fuga and Mt Turlito and in the valley beyond. 43 (Royal Marine) Commando was therefore directed to move from Mt Turlito, and go round behind Mt Fuga to its north-east side, then north-westwards to a position immediately north of Mt Ornito, then on to Mt Ornito itself. After the capture of Mt Ornito, 43 Commando were to exploit south-westwards to Point 711. They were to be responsible for their own right flank protection as they moved up to Mt Ornito, but were to be assisted on this flank by a patrol from the Yorks and Lancs. 9 Commando were to move off from Mt Turlito half a mile behind 43 Commando and were to take the same route round Mt Fuga. They were then to pass Mt Ornito on the north-east side and to push on to the north-east slopes of Mt Faito. They were to attack Point 803 from the north-east and after its capture to exploit north-westwards to the highest peak, Point 828.

From Mt Fuga itself, B Company of the Yorks and Lancs were to make a diversion with fire only, into the valley and across on to Mt Ornito and Point 711. After the capture of Mt Ornito and Point 711 by 43 Commando, the Yorks and Lancs were to clear the valley between their positions on Mt Fuga and these objectives. Extra flank protection was also given by machine guns of the Yorks and Lancs mounted on the extreme right of their Mt Fuga position and covering the hill on the right of Mt Ornito. On the left flank the machine guns of 9 and 43 Commandos had a similar task, covering the important village of Costanzo. The Belgian Troop of 10 (IA) Commando was to remain in reserve and as Brigade HQ protection troop on Mt Fuga.

That was the somewhat complicated plan, and at 18.30 hrs on 2 February, 43 Commando left their assembly position behind the slopes of Mt Turlito and moved round to Mt Fuga. B Company of the Yorks and Lancs could be heard firing from the forward slopes of Mt Fuga to create a diversion, and at the same time gunfire on 56 Division's front to the left indicated that the feint attack by this Division had begun. Soon afterwards the enemy patrol which had been seen at 16.35 hrs moving down the forward slopes of Point 711, came in contact with one of the platoons of the Yorks and Lancs. A sharp fire fight ensued, after which the enemy patrol withdrew. 9 Commando, meanwhile, moved round Mt Fuga without incident and, taking advantage of the work already done by C Troop and E Troop of 43 Commando, pushed on to the eastern slopes of Mt Ornito without opposition. 4 Troop went in front of the rest of the Commando as advance guard and were followed by 2 Troop and 1 Troop. The Commando HQ came next with 5 and 6 Troops in the rear.

9 Commando pushed on north-westwards from Mt Ornito towards a hill some 500 yards north-east of Point 803. From this hill they were met with considerable small arms fire and it was necessary to capture it before they could proceed to attack Mt Faito. 4 Troop supported by 1 and 2 Troops attacked the hill and eventually captured it in spite of heavy mortar and shellfire which came down on the whole of the unit and caused many casualties. After the capture of this feature in which a number of prisoners were taken, the Commando was reorganized and Nos. 5 and 6 Troops became the Advance Guard, while 2 and 4 Troops went to the rear. During this reorganization, artillery fire fell repeatedly among all the Commando troops and further casualties were sustained.

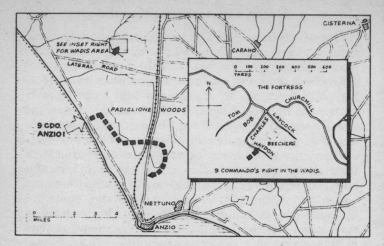

Anzio

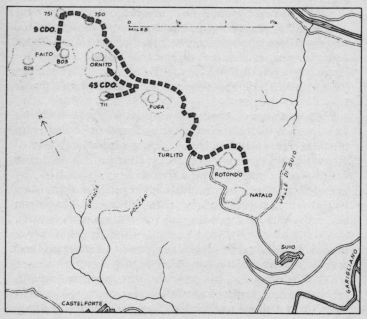

Monte Faito

Leslie Callf was then a Lieutenant in 9 Commando and takes up the story: 'This was an unwieldy two-Commando attack, with no chance of surprise, especially for the furthest objective, Mt Faito. The codename for Ornito was "Laycock" and for Faito it was "Charles". Information about these objectives was limited, to say the least. In the event, neither was defended in any strength. There were, however, many well-sited machine gun posts covering the approaches, especially to Mt Faito. Most importantly, there were several well-sited observation posts, which could, and did, call for stonks of artillery and heavy mortars in a most concentrated manner.

'No. 43 put in their attack and took Ornito with little opposition, while No. 9 followed on, meeting several isolated posts to the north of Ornito. No. 4 Troop, supported by 1 and 2 Troops, attacked and captured prisoners at these posts. The Commando was now strung out on two very rocky promontories joined by a saddle, to the north-east of our objective, Faito. 5 and 6 Troops now took over the lead for the final attack. During most of our advance round the east side of Ornito, the whole column had been continually shelled and mortared, together with spasmodic small arms fire. As 5 and 6 Troops moved up, an extremely heavy stonk covered the whole promontory and seemed to continue for ages. 5 and 6 Troops were moving, the remainder of the Commando were trying to scratch some cover in the rocky ground. I don't know which was better, but I preferred to keep moving as fast as possible. This was the most vivid picture of the war, which remains very clearly in my memory. The shells and mortars were exploding on the rocks which covered every foot of the ground. The sight of the almost horizontal flashes with tearing pieces of rock and shrapnel, and the cries of the wounded, was horrifying.

'At the same time, two machine gun positions sited in derelict stone houses or huts to the front and to the right were firing tracer into the Commando column. 5 Troop (or what was left of us) attacked the front post, taking two prisoners. 6 Troop sustained one killed and two wounded before they silenced a very determined enemy in the right-hand post. A very depleted 5 and 6 Troop now pushed on to the lower slopes of Mt Faito and the assault team advanced further up the hill as forward patrol. Due to the heavy casualties, now about fifty per cent, including the CO and the second-in-command, the CO gave the order to withdraw and consolidate on the slopes of Mt Ornito.

'It was not until 12 May that Mt Faito was finally captured, that is, three and a half months later, by the *Goumiers* of the French Moroccan Mountain Division. During our consolidation at Ornito we found that the Germans were listening in to our radio communications, so when Captain Mike Allen and myself were speaking, we spoke a school backslang called "agee pagee". I can't remember how we both came to realize we knew it!'

Captain Harry Lucas gives another account of the Ornito battle. 'About 20.00 hrs on 30 January 9 Commando embussed at Bacoli to join 43 Commando at the assembly area just north of the Garigliano river. Around 06.00 hrs on the 31st we arrived at the debussing point south of the river, crossed by pontoon bridge and marched to the assembly area. That night we marched to the forward assembly area (Suja). The attack was postponed to the next night, so the Commando rested. Shellfire hits during the night killed five from 1 Troop and wounded several, including Sergeant Bilborough who died in the CCS at Sessa Aurunca after I arrived there.

'At 02.02 hrs the CO and Troop Commanders went forward to positions where some of the ground we were to advance over could be seen. Our own medium artillery fire ranged shots to ascertain whether they could clear the crest. Two shells bursting close to us suggested they could not. At the CO's briefing it was decided that 9 Commando would advance round E flank of Ornito and seize Mt Faito, while 43 Commando would secure Ornito and Point 711. This would be a night attack with no air or artillery support available. Our only hope was to surprise the enemy. Orders were given to 3 (Heavy Weapons) Troop to remain in Brigade HQ area until called forward to consolidate the defence on capture of the objective.

'I recall that I was at this time, and had been for some while, extremely worried about the special problems of the Heavy Weapons Troop, and my Mortar Section Commander, Lieutenant David Balls, was no less so. We were armed with two Vickers MMGs and two three-inch mortars, all of which together constituted at least ten heavy manloads. The mortar bombs weighed 10lbs each and were carried in cases rather like medium-sized suitcases, three to a case, two cases to a man – a 60lb load. The MMG ammunition was heavy and the gun was a thirsty fighter – about 250 rounds a minute, or one belt, normal firing. All this, in addition to the normal equipment and personal weapons we carried, constituted a very heavy load to be moved by a total of thirty-six all ranks. This factor really made it impossible to employ us on short raids, which had been the original role of Commandos. (We had been left out of Operation Partridge, for example.) For the more normal field operations in which we were expecting to be employed increasingly in future, we had been equipped with canvas wheelcarts, rather like deckchairs on wheels, which really did enable us to keep up with fast-moving assault troops on any road or even reasonable track. Whenever the going was really soft – mud or sand, for example – the low-radius wheels sank in, and we had to find alternative means of transport. At Anzio, for example, we had commandeered a bullock cart, and actually arrived at the Forward Assembly Area in time to join the party! In these mountains, operating over very steep, rough and stony mule tracks, conditions were infinitely worse. So far, it is true, we had been relieved of most of our load-carrying problems by the provision of a mule train, with Italian muleteers. This, though, created further difficulties; these mules were not trained to the gun, and one of them, startled by shellfire, had bolted carrying a mortar baseplate and was never seen again. This rendered one of my two mortars useless. The Mortar Section spent a whole day searching the hills for the lost baseplate, in vain. In any case, from now on, no mules would be available, and everything would have to be humped. The problem of replenishment was daunting.

'I had another reason for anxiety too. The Medium Machine Gun and the three-inch mortar were very useful weapons in support of an attack, as well as in defence, provided their fire could be controlled by officers in a position to observe the fall of the shot and the position of our own troops, selecting precise targets and determining fixed lines for night firing. Otherwise they could be very dangerous to our own troops. In our present situation, with a night attack over extremely rough and mountainous country, without reconnaissance, these dangers and difficulties would be magnified. Francis Clark, second-in-command of 9 Commando, a machine-gunner and experienced in handling mortars, well understood this, and it was in consideration of these factors that we were not ordered to go forward with the assault troops. Colonel Tod also said that we would make such a bloody row that the essential element of surprise would be lost. There was no answer to this. However, when the leading troops moved out to attack, we did feel rather like the young lady who sang, "I brought my harp to the party but nobody asked me to play."

'Meanwhile, the remainder of the Commando had occupied a position on the east flank of Mt Turlito, dug in and built sangars. 3 Troop and Brigade HQ established themselves in the valley on the east side of Mt Fuga and built sangars. Francis Clark took some officers on a pleasant scramble in sunshine, with views of the Garigliano valley and mouth, and Mt Cassino to the east.

'Around 20.00 hrs Commando HQ and Assault Troops passed through 3 Troop's positions and advanced to attack, with much badinage between 3 Troop and the rest. "Good old 3 Troop, dodging it again" etc. But we were very anxious. It was thought that the enemy held these hills with relatively few troops on the ground, but had massive concentrations of artillery fire, so all depended on quick success and digging in before the enemy could react. This was confirmed when, in 1955, I was host at the University of Nottingham to a Professor Schmidt of the Free University of Berlin, who claimed to have been the officer of the German Artillery Observation Corps who controlled the fire of the whole Divisional Artillery of the German Division opposite us that night. He produced his personal war diary to prove it, and clearly regarded the effect on 9 Commando as a personal success. We examined the war map which I had been carrying, and he showed me in some detail the disposition of their Artillery DF tasks, which covered every possible approach and gave details of the system of switches which could be made on call. Arrangements also existed, he said, for the fire of mortars to be co-ordinated with that of the artillery (88mm). He told me that he and his men from the Observation Regiment were provided with quite light infantry support for local defence, and that they themselves were regarded as "disposable". It is interesting to note that all the POWs who carried my stretcher after I was hit were from this Observation Regiment. He also said that although his OPs came under fire on that occasion, his batteries were not shelled.

'Visits were made to Brigade HQ for news but radio silence was solid and there was little to hear but occasional shellfire, some of it quite heavy. Then the first POWs came in, and Ornito was taken. Later, with David, I climbed the flank of Fuga to see whether there was any sign of activity towards Faito. On arriving at the forward northern edge of Fuga, we observed, through a gap between Point 711 and Ornito, an exceptionally heavy bombardment, lasting several minutes, on the far side of the valley leading north-west to the lower slopes of Faito. Continuous gunfire, hundreds of shells/mortar bombs (probably multiple-barrel mortars as well as 88s) – clearly, 9 Commando had not achieved surprise. We learned later that this stonk killed or wounded more than half the members of HQ and the four troops caught in it, including the CO, second-in-command, Intelligence Officer and at least four other officers and several senior NCOs. We returned to 3 Troop and I reported what we had observed to the Brigadier.'

Mike Allen was out on the mountain at this time. 'I remember being heavily shelled by our own supporting artillery as the Commando was recovering its wind and licking its wounds on the forward slope of Monte Ornito, after having endured similar and devastating enemy shelling during an approach attack on Monte Faito. The mistake by our artillery arose from a faulty map reference signalled to his gun lines by an FOO. He was soon persuaded to correct the error of his ways.'

Harry Lucas continues: 'At 03.02, shortly after day-break, I went forward with Ted Healey, my orderly, to recce a route forward and attempt to contact Commando HQ. We met many walking wounded, including Captains Mike Long and Harry Kither, and Lieutenants Martin Ferrey and "Ally" Wilson – the latter with a gaping eye-socket and a battered face – as well as stretcher parties carrying more serious cases. Having rounded the east shoulder of Ornito and entered the long valley leading north-west towards the lower slopes of Faito, we could see many dead, especially on the hillside flanking this valley (the hillside, I judged, where the stonk had occurred which we had observed earlier that night). We remained in that area for perhaps twenty minutes without seeing

or, apparently, being observed by either our own troops or
the enemy, from which I concluded that either our troops
were in possession of Faito, or at least that the enemy's
were not. Returning to 3 Troop, I found an order to report
to the Brigadier, who ordered me to take 3 Troop forward
to the forward slopes of Ornito, where what was left of 9
Commando had been withdrawn, and where a counter-
attack was expected. On the Brigadier's instructions, I
first went to see if I could get any volunteers from among
the walking wounded who were hanging around the RAP.
I did not see any who were clearly unwounded, though
there were several men there whom I knew. I walked
among them and called for volunteers, saying I was going
forward with 3 Troop and that every man was needed to
hold the ground they had won at such cost. Corporal
Walsh of my old Troop, 4 Troop, whom I knew to be a
first-rate soldier and a brave man (he later won the MM,
and when I next saw him, at the end of the war, he had
three wound stripes) was the senior NCO as far as I could
see. He said, "Ye cannae ask these men to go back there
the day, Captain Lucas, Sir; the morn maybe, but no the
day." I believed him and went to rejoin my troop.

'It must be said for these men, that every one rejoined
the unit within a day or so, and that before the end of the
month they were again fighting gallantly in the Anzio
beach-head. They were the bravest of the brave but, for
the moment, they were numbed with the shock of the
bombardment I had witnessed. I then went on ahead with
my recce group, including Lieutenant David Balls, to
make contact with Commando HQ and select defensive
positions for the MMGs and the remaining three-inch
mortar in preparation for the expected counter-attack,
leaving the Troop Sergeant Major to bring up the rest of
the troop, laden as they now were, manhandling the heavy
weapons and as much ammunition as they could carry.
Morale was high, despite the rather depressing situation.
We were, at last, going to get our chance. Occasional light

shelling merely served to get the adrenalin going. One shell, however, had an unfortunate effect, at least I thought so; it fell more or less in the middle of the recce group, badly wounding me. I departed on a stretcher on my way to Blighty, three months in hospital and eighteen months in Holding Operational Commando. Luckily, no one else was hit, and 3 Troop went on under the command of Lieutenant Balls. Their subsequent fortunes must be told by other witnesses, but they performed gallantly until the end of the war. David Balls was killed at Anzio, and one of his successors at Comacchio.

'My experience after I was hit may be of interest, as exemplifying the difficulties met with in evacuating wounded from this rather inaccessible battle area. I received immediate attention from the Troop Medical Orderly, who dressed my wounds. David gave me a morphine injection and wished me luck. I was a bit depressed, because I had no sensation below the hip level, and believed (rightly as it turned out) that I had been hit in the spine. A troop stretcher party carried me to the RAP near Brigade HQ, where the doc, John D'Arcy, gave me thirty sulphathiazola tablets, redressed the entry wound, packed it with drugs to prevent gas gangrene, and turned his attention to more promising cases.

'I was then carried by four German POWs, who did not seem at all depressed by their present fortunes, to an area just behind the crest where a long line of wounded were lying on stretchers under the dubious shelter of a drystone dyke, waiting to be collected by one or other of the Field Ambulance stretcher parties which had been allocated to the Brigade for this operation. I was lying on my face, so I could not see much of what was going on. Shells still fell from time to time, some quite near, some in the distance. I wondered how David and 3 Troop were getting on. A padre (it may have been ours) came along at one point and offered to say a prayer with me. In answer, perhaps, to my prayer, Sergeant Miller of 2 Troop, whose mother lived next door to my aunt in Bournemouth, came along and asked if I would like a drink. "The CO is two stretchers away from you," he said. "His flask is sticking out of his pocket and he's fast asleep. I'll borrow it." And he did. I asked him the time and he said, "About 16.00 hrs." I had been hit at about 13.00 hrs – it was clearly going to be a long job. Happily, I was only conscious for half the time; and I was strangely relaxed about the whole business. I was certain by now that I was not going to make it, and it didn't seem to be my problem any more. My turn came at last to be borne on the next stage, and there began a seemingly endless trail of discomfort, mostly in the dark. My bearers, for whom I was by no means the first customer, struggled, slipped, fell, swore, dropped me, picked me up again, carrying me with my head sometimes above and sometimes below my heels. One party were very jolly Gurkhas, who never stopped laughing, and who, whenever shelling came close to the track, put me down and lay on top of me. I was lucky, however; some of my comrades were carried on stretchers strapped to our old friends, the mules. All this time, units of the Hampshire Regiment were struggling past us up the narrow track, on their way to relieve our Brigade. One of them was my cousin, but at the moment he actually passed me, I was asleep or unconscious.

'At last we came to our original Advanced Assembly Point, where the Admin Officer, Andrew Cochrane, who had remained there with our B echelon, bent over me. "Who's this? Ah, Harry, my poor fellow. I am sorry to see you like this. Well, you'll not be needing your G1098 any more. I'll just have your boots, helmet, compass, revolver and field-glasses." I persuaded him that the glasses were my own, but he had the rest. A most efficient Admin Officer, our Drew.

'One more stretcher party down to the road, a short ride with my stretcher strapped on a jeep, over the pontoon bridge, thence by ambulance (a converted three-tonner) to the Casualty Clearing Station at Sessa Aurunca. By this time I was pretty wide awake, and I was very conscious that Sergeant Albert Cruickshank of 4 Troop (whose leg had been shattered some twenty-four hours earlier and whose stretcher was just above mine) was having a haemorrhage. I tried in vain to make the driver hear. Fortunately Albert survived, and only died in 1987.

'I was operated on immediately, and successfully, by Major Robb, MC, RAMC, and his surgical team, to whom I am eternally grateful. He removed some shell splinters and a handful of bits of map and mapcase, flowers and Italian real estate from my abdominal cavity, but told me he had had to leave one splinter embedded between two of my lumbar vertebrae, but that I was a lucky chap, and I would make a very good recovery. He was right on both counts.'

During this Ornito operation, 2 SS Brigade had been rejoined by the doughty Admiral, Sir Walter Cowan. After his capture in North Africa, where he was last observed attacking a tank while armed with a ·38 pistol, he had been released by his Italian captors as 'being at 71, too old to take any further part in the war' and promptly made his way back to the Commandos. While at Ornito he assisted the wounded Colonel Tod to make his way from the battlefield. No. 9 Commando lost a quarter of its strength at Ornito including fifty per cent of the officers.

On 29 February, Nos. 9 and 40 Commandos found themselves en route for the Anzio beach-head, where the situation had deteriorated sharply in the previous three weeks. On 2 March, 40 joined 169 Brigade ten miles north of Anzio town, while on the same day 9 Commando took up position in the 167 Brigade area, a region of deep gullies or wadis which seamed the central plain west of Anzio town. Lieutenant Colonel Tod, now recovered from wounds received at Ornito, returned to the command and in the first eight days at Anzio, apart from holding their share of the line, No. 9 sent out eleven fighting patrols, killing or capturing sixty-two of the enemy, losing nineteen men themselves, killed or wounded.

On 10 March, Colonel Tod was ordered to mount an attack, codenamed Operation X, to clear three wadis, only 500 yards from the beach-head perimeter, which the enemy were using to form up before attacks. These lay about eleven miles north of Anzio town. The three wadis were codenamed Haydon, Laycock and Charles, and in the centre of these stood a small hill called Beechers.

Colonel Tod's plan for the attack was divided into three phases. The first phase was to be carried out in darkness. The unit was to cross the start line in two waves. The first wave was to assault and clear Haydon, and to be joined by a second wave and the Commando Headquarters. The second phase was to be carried out at first light and during it Charles was to be cleared and occupied, and the junction of Charles and Laycock was to be consolidated. In the third phase, Laycock was to be cleared and occupied and the whole force was to consolidate in this wadi and form a defensive position. To carry out this plan the Commando was divided into three squadrons each of two troops, called A, B and C squadrons. Support was to be provided for all three phases of this attack by 91 Fd Regiment RA, the machine guns of A company, 7 Cheshires and by 13 Brigade's support company mortars.

Corporal Clifford Searle begins the story. 'We had gained the impression that if there was an unusual task on hand, Captain Callf was sent for. During the difficult days at Anzio, it was said that companies of line troops were surrendering to inferior-numbered German night patrols so 10 Section of 5 Troop was sent up to a wadi where a company had recently disappeared, to investigate and test the enemy strength there.

'At the approaches to the wadi and near the forward troops I heard whimpering and found a young lad, deeply distressed, in a dugout. He told me he was sixteen years old and had only arrived in Italy that day having been immediately sent to the front. All I could say to him was that he had little to worry about – especially while we were around – and as soon as possible he should disclose his correct age to his superiors. Shortly afterwards we found the ration-dump of the missing company. As usual, the Mortar Section covered the rear of the formation as we moved into the wadi – we were fired upon from the high ground to our right. Automatic fire hit Tommy Bostock's hand and we went to ground. I called upon the mortar man to range a few rounds on to the high ground and in the meantime Captain Callf quickly reorganized us for an attack to rout those holding the high ground. We attacked up the side of the wadi and over the top with bayonets fixed, yelling and shouting as we moved in extended formation. On reaching the top with Captain Callf well to the fore, I was surprised to find one German only standing up in his trench attempting to fire his pistol. The backs of a number of other Germans, in a crouching position, could be seen just below the tops of their trenches and they soon surrendered without putting up a fight. In all probability our noisy approach gave the impression that a regiment of men were about to descend upon them. One of the eight or nine prisoners who spoke English said to me, "We shall be fighting alongside you one day, against the Russians." It was a quickly devised plan and a successful one, underlining that one's section was being well led and with decisive ability. It was, for me, the most exhilarating moment of my service, going over the top. Although others do not agree, I seem to recall a Tiger tank coming from our right on the high ground with its guns blazing. This was at the point of our withdrawal.'

Captain Leslie Callf, MC, takes up the story. 'My most thrilling and proudest moment of the war was in leading

my troop in an attack against a superior force of paratroopers at Anzio. We had hardly recovered from our
attack on Mt Ornito/Faito, suffering about fifty per cent
casualties, when we were called back to Anzio as the
situation there was critical. We landed on 3 March and 5
Troop was ordered straight into the front line sector held
by the 9 Royal Fusiliers with orders to deal with a troop
of German paratroopers who had infiltrated and taken
over part of our lines.

'5 Troop was about half strength, mustering one officer
and twenty-eight ORs. We arrived at first light (05.15 hrs)
and contacted the officer-in-charge for information as to
the enemy's whereabouts. The only information was a
vague wave of his hand down the wadi with the words,
"There . . . somewhere down there . . . I've just been
promoted Major!" With these words the officer disappeared down his dugout and left us to it. The wadi was a
deep ravine with stunted trees and foliage, about thirty
feet down to mud and water, but it was the only cover
available, so we had to use it. The assault team under
Corporal Bostock pushed ahead with covering from the
Bren-gun team on the highest part of the wadi. We usually
did our raiding and fighting patrols in the darkness but
this was special and urgent and we had to find them
quickly, which we did, rather too quickly, in broad
daylight. The enemy were well dug in on high ground
overlooking the wadi and they opened fire with automatic
weapons, slicing Corporal Bostock's trigger finger off as
he returned fire. Casualties occurred through the troop.
Corporal Searle quickly replied with mortar smoke as we
regrouped. Corporal Bostock, assisted and covered by
Hopkins and Belasco, reported back to me, and standing
rigidly to attention, asked permission to fall out as he'd
lost a finger – all this during enemy machine-gun fire!
The only way was a good old-fashioned bayonet charge.
We left the wadi and spread out in the dead ground below
the enemy positions, with Brens on the flanks giving

covering fire. Fusilier Storey, who was lying just behind me, was killed instantly as we were getting into position.

'Every man always carried two No. 77 smoke grenades, so that a smoke screen could be created for about two throws of about forty yards. They knew the drill; throw and run through the smoke. This was the moment, and one I shall never forget. In broad daylight we had to cover about sixty yards of open ground against German paratroopers, well dug in. I looked to the right of me and the left and to CSM Walsh next to me, and gave the order, "Throw!" and as the smoke formed, "Charge!" and in we went, hard. I think we must have looked a fearsome body as we came through the smoke onto them. Many of them were killed and others put their hands up. We suffered three killed and nine injured. I'm not sure of the German casualties, but the official report gave twenty-five killed and twenty-three POWs, which was approximately twice the strength of No. 5 Troop on that day.'

Corporal Hankinson took part in Operation X. 'During the latter period we made a frontal attack on a wadi held in some strength by the Germans. We attacked late in the evening, and after some fighting we found ourselves occupying what had been the enemy positions. This operation was intended to be a feint and a forerunner to a Corps attack the following dawn. When the main attack, for whatever reason, was cancelled, this left us with the enemy on three sides and some several hundred yards of open ground (over which we had attacked) between us and the forward posts of the Green Howards.

'We came under sporadic fire throughout the night, making several sorties and attempting to improve our position, and at dawn, together with my section, I found myself on the front edge of the wadi. We beat off with rifle fire and grenades an immediate attack, and as the sun rose it became apparent that the enemy was holding a position in some broken ground under a few broken and stunted trees, and in what had probably been their reserve line, some thirty or forty yards to our front.

'All through that day we came under heavy mortar, shell and small arms fire, and although we were exposed and suffered repeated casualties, it was impossible to drop back further into the wadi without losing our field of fire. We were in an uncomfortable situation; it became a very long day! I could visualize no successful ending to our predicament but, as I later discovered, after dark it was intended for a barrage to be laid down around and almost upon our position, under which the unit would attempt a withdrawal. Before this plan could be put into effect, at dusk and under a smoke screen, we received a frontal assault from the enemy and the situation became very confused. I remember hearing enemy cries of "Hands up," and of firing at figures seen dimly, but only a few yards away. Somewhere behind me in the wadi the bagpipes were playing. I sensed, heard, felt or whatever, something land on the ground next to where I was lying, and as I turned I saw a stick-grenade. Without consciously thinking, I put out a hand to throw the thing further away, but it exploded, and although I felt at first no more than a blow on my arm, I soon discovered I had been wounded in the right upper arm and hand, and slightly, no more than scratches, on the ear and face.

'Eventually, under cover of the creeping barrage which had by then been started, I was able, with the other walking wounded to regain the comparative safety of our own lines, and at last, by jeep ambulance, was taken to the tented hospital at the rear.

'On that day the Commando, with a strength of little over two hundred all-told, sustained casualties of twenty-three killed and fifty wounded. Of the dead, three were from my own section and included the then Troop Commander, Captain D. Balls.'

It had been intended to bring supplies forward by first light from the start line to Haydon by porters, but enemy artillery and mortar fire on the start line before first light caused considerable casualties among the waiting porters. An attempt was made by Commando drivers to cross the open ground between the start line and Haydon in daylight on foot, but only one of these men got through. Throughout the day the supply position gave rise to some anxiety. Meanwhile, the failure of the porters to reach Haydon made evacuation of casualties extremely difficult. An attempt was made to evacuate some under cover of smoke, but heavy enemy fire caused the attempt to be abandoned. At 10.00 hrs, twelve stretcher casualties were evacuated under a Red Cross flag, but this procedure meant that twenty-four men had to be away for some time and this depleted the Commando's strength considerably. The enemy respected the Red Cross flag and allowed the party to cross the open ground between Haydon and the start line unmolested. Once the party had disappeared behind cover at the start line however, they were subjected to a heavy artillery concentration.

Mike Allen, MC, who later commanded 9 Commando, gives his version of events. 'Of all the various battles, I reckon few will dispute that the battle of the Anzio wadis was the Commando's "Longest Night and Day". The operation involved a series of attacks for the occupation of three wadis, from which the enemy were in the habit of launching counter-attacks. After the principal wadi was taken and held, it became evident that we had disturbed a bees' nest, which the enemy had no intention of vacating, and repeated counter-attacks, interspersed with deadly accurate artillery fire at what was no more than a large hole in the ground, meant that the Commando would have been annihilated unless reinforced or withdrawn. As the operation plan had made no provision for back-up support or relief, Ronnie Tod (CO) suggested to 5th Division, to whom we had been attached for the operation, that 2 Commando Brigade would be displeased if 9 Commando was left to be expended as the Division's protection against counter-attacks. We accordingly received orders for disengagement and withdrawal to the start line, at which point wireless contact with Divisional Headquarters broke down. As second-in-command, I was consequently dispatched back to warn the front line, through which the Commando had advanced, of our impending return, to arrange defensive artillery fire during the withdrawal, and to marshal and guide the Commando in as it reached our own start line. We took particular pride in the fact that, apart from those killed or known to have gone missing through direct hits, the Commando brought back with it all its wounded casualties, through both enemy and friendly wire and minefields.'

At about 18.00 hrs the enemy fire falling on Haydon increased considerably, and at last light, which was about 19.00 hrs, smoke was put down along the whole length of the wadi. A strong enemy attack developed from the direction of Beechers onto 3 Troop's position in the centre of the wadi and directly opposite the Commando Headquarters. At the same time two weaker attacks, each about a platoon strong, were out on the left and right flanks. The attacks on the flanks were quickly driven off and the enemy contented itself with establishing small groups three or four hundred yards away from our troops on each flank and firing into our positions. In the centre meanwhile, the attack was pushed home with determination. A wave of the enemy assaulted over the crest of Beechers, throwing grenades and firing their weapons as they came. This first wave was followed by a second, armed mainly with automatic weapons, which tried to overrun 3 Troop's positions. A third wave came in behind the second, apparently to consolidate the positions won by the first two waves. The first wave achieved some success and drove a wedge into 3 Troop's and HQ's positions. All the wireless sets at HQ were put out of action by grenades, and half the HQ became fully engaged in the battle. The second wave, however, was unable to take advantage of this initial success as it was mostly broken up by concerted fire from the whole of the Commando. The remainder of Commando Headquarters and 4 Troop moved forward to take part in the battle while 3 Troop's line was stabilized. Lieutenant Colonel Tod ordered a troop from 'A' Squadron on the right flank to counter-attack the enemy, and this counter-attack met the third wave of attackers as they came in to the assault. With pipes playing and all weapons firing, 3 Troop and HQ, with the help of the force from 'A' Squadron, re-captured their original positions and drove the enemy attackers back again over the crest of Beechers.

Lieutenant Colonel Tod ordered all the riflemen in the Commando to withdraw first, carrying the wounded as best they could on improvised stretchers made from rifles and groundsheets or greatcoats. Once the wounded were safely away, the machine guns of all troops were withdrawn. No opposition was encountered during the withdrawal, which was completed in the nick of time and followed closely by our own artillery fire. The start line area was again heavily mortared and shelled and some casualties were inflicted on the Commando as it passed through the area. 9 Commando was withdrawn within the next few days to Anzio town where it joined 40 (Royal Marine) Commando, and with them re-embarked for Naples.

Operation X had cost 9 Commando two officers and seventeen other ranks killed, two officers and forty-eight other ranks wounded, and four other ranks missing, of whom two were believed killed. Careful enquiry from prisoners allowed the number of casualties inflicted on the enemy to be estimated at over 105, including at least one officer. The Commando had therefore inflicted considerably more casualties than it had received, but it had also achieved a remarkable success in that its offensive action had been carried out against a superior enemy who had been considerably reinforced during the day. They had maintained their initial successes against heavy counter-attacks and had extricated themselves from a difficult position without undue casualties.

Anzio, Comacchio and Monte Ornito were 9 Commando's greatest battles and Captain Harry Lucas remembers the men who fought them. 'I am sure you will have heard all about that legendary, heroic and original character "Mad Jack" Churchill of 2 Commando, but less, perhaps, about his brother Tom, who was our Brigadier in Italy when I was with No. 9. He too was a regular officer, but of a more conventional kind. He was undoubtedly a very fine soldier and when he did get his Brigade, he was soon recognized by all who served under him as an outstanding Commander, in whom we had complete trust, and the Brigade had a brilliant record under his command. I have always felt that Commandos, by their very nature, needed a sobering hand at the top. At that stage in the war, and perhaps especially in the Mediterranean theatre, we were in some danger of being used in field operations for which we were well qualified, but ill-equipped, having no administrative tail or combat transport to speak of. This had cost other Commandos dear – No. 6, for example, in North Africa. We certainly believe that Brigadier Churchill, while eager to see us play our full part in defeating the Germans, would do his best to ensure we were properly employed. Like all Commando leaders, he was a front line Brigadier, and much liked and respected for that. He is always associated in my mind with Brigadier Haydon, the very first Commando Brigadier, who also had that cool, professional approach, and who, no less than "Brigadier Tom", greatly cared for his men.

'I expect others will have told you, for example, of MT Sergeant Coupe, mortally wounded at Anzio, singing "Here's to the next man to die"; of the Cook Sergeant, manning a Bren with the CO, Ronnie Tod as his No. 2 in the same battle; of Lieutenant "Ally" Wilson of 5 Troop, at Ornito, who fought on after his eye had been knocked out, until he was ordered to fall out; and of Troop Sergeant Major George Drury and "Piper" Ross of 4 Troop going out, on the morning after Ornito, almost up to the German positions, in broad daylight, to bring in Sergeant Albert Cruickshank, who had been lying there all night with a smashed leg . . . and many others, whom I never knew about.'

Captain Mike Long, MC, takes up the story after 9 Commando returned to their base: 'After our casualties at Ornito and Anzio, the whole Commando moved across to the east side of Italy, to Molfetta. Colonel Tod called up all the officers for a conference and said that our casualties were similar to those suffered by 2 Commando at Salerno. He told us that they were shortly made up by intakes from home, but it had taken three to four months to get back the true 2 Commando *esprit de corps* which was very high before Salerno. Colonel Tod said this was not going to happen to 9 Commando. On no account were the men to start feeling sorry for themselves because their friends had been badly wounded or killed. To prevent that, he ordered two daily drill parades, one in the morning, one in the afternoon. In ten days the standard of drill was so high – it was organized by Captain Davies, MC, ex-Coldstream Guards – that the Colonel said if there was a good drill in the morning, the men could have the afternoon off.

'When the new intake arrived, they drilled morning and afternoon, the old No. 9 mornings only. When the new intake were up to our standard, and only then, they were allowed to put up the 9 Commando black hackle. This created a pride and self-esteem in 9 Commando which continued until the end of the war, and even continues to this day.'

From Molfetta, Captain Long's 4 Troop were sent on two operations along the coast of Italy, to bring out escaped prisoners of war. 'We were first based in tents near Bari, and it was fairly hot, so every day I took the men to the sea and we had swimming lessons. At the time, only about half the troop could swim, but we soon had everyone swimming at least fifty yards. We then went to Manfredonia and embarked in an LSI (Landing Ship Infantry) and sailed to rescue 150 escaped POWs from a beach near the mouth of the River Tena, near Ancona. On our first expedition we brought off 132 men, having some difficulty getting the fully-loaded craft off the beach. On 14 June 1944 we sailed again for the same beach on an LCT (Landing Craft Tank). On board were six or eight heavily armed jeeps, two machine guns in the front, another two in the back. These belonged to Popski's Private Army, who were to go ashore and raid from the Tena area while we returned with the prisoners.

'Anyway, I thought we were going in very fast and we hit the beach so hard that we got firmly aground and couldn't get off again, even though the Navy put out kedge anchors and did all they could. We had been escorted by an armed motor patrol vessel, which now came in until it struck a sandbank. It then withdrew to wait, 200 yards offshore, and Major Popski, abandoning the operation, ordered us all to swim for it. His people stripped off, but all of us from No. 9 swam with our weapons and ammunition. After our swimming lessons and wearing Mae Wests, they were all confident, but on the way out one soldier turned to Troop Sergeant Major Scott and said, "Sar'nt Major . . . I'm going to drown . . . tell my mother I was thinking of her before I died."

'"Steady on, lad," said Scott. "Keep going, it's not far."

'"No . . . I'm going to die now," said the soldier – and then stood up – in two feet of water! They had arrived over the sandbar.

'Major Popski was furious that the 9 Commando men had brought their weapons to the heavily-loaded launch, but Colonel Tod insisted that whenever we crossed a river, we swam or crossed with our arms, and we would much rather have faced the wrath of Popski than an RTU from Colonel Tod.'

In August 1944, 5 Troop of 9 Commando mounted a raid, Operation Gradient, on two islands, Chesso and Lussin in the Adriatic. Captain Callf tells the story. 'Our troop task was to destroy any German garrison and to blow the bridge between Lussin Island and Chesso Island. It was said that a high-ranking General was visiting the island of Chesso and we were to capture him. The distance from Ancona to Lussin was seventy-five miles across dangerous waters, passing rather too close to Pola, an E-boat base. We carried Goatley boats, two canoes and a folding bicycle for each man. We were on the point of leaving, fully armed and black-faced, when the young doctor, who was armed with a ·45 automatic pistol, suddenly asked how it should be carried – cocked, or safety catch on etc. (It was not usual for MOs to be armed.) One of the two Lieutenants, in almost a reflex action, drew his Colt and accidentally shot the other Lieutenant in the left wrist, the bullet coming out near the elbow. Happily the injury was not serious, but we had to reorganize quickly, being one officer short. Private Lancaster, a regular soldier of many talents, took over the canoe, now without a paddler. The Naval Officer in charge made an excellent job of navigation, and we launched our assortment of boats well offshore and paddled in. I was loaned the ship's bugle for luck and I slung it round my neck. Once on shore we assembled the bikes and pedalled off to the bridge. The Italians guarding it ran off when they saw this crazy bunch of cyclists, and explosives were laid on the bridge. In bright moonlight we cycled to the north of Chesso but could find no garrison. At least two bikes broke down, so two others had double riders, and it was said the visiting General had left the previous day. We planted anti-personnel mines near our landing area, found our boats, and waited until we heard the bridge explode, and paddled out to the waiting MGBs, bringing with us some civilians who wished to leave occupied soil ... the bugle was duly returned. On the return journey to Ancona we picked up a German airman who had been drifting in his dinghy for ten days, and very glad he was to see us.'

We must now leave No. 9 for a while, resting after their exploits in Italy, and follow Jack Churchill's No. 2 Commando across the sea to fight with Tito's Partisans against the German garrisons occupying the Yugoslav islands of the Adriatic.

9

Yugoslavia, Greece and Italy, 1943–45

'What shall we tell you? Tales, marvellous tales
Of ships and stars and isles where good men rest.'

JAMES ELROY FLECKER

When the German Army entered Yugoslavia in April
1941, they found a nation deeply divided and a country
apparently ripe for conquest. Yugoslavia is not a homogenous nation, numbering Croats, Serbs, Montenegrins and
Macedonians among her disparate ethnic communities.
In 1941 these differences were compounded by faction
fighting between two political groups, the Royalist Cetniks under Draja Mihailovitch and the flourishing Communist party under Josip Broz, who later became known
as Marshal Tito. United only in their opposition to the
Germans, both parties took to the hills after their
National Army was defeated, and began a ruthless guerrilla war against the invader. In the early months following the German invasion, the two parties worked
together, but their basic differences soon drove them apart
and the Cetniks began enlisting German help in their
struggle against Tito, while the Communist Partisans
struggled on virtually alone against the German Army,
which was now ruling Yugoslavia with a hard and heavy
hand. In the beginning, the British supported Mihailovitch, but as his German connections became more clear
the British and United States forces switched their aid to
Marshal Tito. In spite of this assistance, the Germans

tightened their hold on the country and by mid-1943 had driven Tito's Partisan army from all but a few mountain strongholds on the Yugoslav mainland, and a handful of islands in the Adriatic, Vis, Hvar and Brac.

In 1942, the British sent a military mission to the Partisans, commanded by Brigadier Fitzroy Maclean. In December 1943, Fitzroy Maclean returned to Bari with the request – the demand – that military assistance be sent at once to reinforce the Partisan garrison on Vis, and help them to raid and if possible retake the other islands off the Dalmatian coast and forestall further German expansion. On 16 February 1944, men of No. 2 Commando, commanded by Lieutenant Colonel Jack Churchill, began to arrive on Vis.

Ted Kelly was among the first arrivals. 'We travelled by Partisan schooner and were carefully schooled in how to answer a Partisan challenge in Serbo-Croat. At the time it seemed to us to receive undue emphasis, but when we came to know and work with these dedicated, trigger-happy people, we saw the point. The script is engraved for ever on my memory:

"Stoi!"	(Halt!)
"Stoi san!"	(I have halted!)

The timing of the response and absolute cessation of movement after *"Stoi!"* was critical and measured in milliseconds.

"Choi de?"	(Who goes there?)
"Drugovi Ingleski"	(English comrades)
"Naprid"	(Pass)

'Again, timing was of the essence. Do not stir an eyelid until you are sure that the last word was what you thought it was.

'The British sense of humour, particularly that of the licentious soldiery, does not travel well. It created problems. The Partisans rejoiced in singing patriotic and political songs which they took very seriously indeed. The British soldier who finds a good tune likes to set his

227

own irreverent and obscene words to it, and I fear our hosts took great offence at our version of one of their most cherished songs, when a translation from the vernacular was obtained. I am not sure that they were any less offended when we taught them to sing dead-pan what we said was one of our most patriotic songs: "Please don't burn our •••••• house down; Mother has promised to pay." We drank a lot of vino with them, admired them and in an odd sort of way, loved them, but we never really understood them at the time. It was much later, when the atrocities perpetrated on their people were revealed as truth, not propaganda, that we understood their fanatical hatred of the enemy, their all-consuming lust for revenge and their total disregard for their own lives.

'The world of the Partisans was very strange to us; it had an almost theatrical quality. The walls of buildings were daubed with slogans and Communist symbols. "*Zivio Drug Tito*" (Long live Comrade Tito) took pride of place over "*Smrt Fascismo*" (Death to Fascism) and "*Slobodu Naroda*" (Freedom for the People). Women soldiers carrying guns were a novelty, and the Serbo-Croat language, with unpronounceable collections of consonants like "*crvna*" was totally incomprehensible to the great majority of us.

'From our point of view there were several obstacles to close understanding. Communism was a difficulty not only because it was foreign to our thinking but because of their total commitment, not to say obsession, towards it. Their intense patriotism, constantly expressed and demonstrated, seemed to us overdone, frankly boring and not in the best of taste. The British habit of understatement was deeply ingrained in us and demonstrations of patriotic emotion embarrass us except on very special occasions. The British soldier's habit is to make fun of what he sees as pretentious and his sense of humour was not welcome in this particular environment.

'The Partisans' attitude towards us was not unlike our

attitude to the Americans. They welcomed our help both in manpower and in material but they didn't actually like us. They regarded us as pampered, with our fancy equipment and uniforms and our fancy food tastes, and lacking in commitment to defeating the Fascists. "Overpaid, oversexed and over here" probably summed us up to them.

'Nevertheless, we drank coarse red vino with them in the little dimly-lit bars and learned to sing their songs. They had some stirring tunes and we learned the words phonetically. One particular song, *Domovina*, was especially loved by us and we adopted it to our own words – "No more vino . . . someone's drunk the ••••ing lot!" This nearly caused an international incident when an interpreter heard it. The reaction was much as ours would be if someone sang vulgar and disrespectful words to our national anthem. We meant no disrespect – a good tune was just a good tune to us – but one man's humour is another's insult.

'In the mixed Partisan army, sex was strictly taboo and transgressions were punished by death. There were many good-looking girl soldiers and we did not take kindly to being forbidden even to chat them up, but who would risk the life of a Yugoslav girl to satisfy his own ego? Somehow humour and sex will survive, however, if only on a petty scale. At one point I was in the hospital with a recurrence of the malaria which I had contracted in Italy. A beautiful and buxom girl in Partisan uniform nursed us. In fractured English, she attempted to impress us with the beauty of her home town, Split. She probably thought we were quite mad at the efforts we made to get her to repeat, in her romantic Slav accent, "I would love to show you my beautiful Split."

'Drilled in the ethics of the Geneva Convention, we also found their treatment of prisoners barbaric. The German prisoners we took ourselves were terrified that they would be handed over to the Partisans, and much friction was caused by disputes over who captured them. Our prisoners were shipped back to Italy as quickly as possible. We could not condone the Yugoslav ill-treatment and summary execution of prisoners but we understood it. Although many of the stories which we heard from the Partisans may have been exaggerated, we had no doubt that their people had suffered the most appalling atrocities under the Germans and especially from their own hated Ustachi, Yugoslav Fascists.'

The war in Yugoslavia was never a gentle affair. Neither side was very interested in taking prisoners, and the Partisans tended to shoot any Germans out of hand, and were equally ruthless in executing Cetniks, or Ustachi traitors or collaborators. The Germans murdered the Yugoslavs indiscriminately, burned villages to the ground and refused to grant captured Partisans prisoner-of-war status. This was total war.

'I can sum it up best with one story,' says Bishop Ross Hook, MC, then padre with 43 (Royal Marine) Commando. 'I visited a field hospital and found it full of wounded children, many with feet blown off and terrible injuries to their legs. Some of these children were no more than ten years old. It transpired that the Germans were laying *Schu* mines – small anti-personnel mines – in front of their defences. Before an assault, the Partisans sent waves of children running across these minefields to set off the mines and create gaps. I was shocked. I told our interpreter I thought it barbaric to send young children into battle, but he was quite unrepentant. 'It saves the lives of our soldiers,' he said, 'and we have plenty of children.'

'The Partisans were fiercely disciplined, shooting people for minor infringements. Since their armies contained women, sexual irregularities were not tolerated. Some months after arriving on Vis, some men of No. 2 Commando had to watch while the Partisans shot three women before their eyes for the crime of pregnancy.'

Colonel Jack Churchill's much depleted No. 2 Commando was still not up to full strength after Salerno, and so, in addition to No. 2, the force sent to Vis included a mixed bag of troops; Americans, many of Greek or Yugoslav stock, or speaking at least one of the many Slavonic languages, the Yugoslav troop of 10 (IA) Commando, and some Royal Engineers and Royal Artillery, plus naval units in MTBs. This force landed at Komiza, on the island of Vis, on 16 January 1944. 'Beauty was everywhere,' records Brigadier Tom Churchill. 'Grey stones set against the blue sea, red earth and green vines climbing up the terraced hillsides, and flowers everywhere, pink cyclamen, blue gentian, purple orchids, all standing out clearly in that rich, clear air.'

Operations began at once. The Germans were determined to recapture all the Dalmatian Islands and reinforce their scattered garrisons, and diverted a division of mountain troops, the 118th Jaeger Division, from the mainland for this task. Colonel Jack rightly believed that only by constant activity and raiding could the Allies' slender hold on Vis remain secure, so ten days after landing he led the Americans and three troops of No. 2 to Hvar, a large island just off the Yugoslav coast, attacked a garrison near the port of Milna, and returned with four very frightened prisoners. Hvar was raided again, twice in swift succession, and in early February No. 2 Commando expanded their operations to the island of Brac, where Second Lieutenant Barton stayed ashore with a small party for several days before shooting and killing the German Commandant.

On 27 February the American Operations Group returned to Hvar to fight a gun battle with a German patrol, and on the same day the redoubtable Second Lieutenant Barton took another patrol back to Brac and killed a number of the garrison with grenades before returning to Vis with many prisoners. For these two actions Barton received the DSO, a rare award for a junior officer. He also went on a German death list, to be shot if captured, and was therefore transferred back to Italy.

After these successful beginnings, the Commando contingent on Vis began to expand. On 5 March, Brigadier Tom Churchill and his Brigade HQ arrived, taking over command of two Commando units, for No. 43 (Royal Marine) Commando under Lieutenant Colonel R. W. B. Simmonds had arrived on 20 February. On 17 March two troops of No. 2 plus some Americans and the Heavy Weapon Troop of 43 attacked the island of Solta. The enemy garrisons were now alert to the possibility of raids and the defending Germans engaged the Commandos with rifle fire as they scrambled up the terraced hillsides around the town of Grohote. Kittyhawk dive-bombers pounded Grohote at dawn before the attack went in, the two fighting troops of 2 Commando supported by 43's mortars and MMGs. Ted Kelly was there: 'We were briefed from photographs as usual. The plan was to surround Grohote in a horseshoe formation, the open end leading to an open space to be used as the killing area. It was understood that the German forces on the island were due to be relieved on the day after the raid. Our objective was to present the relieving force with an island totally empty of Germans. It was a true combined operation involving Army, Navy and Air Force.

'We landed on the night of 17/18 March from LCIs onto a rocky beach, making a ridiculous amount of noise. Every dog on the island barked to warn their masters of the intrusion and we expected trouble. The Partisan guides who met us included a shepherd who had brought his flock of sheep with him. Their bells tinkled and apparently convinced listeners that the dogs had been disturbed by the flock. We tiptoed along behind our guides and arrived at our prearranged positions without incident.

'We waited in as near silence as we could manage – dying for a cigarette – until first light when our CO ("Mad

Jack" Churchill) had a German-speaking member of the Commando announce our arrival over a loudhailer and invite the Germans to surrender. Sporadic small arms fire was the response. The announcement indicated that failure to surrender would result in Grohote being bombed.

'At the appointed second, the Kittyhawk fighter bombers arrived and proceeded to give a demonstration of precision bombing and strafing which had us virtually throwing our hats into the air in admiration. Our ring around the place was fairly tight and debris from some of the bombs exploding in front of us came over our heads and landed behind us. Immediately the last bomb dropped we closed in to the village to take our prisoners and do a house-to-house clearing operation. Everything went according to plan. From captured documents a roll call was taken of the German garrison and every man was accounted for. The dead were buried, the wounded treated and all German survivors, numbering over 100, accompanied us back to the embarkation point. Our own casualties had been very light – I think two of No. 2 Commando.

'Most military operations seem to have an essential element of shambles, sometimes on a truly grand scale. Solta stands out like a good deed in a dirty world, and I know that this raid was as near perfect a combined operation as possible. To take the whole of the German garrison off an island hours before they were due to be relieved was a masterstroke of intelligence, planning and execution. The reprisal on Komiza with Stuka dive-bombers showed that they agreed.

'In between raids, another edition of our show *Razz-Berets* was organized, this time as a touring version to be performed in Komiza, on the central plain, and in Vis. This barn-storming production was notable for the electrical genius of Sid Crane who worked wonders with signal lamps to provide some really professional-looking lighting.

'One of the available volunteer duties was to go on

operational sorties with the MGBs and MTBs which patrolled the Adriatic. Our role was that of boarding party and a number of prizes were taken, including a schooner loaded with butter which enhanced our diet for some time. There was never a shortage of volunteers. This had nothing whatever to do with bravado. It was simply that the food on board Navy vessels, especially the freshly-baked white bread, was so good. After six eventful months with the Partisans we were relieved and returned to Italy, minus our beloved "Mad Jack" who had been taken prisoner on Brac.'

Dudley Cooper, MM, was close to Colonel Jack on the Solta raid. 'Colonel Jack had a radio for directing aircraft onto the enemy positions. We were about fifty yards closer than we should have been, and saw a German mortar team setting up near a tower. I could hear the dialogue between Colonel Jack and the pilots, and a plane dive-bombed the mortar crew, putting one right in the middle of them. But the next bomb fell right on the position we should have been in. I heard the pilot apologize for this error. Then we went in with little opposition; it was copy-book stuff. Vis was also an MTB base, and on one occasion my section was ordered to assist on a job. We went on board an MTB lightly armed and sailed to destroy a small German destroyer, aground and damaged on the beach near Split. When we arrived at the target we lowered fuel drums set with explosive pencils inside the enemy craft.'

Leaving Solta, the Commandos and their Yugoslav and American allies returned to Vis with over 100 prisoners, and from then on the force on Vis mounted raids right across the Dalmatian Islands with ever-increasing strength and regularity.

Six days after Solta, the Commandos went back yet again to Hvar to attack the garrison of Jelsa, the island's port. This was a considerable landing, with Lieutenant Colonel Simmonds taking his complete 43 Commando, plus a 3,000-strong Partisan brigade. In spite of communication problems, and the fact that the Partisans were a law unto themselves, attacking only when and where they wished, the raid went off as planned. A German counter-attack was beaten off. Their garrison lost about fifty men killed and 100 taken prisoner before the Commandos and the Partisans withdrew on the night of 24 March. The Commandos experienced considerable problems keeping their prisoners alive, for the Partisans often demanded that they be handed over for interrogation – an interrogation that inevitably led to execution, so most prisoners were hastily shipped across to Italy.

During this period, life on Vis, if never orderly, became much more organized. An airstrip had been built by the Royal Engineers, and when not on operations the men lived in small tents set in the hills around the airfield, where reinforcements came in every night from Italy; there was a squadron of Spitfires on the island now and a squadron of MTBs and MGBs in the harbour. There was even an island newspaper, *Vis a Vis*. Vis was now rightly named 'The Malta of the Adriatic', and considered able to resist even all-out attacks. Meanwhile the raids continued.

Patrols from No. 2 Commando went with Partisan brigades to raid Korcula, Mljet and many other small islands, while Commando sections, notably from No. 2, took up patrolling with the Royal Navy, boarding the small caiques and German coastal craft trading between the islands. The Royal Navy craft would lie close inshore, hidden in the dark by the loom of the land, until an enemy supply ship or schooner convoy slipped quietly by. Then they would roar out of the dark, guns blazing, to swoop alongside a ship. The Commando boarding party would leap over the rail with pistols and grenades and swiftly overcome the crew. This activity brought some rich cargoes back to Vis, most memorably that shipload of butter which several Commandos mention in their letters. All in all, it was an exciting piratical life.

In May the island received further reinforcements when the veteran Royal Marine Commando No. 40 arrived from Italy, still commanded by Lieutenant Colonel 'Pops' Manners. On the 23rd, Nos. 2 and 43 Commandos sent a party, including the indefatigable Admiral Sir Walter Cowan, to Mljet, which was said to have a garrison of 150 German troops. In spite of an extensive and exhausting search, the Commandos failed to find the enemy, lost a number of men to snipers and heat exhaustion, and withdrew, disappointed. Dudley Cooper again: 'We landed at dawn to sporadic gunfire and sniping and began to climb up the island which appeared to go straight up from the sea. We reached the top, where the basalt rock stood up like fingers, and stopped while patrols went out. Time was running on and a naval patrol went round and round the island calling to the Germans to give themselves up. We sat playing cards with the occasional sniper having a go at us until it was deemed necessary to leave before German reinforcements arrived. We re-embarked and left. Talking to the Partisans later, we found that half an hour after we left, the garrison came out of a cave we had not found and were looking for us to give themselves up. The Germans did not surrender to Partisans, and so the garrison went back into hiding.

'Vis was transformed during our stay. A light ack-ack battery was next to us, and their story was that they first set up in and around the harbour at Komiza. They received a sudden and unexpected visit of several Ju88 bombers, which came in low over a small hill, and there was no doubt they knew the gun positions. All four guns were bombed in the very short attack and received casualties and damage. One lost its crew, and the gun at the canning factory received a direct hit, destroying both gun and crew. After that they moved in to a wider area up on

the hills. In another incident some time later, an uniden-
tified plane came without warning from between a saddle
of the hills behind Komiza. Unfortunately for him the
gunners had a score to settle, and he was quickly hit.

'Things progressed all the time and an airstrip was
built. The American Rangers joined in mounting guns
and helped in defence and attack. The friendship made
with the naval coastal ships continues to this day, with
both our Associations continuing in return visits to Vis.
There were many other things I remember of the island's
first fortnight: living on one tin of bully beef and biscuits
a day while the Partisans had white bread and American
rations; the childish plays put on in the local hall by the
Partisans; and the songs we learned without knowing the
meaning of the words we sang. We still sing them on our
visits to Yugoslavia.'

On 25 May Brigadier Tom Churchill left for a visit to
the UK, handing over the command to his brother Colonel
Jack of No. 2 Commando. On the same day German
parachute and mountain troops mounted a fierce attack
against Marshal Tito's headquarters on the Yugoslav
mainland. This attack forced the Marshal to flee and put
all the Partisan forces on the defensive, so in an attempt
to divert the German forces from their sweeps on the
mainland and prevent the island garrisons crossing to join
in these operations, the forces on Vis were ordered to
mount a major attack on Brac. A large force, consisting of
Partisan brigades and both the Royal Marine Commandos, led by Colonel Jack Churchill, landed on Brac on
2 June. This landing went tragically wrong; communications broke down between the units, they attacked the
Germans in succession rather than together, and although
the main German position was briefly captured, Colonel
Manners of 40 Commando was killed and Colonel Jack
captured, the total Commando losses coming to eleven
officers and over 100 men, the worst casualties suffered
by the Commandos since the operations from Vis began.

Fortunately the Brac raid succeeded in its overall objective. The Germans kept all their garrisons on the islands and even reinforced them, with no troops crossing to the mainland.

Dudley Cooper again: 'When the news reached No. 2 that Colonel Jack was a prisoner, volunteers went to Brac to try and get him back, but we landed on Brac only to hear that Colonel Jack had already been moved to the mainland.'

Brigadier Tom Churchill returned to Vis on 12 June, and when Marshal Tito arrived from the mainland on 23 June, he inspected No. 2 Commando, and thanked the British forces for their efforts on the islands. This was very gratifying and well-deserved, but relations between Partisans and the British gradually deteriorated as the Russian Army advanced into the Balkans and support from the West became less important.

It was decided to keep up the raids, but also to station patrols, each of two officers and thirty men, among the various islands. At the end of June, 43 Commando attacked Hvar, killing eighteen out of a twenty-strong German patrol, while 40 Commando concentrated on making life wretched for the Germans on Mljet. At the end of the summer, the Germans began to withdraw from the islands, first from Brac and then from Solta, but while 43 Commando stayed on Vis to harass the departing enemy, Nos. 2 and 40 Commandos had returned to Italy in May 1944 to meet up again with No. 9 Commando, which had been kept busy along the coast of Italy. In October 1944, the last Commando unit, No. 43, returned from Vis and rejoined the Second SS Brigade. In ten months of operations they had raided almost at will around the Dalmatian Islands and tied down three German divisions, while inflicting steady losses on the island garrisons.

These exploits were not managed without loss and some bad feeling. When British and American help was needed, the Communists were all smiles; now that the Russians were on hand, the Partisans became sullen, unhelpful, even hostile. 'Although,' says Ross Hook, 'their faith in the Russians took a sharp knock when the advancing Red Army raped and pillaged its way through their capital, Belgrade.'

Since the war the old Commando soldiers have returned to the islands many times and built up warm friendships with the former Partisans. At the time, though, the Commandos were glad to leave and turn their attention to Albania and Greece.

On the night of 28/29 July 1944, Lieutenant Colonel Fynn, the new CO of 2 Commando, landed at Spilje in Albania at the head of a considerable force totalling, with his own 250-strong Commando plus attached ranks from No. 9 Commando and the Highland Light Infantry, some 700 men, almost a host in Commando terms. For once they outnumbered the Germans, but they attacked four German positions which were in a state of total defence and stubbornly defended. The German garrison beat the attack off, inflicting about sixty casualties, before the Commando returned to their ships. Spilje fell two days later to a full Partisan brigade.

Two months after Spilje, 2 Commando were sent to attack the town of Sarande on the coast of Albania opposite Corfu, through which the Germans were now withdrawing, urged on by local Partisans. 2 Commando landed in a cove, codenamed Sugar Beach, six miles north of Sarande on the night of 22 September, but the landing stalled when it became apparent that the Germans were still prepared to defend Sarande at all costs and had over twenty artillery positions ranged on the only road the Commando force could follow from the beach towards the town. Intelligence work had also been faulty, for the total enemy forces at Sarande stood at nearly 2,000 men, not the anticipated two to three hundred, and the terrain was extremely rugged. Brigadier Churchill moved his men into a defensive position close to the beach and sent for reinforcements. 40 Commando, now commanded by Lieutenant Colonel R. W. Sankey, RM, plus some field guns, arrived from Otranto on the 24th, but meanwhile it rained . . . and rained. The Commando troops who were out on the hills around Sarande remember the next week well. They suffered over 200 cases of exposure before the weather improved on 4 October. By now the guns were ashore and, with artillery able to range on Sarande, the attack went in on 9 October with 2 and 40 supported by artillery and the Royal Air Force Parachute Levies, who mounted a diversionary attack. The town fell after a stiff fight on the afternoon of 9 October.

Eric Groves of 2 Commando recalls Sarande: 'During the afternoon of 22 September, in bright sunshine, we boarded three LCIs tied up in a small fishing harbour just south of the town of Bari. By the early evening the previously clear sky had clouded over, a strong wind was blowing and the sea was looking decidedly unfriendly. Soon we were into one of those notorious Adriatic storms, the *bora*, which come up without warning – a monstrous sea, spume, rain and tearing winds. We quickly lost sight of the other vessels as our own craft pitched, rolled and corkscrewed through troughs and peaks of water. My companions on the troop deck, including the happy-cardschool, were all looking the worse for wear and most, including me, had already parted with their recent meal. At this point I decided it might be more comfortable on deck. No luck there, so I tried the engine room which was certainly warmer. But the engineer didn't look too happy and was stretched out alongside his thumping GMC diesels. Eventually the storm abated and unbelievably we were still on course for our landing point, a sandy cove about five miles north of Sarande. The time was now after midnight and the moon had come out. Having recovered somewhat, we prepared our weapons and ammunition ready for landing. The run into the cove commenced with the ramp partly dropped. At this point we hit a sandbank in the middle of the lagoon and stopped. Keeping our fingers crossed that no enemy artillery was in the vicinity, we backed off and had another go at a different point. Better luck this time, straight onto the beach, ramps right down and off at the run through soft sand to take up defensive positions about a hundred yards up, among scrub and stunted trees, somewhat reminiscent of the Dorset coastal chines.

'Captain Parsons (later killed in the main attack) who had signalled us in, told us that an 88mm gun had been positioned at the head of the valley earlier in the evening, but had fortunately moved off before our arrival. Supplies of ammunition and other items were unloaded, while from one of the other vessels, mules were taken off. These had been brought over to carry ammunition up the valley and across the volcanic hills to our proposed attack start point about five miles away. These animals proved useless and pending the purchase of small, sturdy local animals, men were employed carrying bombs and ammunition to the top of the pine-covered cliffs, an exhausting operation.'

Bob Bavister, No. 2 Commando's Administrative Officer, also remembers the mules. 'Seventy-five mules were landed altogether, some belonging to the Raiding Support Regiment. We had to learn to handle them after landing, so it was as well that the RSR were there to teach us. The beach party was responsible for loading them and leading them into the hills, but when some mules were killed, their fellows would not go past the spot where it happened. They were much fussier than horses about water, and if they decided the path was too difficult, they would just lie down and have to be unloaded and their loads man-packed to the destination.'

Eric Groves again: 'The local mule purchase was an interesting affair. This involved an officer seated behind some piled-up ammunition boxes, on the top of which lay

241

a bag of new "Victorian" sovereigns. A tommy-gunner stood by with a suitably ferocious expression. In front stood the villainous-looking Albanian, proclaiming the outstanding virtues of the bag of skin and bone held at the end of a length of grass rope. Apparently the only payment these people would accept was in Victorian gold sovereigns. (I understood later that they were still being minted in England for such special purposes.) Much to our surprise these seedy-looking animals performed very well.

'Active patrolling towards Sarande across volcanic split rock became a daily activity, which destroyed the boots we had been issued with for what was supposed to be a forty-eight-hour operation. With a deterioration in the weather and useless boots, men started going down with trench feet. The problem of water became acute for those of us in the forward area. Usually, first thing in the morning, water could be found in small depressions in the rocks – at the most half-a-cup at a time – but the problem was getting it out. So mostly we drank it to last for the next twenty-four hours or until something could be brought forward from the beach.

'I believe 40 (Royal Marine) Commando, sent to support us, landed on the 24th and took up the coastal sector on our right. During a brighter period after the arrival of 40 RM, 2 Troop moved towards Sarande and left a small observation group, comprising a Bren section under, I think, Sergeant Bullock, to keep an eye open for enemy movements in the direction of the landing beach, with a reserve of my mortar section strengthened by two riflemen. We would change position every two hours. (We lay about 100 yards behind our forward position.) The balance of the troop then made its way back to the beach-head for the evening where, I believe, we were to be relieved at nightfall. During the early afternoon, just before we were due to move up and occupy the forward position, a terrible roar of machine-gun fire and explosions broke out from the direction of our Bren position and a German in a huge helmet appeared in front of me. I fired at him and he disappeared. We quickly got back to a stronger position and sent one of the riflemen back to our base to report what had happened. The row in front subsided and the enemy showed no signs of advancing any further, and in fact could no longer be seen. Eventually 2 Troop came steaming back, having heard the firing and about-turned immediately, meeting our messenger on the way. The forward position was empty and the men manning it had either been taken prisoner (subsequently freed after the capture of Sarande) or evaded the enemy in the excitement (the Bren gun had jammed). We learned later that 40 RM Commando had seen an enemy fighting patrol of about 100 men leave Sarande and move towards our position through a defile out of our sight until it came into view from behind a rocky outcrop about 100 yards in front. The Marines had tried to signal us but this was not observed. It seemed that after overrunning our position, the enemy decided not to advance further in case of a trap, and immediately retired to Sarande.

'The weather started deteriorating and we returned to the base, where by now evening had set in and a steady rain was falling. Near the head of the valley we found a ledge some eighteen inches above a dried-up water course. Here, with a groundsheet underneath and a gas cape stretched over the top across some pieces of branch held down with rocks, we were able to crouch and brew up on solid fuel burners. This cheerful pursuit out of the way, we got down for a good night's sleep. The first inkling that things were not going to be as good as was hoped for was an increase in rain, followed by thunder and lightning. The gas cape flapped and tipped water down my back. I crawled out and without much hope rearranged it so the drips now went somewhere else, but the ledge seemed to be getting unaccountably muddy. I tried ignoring this for another hour when a new noise became apparent, something like a waterfall. I sleepily thought if I ignored it, it would go away, but it didn't. Deciding that there was no longer any point in keeping my eyes closed, I thought I might as well see what was going on. I found that the gulley had filled with a torrent that was lapping over the edge of my crumbling ledge. My companions were all experiencing the same unpleasantness. Dawn was breaking, so we retrieved our mud-filled coverings and equipment and made our way towards the beach some three-quarters of a mile away.

'With the full dawn came the sun, and our clothes started steaming. On the way down to the beach we were told that a good breakfast awaited us, plus (just as welcome) a supply of boots which had arrived. This was a great day of recuperation. We swam in the clear waters of the bay, lay in the sun, dried out and watched the landing craft unloading further stores. All the earlier misery was forgotten, our clothes were dry, we had clean socks and, most important of all, well-shod feet.

'We learned that the supporting 25-pounders had been landed further along the coast, and that night moved forward again across the rocks to our start point some 400 yards short of the enemy inland gun positions; 25-pounders and 20mm cannon. 40 Commando were on our right along the coastal stretch. Just before dawn our artillery laid down a short barrage and we advanced to our objectives. Short of our objectives, the enemy fire became heavier in our direction, mostly caused by the considerable noise from Albanian Partisans, who had decided to join in. They were shooting dangerously over our heads from far too great a distance. The problem eventually became so serious that Colonel Fynn threatened to arrest the Partisans' leader unless he called them off and allowed us to get on with the job. We were into mid-morning now, and Captain Parsons (later killed in this action) at the head of his troop, took the 20mm cannon position. We were now into the main defence position and the enemy troops were surrendering. Firing died away and we started to move slowly down the hill into the town, keeping to the few paths as a considerable number of mines had been laid.

'Reaching the outskirts of the town, we were halted at a white-painted, four-storey building, heavily covered with Red Cross emblems and also heavily damaged from shellfire. The Marines were already in the town and were looking for a massive demolition charge which was supposed to be somewhere in the centre. It was found, and I cannot recall whether it was blown or not. Captain McWilliams' medical team, together with enemy medical personnel, had finished treating the wounded and were now sewing the dead of both sides into blankets for burial a few yards away in a plot being excavated by prisoners. A service was conducted by the padre, attended by some prisoners and ourselves, a volley was fired over the graves, and these were filled in with a marker at the head. It was, I understood, the intention to return at a later date to remove the bodies to Italy, but the burial party was not able to land, being fired upon by the Albanians who, by then, had become well established due to a general enemy withdrawal inland from the coast.

'Following this, we retraced our steps the five miles back to our landing beach. The following morning, in bright sunshine, a group of us boarded a landing craft and set off for Corfu, where white flags had been observed. I should also mention that patrolling towards the inland town of Delvine some seven miles across marshy land produced information that it was strongly held. This place was suggested as a secondary objective by LFA (Land Forces Adriatic), after the taking of Sarande, and resulted in Brigadier Churchill resigning his command and returning to England, as he was not prepared to commit what was left of his force after Sarande to an attack across appalling terrain without considerable reinforcements of men and artillery, which were not forthcoming.'

The successful operations on the Albanian coast following the fall of Sarande led to the fall of Corfu just across the straits, where 2 and 40 landed in mid-November. Then 2 SS Brigade suffered the loss of its Brigadier, Tom Churchill. With 40 Commando detached to garrison Corfu, the useful RAF Parachute Levies removed from his command, No. 9 Commando now in Greece and 43 Commando still in Yugoslavia, and with no transport, Tom Churchill was ordered to pursue the retreating Germans across Albania with his much depleted No. 2 Commando. He replied to this order with a one-word signal: 'How?' There was a short dispute and the Brigadier resigned with the command of 2 Special Service Brigade falling to Brigadier R. J. F. Tod of No. 9 Commando, which had been operating in Greece, at Kithera and Skiathos in the Sporades. Their task now was to prevent civil war breaking out between the Royalists and the Communist Greeks of Elas, a far from easy task. 9 Commando formed part of Foxforce, which also included men from the SBS, the LRDG of Western Desert fame, some Royal Engineers and Greeks and the guns of the Raiding Support Regiment.

Captain Mike Long of 4 Troop, 9 Commando, takes up the tale. 'We sailed to Skiathos on caiques and it took six or seven days from the first boat reaching Skiathos until the last one arrived. Then the rest of the Commando went off to Salonica and 4 Troop were left on Skiathos, with orders to protect the naval base. The "navy" consisted of four destroyers, which soon left, but then in came HMS *Ajax*, the cruiser of Battle of the River Plate fame, when she and other ships had fought the battleship *Graf Spee*. I paddled out to HMS *Ajax* in a canoe, accompanied by TQMS Graves, and we were supplied with showers and fresh bread for the troop, which was very welcome.

'On one occasion we decided to hold a display of Highland dancing on the quay, under Piper Ross, with eightsome reels and so on. The Captain of HMS *Ajax* ordered the Royal Marine band to put on a display, and not to be outdone, the Mayor of Skiathos organized Greek dancing. The whole afternoon went down very well. The troop medical orderly, Lance Corporal "Doc" Quigley, ran a daily clinic for the local people, and we all got on very well.

'I also remember that we had left a very dispirited Italy, but when we got to Greece, where people had had a much harder time than the Italians, we found the most amazing and impressive morale and national pride. In Athens we collected a week's supply of sweets from the troop and gave it to a local orphanage. All the children came and sang for us "It's a long way to Tipperary". The men were standing about when I realized that the Greeks must think that "Tipperary" was our national anthem, so I quickly called them to attention until the children had finished. No. 9 Commando entered Athens on 12 October 1944, where the Colonel received the Freedom of the City.'

In March 1945 the much-travelled units of No. 2 Special Service Brigade, which had become No. 2 Commando Brigade in December 1944, finally came together again at Ravenna in Italy. In mid-March, Brigadier Tod was ordered to lead his brigade against the German positions astride Lake Comacchio, a few miles north of Ravenna, a natural obstacle which barred the northward advance of the Eighth Army towards Venice.

Lake Comacchio is a very shallow lake, separated from the Adriatic by a narrow spit of land and fed from the south by the River Reno. Brigadier Tod's plan was for No. 2 Commando to cross the lake in small boats, land a third of the way up the spit and seize two bridges which carried the only road across drainage ditches. No. 9 Commando would also cross the lake and clear the western half of the spit, while No. 43, now under Lieutenant Colonel

Ian Riches, RM, attacked up the spit from the south. This meant three Commandos would clear the spit, while the last unit, No. 40, were to hold the south bank of the Reno at the base of the spit, and then cross the river to seize the north bank, after which the whole force would advance, clearing German positions and opening a way round the lake for the advancing British divisions. All the German positions were given biblical codenames – Acts, Joshua, Ezra, Leviticus, and so on, and were garrisoned by German and Turkoman troops, equipped with machine-guns and field artillery.

9 Commando, totalling 368 all ranks, excluding attached personnel, moved from Ravenna at 16.00 hrs on Easter Sunday, 1 April. For their part in the operation, 9 Commando were allotted six Fantails (LVTs), one Weasel and twenty-six stormboats, plus six assault boats to be used in case of breakdown. The loaded Fantails bogged down in the shallow water and mud had to be abandoned, the Commando landing in the stormboats and Goatley boats. The Commando had once again been organized into two-troop squadrons, A Squadron consisting of 1 and 2 Troops and B Squadron of 5 and 6 Troops under Major L. S. Callf, MC.

Major Leslie Callf gives his story of the Comacchio battle, Operation Roast, which began when the war in Europe had just five weeks left to run. 'There was some confusion at the stormboat area prior to wading off, as no blue guiding light was visible and no clear order given for setting off. However, the word was passed down to "follow your serial" so the squadron moved off, pushing their boats and keeping within voice control. There was still no blue light visible, and it appeared that the blind were leading the blind. Various degrees of difficulty were experienced by the boats owing to different loads, and we soon became very spread out. 6 Troop appeared to keep together, and went out into deep water, while 5 Troop's lighter boats kept inshore. My own boat travelled midway and became stuck in the mud on three different occasions and fell slightly behind. Information from a Folboat manned by SBS resulted in our pushing and wading into deeper water, where it was possible to paddle. The drivers had orders not to start their engines before reaching the blue light, but upon receiving the okay from HQ, we had several attempts to start ours while still half a mile from the light. By putting most of the weight in the bows, we managed to gain sufficient clearance for the propeller to start, and soon made the FUP, where Major Porter was waiting in a Folboat together with the complete three boats of 6 Troop and several serials of 2 Commando.

'Eventually, the remaining boats were complete and tied together, and we set off. 4 Troop went westwards wide of the islands en route, and 5 Troop, going in between the islands, took the lead. The mist became thicker near the coast, and we strayed slightly to the north, hitting the Argine at 601591. We became stuck in the mud, and had to untie all four boats and push and paddle and allow each boat to find its own way in. The smoke screen was perfect and the phosphorus smoke bombs lit up the house opposite our landing beach. Mud within 300 yards of the shore was especially sticky, and the last wade was very tiring. On shore we found that 4 Troop had organized the beach-head as practised and we quickly formed up near the road, ready to move when all the squadron reported. Time of landing was approximately 05.30 hrs. I reported on wireless about 05.45 hrs (first light) that the squadron was ready to move, and that we already had three prisoners who stated that there was a company of the enemy with three machine guns covering the beaches and approaches. I gave orders to proceed to bound one, and B Squadron moved off in extended order. In 5 Troop, 9 Section led and put down smoke opposite the house at bound one and overran it, leaving 10 Section to search in detail. No prisoners were taken here. A very heavy mist came down at this time and I decided that we could take advantage of it to cover our advance and endeavour to overrun "Leviticus", where the bulk of the enemy defenders seemed to be. Two 38 sets were "dis" owing to the water. I could not get into contact with 6 Troop by walkie-talkie at that moment, but hoped 6 Troop would push on in the same manner. Visibility in the mist was about six feet. I gave the order to advance as far as Smarlacca House, or to such a time as 9 Section in the lead were forced to cease their advance. We proceeded at good speed over the ploughed ground down the vine lanes south of the house at bound one, in extended order, 9 Section leading, covering the road to within fifty yards of the beach. 9 Section bumped the enemy who were dug in, and facing our direction on the edge of sand dunes at 608583 (about 400–500 yards north of the aforementioned house). The enemy opened up with all their automatic weapons, firing down the vine lanes, and threw egg-and-stick grenades; at the same time further down the coast, automatic weapons were firing on the remaining boats putting in to the shore. Lieutenant Long's section swept into the enemy and overran them, but sustained eight casualties in doing so, including Lieutenant Long and his batman. 10 Section and Troop HQ came through 9 Section, and still in the thick mist the whole Troop pushed to the gun lines, with Sergeants Searle and Stephens pushing round the beach flank to engage and silence the Spandau firing on the beach. One 75mm gun was blown up just before we reached it, and another was captured intact (it had a demolition charge ready to be ignited). A German about to blow the charge was killed.

'It was impossible to go on without reorganizing the squadron, as we were now mixed up, and pushing before us about ten prisoners. The mist was just lifting, and I gave the order to consolidate and reform the line. I could now see that two sub-sections (depleted) had pushed ahead on the right flank nearest the beach, and had stopped the Spandaus firing on the boats coming in. Troop HQ had pushed ahead of the remainder of 9 Section and were in the middle of the dunes between the road and the beach. 10 Section were slightly behind, finishing their mopping up process. Prisoners were being pushed up to Troop HQ and were coming back from the forward sub-sections. The enemy, in ones and twos, were being pulled out from dug-outs near the guns. Thinking that an obstinate enemy still remained in a dug-out, CSM Walsh, MM, rushed up and used his flame-thrower, setting alight the camouflage which raised a smoke column. At exactly this moment, the whole area from the road to the beach was subjected to mortar stonk of disastrous accuracy, followed by two or three more in quick succession, covering the whole area from the dug-in positions to the gun positions (obviously a DF task). The fire came from both south and north, the northerly fire mainly covering the outer edge of the dunes overlooking the beaches. Troop HQ was situated in a large shell crater, and two direct hits during two of the stonks killed four, Sergeant Dickenson, Sergeant Porter, Private Drummond and Private Urquhart, together with one prisoner. It also put the wireless out of commission and wounded all Troop HQ except Private Lancaster. Total casualties during this stonking were four killed and eleven wounded. The passage of time from overrunning the FDLs of the enemy to the stonking was very short, a matter of five minutes or even less.

'Realizing we were in a DF task, I ordered the remaining men to advance to the next ridge and consolidate and reorganize. An extremely trying period ensued under Spandau fire from front and left flank, while wounded were accounted for and LMGs got into action. All wireless communication, together with walkie-talkie, was dead, and I had no knowledge of 6 Troop's whereabouts. Lieutenant Robinson organized his section on the right flank, and prisoners were rounded up and sent to assist Lance Corporal King and the walking wounded we had left behind. Lieutenant Long hobbled up and asked for a task to do. Two runners were sent off to 6 Troop to give them our position and situation report. 10 Section, under Lieutenant Robinson, was ordered to advance again to the next ridge, where they engaged targets to the front. My runner returned with Captain Kennedy's runner, and I decided to visit 6 Troop and make further plans over his wireless. Meanwhile, I detailed Lieutenant Long to organize all prisoners and walking wounded to help the badly wounded back to HQ, and give our situation and try and send up a wireless set. One mortar had been destroyed, and both enemy rifles were out of commission. A sniper was pushed forward to engage and observe. At approximately 08.30 hrs I contacted Captain Kennedy and learned that he had also been subjected to mortar shelling, and had taken up a line level with us east of the road. After sending through our casualty return, I arranged an artillery shoot of HE and smoke on Smarlacca House target 9D for five minutes. 6 Troop would then advance to the line of the house under our covering fire, followed by 5 Troop advancing past Smarlacca, i.e. to the end of bound two.

'I returned to 5 Troop and withdrew the forward section 100 yards as a safety area for our own artillery support, which went down at 08.45 hrs. The smoke quickly billowed up into the air and was thickened by two-inch mortar smoke from 6 Troop, who then advanced but came under an immediate and accurate mortar stonking, killing Lieutenant Morris and wounding eight other ranks. 6 Troop were hidden from view of 5 Troop, and it was a very considerable time before I realized that they had not gained their objective. I advanced 5 Troop forward again to their old positions on a ridge about 200 yards north of Smarlacca House, and at the same time another stonk fell on our lately occupied positions. I sent two more runners to find out what had happened to 6 Troop, and meanwhile dug in on our position with two weak sub-sections on the right flank, and one in the middle with Troop HQ, Lieutenant Robinson being on the right flank. It was impossible for my troop to move until I could again establish contact with 6 Troop. Without command or knowledge of events, I decided to wait where I was. Two Spandau positions, one to our front in the vicinity of a pillbox by the house, and the other on a knoll east of the road, were engaged by our fire. Our mortar was employed without success, and each time a further stonk was returned by the enemy, behind our positions in the vicinity of our previously held line. A further four prisoners were taken on our right flank as they were trying to crawl through our lines. My runner returned with information of 6 Troop and of their positions, which were again approximately opposite, but further east, and hidden from 5 Troop in dead ground. The "cab rank" was being employed by us, but their bombs were dropping behind and nearer to us than the enemy and very close to 6 Troop positions. The mortar operator must have now again spotted our position and two stonks were put down within twenty-five feet of us.

'Captain Bassett-Wilson, MC, had now come up between mortaring and informed me he was liaising between 5 and 6 Troops, and had sent an FOO to 6 Troop. We were both digging deeper positions as we discussed a plan for moving forward, when a direct hit landed by the side of Captain Bassett-Wilson, badly wounding him and injuring one other. A second direct hit immediately afterwards killed Captain Bassett-Wilson and Lance Corporal Lody, and I decided to withdraw the line. Meanwhile, Lance Sergeant Stephens and Private Sherwood had been hit by automatic fire while endeavouring to bring more fire power on the right flank. They had both been evacuated prior to the last stonk, assisted by five prisoners and Lance Corporal

King. 5 Troop withdrew in small groups, and although mortared, did not suffer further casualties. One sub-section remained isolated on the right flank. Our next line was taken up on the edge of the vines, 400–500 yards south of bound one. As we were digging in, two bursts of fire came down the vine lanes and wounded Lance Sergeant Searles, Lance Sergeant McNeil, Lance Corporal Parkin and Private Smith. This fire swept the whole of the vine area and was fired in an indirect role, obviously covering the FDLs guarding the gun lines, which we had attacked in the mist. Our remaining prisoners helped the last of the wounded back after Spandau fire had ceased. We now dug in again and I was quite sure that we would be unable to advance in daylight while the mortar operator was in position. I suspect that his position was south of the actual mortars. It was obvious that the whole of the area of "Leviticus" was easily controlled by the enemy's knowledge of the ground. About half an hour later, the artillery support (fifteen minutes' HE, followed by smoke) came down for A Squadron (1 and 2 Troops), and later still, the welcome sound of bagpipes heralded the appearance of 1 Troop. It was learned later that two mortar operators were hiding, observing 1 and 2 Troops advance, but were captured by 6 Troop, when they tried to crawl through our lines at night. One of the Spandau gunners also ran off, and I believe managed to evade capture.

'All arms and personal effects of the dead and wounded were gathered into one dump and later removed to Q dump. Dead Germans' documents were also collected. Replenishments of expended arms were made up. The Adjutant, Captain Hill, came up and gave me information as to night consolidation. In the mail, which came up later, Private Lancaster received a book called *Bullets for Breakfast*; Lance Corporal Smith's birthday was celebrated crossing Lake Comacchio.'

Lieutenant Don Long, MC, of 9 Commando, recalls his

experiences at Comacchio: 'I remember walking to the lorries with George Robinson, who said, "The one thing I could do with before the war ends is an MC." We were all quite sure the war would be over shortly, so I said, "Don't be bloody silly, just hope we don't get one of those white crosses the Pioneers make." Well, when we landed at Comacchio, it was an awful nonsense. The Fantails got stuck, the stormboats wouldn't float. But anyway we eventually landed and I was going over to talk to Sergeant McCreasy. We were worried about the *schu* mines, which could take your foot off, and as I ran over I was conscious of being blown into the air. I came down with the most awful bump, but was delighted to see I still had both my legs, although I was now pretty useless. It turned out later to have been a stick grenade which was a blind (undetonated) until I kicked it, hurting me and taking off my batman Francis' left cheek.

'My Troop had gone on but I looked in a hole and found a German there, looking rather glum. I pulled my Colt 45, got him out, got rid of his rifle and had him carry me piggyback up to where I found Major Callf and the battle.'

Dudley Cooper of 2 Commando won the Military Medal at Comacchio. 'We were on the start line where, according to the briefing, we would board the collapsibles and be towed by the outboard up the lake. We would then carry them over a dyke and row ashore on the east bank, after a barrage had been laid down at dawn. Some engineers joined us for mine-lifting duties. They had not been briefed by their officer and were in clean fatigue and no weapons. They were soon disillusioned and given rifles and ammunition and told they would have to look after themselves in an assault. We got in the boats and the mosquitoes rose off the lake in millions. The driver of the outboard started the engine and put it in the water, where it immediately stopped. None of the engines would work. Eventually we all got in the water and found mud up to the thigh and water to the lower chest. We pushed and pulled the boats up that lake for hours. The water became deep enough to put the engine on. We all climbed in and away we went, only to stop in five or ten minutes at the dyke. We could have walked the collapsibles up there instead of the heavy outboard. We lay on the dyke and awaited the barrage which was on time. Our eager officer did not wait for the ceasing of the barrage and we were soon too close for comfort. I stopped paddling and the officer told me to keep going. At that moment a large piece of shrapnel passed our heads, and it was a panic back-pedal until the barrage ceased. We went in on a German gun battery and were quickly in control. The officer and my number two and I moved forward and saw the Germans regrouping for counter-attack. I ranged the Piat and sent all the bombs into the woodland where they were. We were out in front of our own lines with only small arms to defend ourselves, and no one knew where we were at that time. I told the others I would cover them as they retired, as there was a machine gun covering our position. I used my ·45 Colt to keep the machine gun owner busy, but once I had emptied the gun, the machine gun kept me from moving or reloading. After a hit on the shoulder-piece of my Piat and holes in my blouse and trousers, I decided to play dead. The slightest move drew fire, until I was so still I closed my eyes and relaxed.

'After what seemed hours but was probably only half an hour, Willy Neil came up behind me, calling my name. I said to him, "If you can get out here, we can get back . . . run!" And we ran back to our lines. My number two had been unfortunate. He was in a shell hole with German prisoners and others when a mortar bomb burst in the hole killing them all. No counter-attack came and ten or twelve Germans were dead where the Piat had sent the bombs. We moved out up the road to a small bridge. The engineers were set to work and found mines on the bridge and on the river bank on both sides. We dug in on the spit, east of Fort Garibaldi. The tanks came up, drawing

gunfire down on us and also a large number of foreign
soldiers from the German lines with their hands up. They
stated that they had shot the German Sergeant and his
aides. We were relieved by men who went on to attack
Fort Garibaldi, so we escorted the prisoners back. We
later learned the Marines had met trouble; the amphib-
ians had grounded in the mud and when the doors opened,
guns shot in at point-blank range from tanks, not known
to be in the area. One Piat gunner fired in full view and
stopped a tank but lost his life, being so exposed. A lot of
men were lost, but the objective was finally taken.'

It took 2 Commando Brigade until 4 April to fight their
way up and across Comacchio, and following Operation
Roast, the Brigade came under the command of 56 Division for their next operation, around the Argenta Gap.
Lieutenant Peter Bolton of 9 Commando takes up the
tale. 'We only had a couple of days' respite until we were
off again on Operation Impact Royal with 24 Guards
Brigade. The plan was to cross the south-west shore of
Comacchio in Fantails, land by day and advance up the
west side of the lake to secure a crossing point on the
Fosse Marina Canal, which would open the way northwards and westwards to the Argenta Gap. We landed as
planned with no opposition but as we deployed on the
lakeside we came under mortar fire. Luckily we had dug
in fast on arrival, so there were no casualties. A bomb
exploded very close to the slit trench occupied by my
batman Private Woodcock. As I stuck my head up after
the bang to see what had happened, I saw Woodcock
rising like an angel out of a cloud of smoke, and wander-
ing off towards a nearby wood. "Come back Woodcock,"
I shouted, but he was obviously in a daze and disappeared
into the wood. A further stonk precluded immediate
investigation, but some ten minutes later he came staggering back asking what had happened. My rucksack,
which was on the edge of my slit trench, was peppered
with shrapnel, and an emergency ration tin of black

chocolate in the top had been completely pulverized. Woodcock was pretty deaf, and had to be left with the MO.

'On we went, I had an objective – a farmhouse – which we marched hopefully towards. It was getting dark as we slogged on. We must have been pretty tired as one of my lance corporals walked off the side of the track and fell into an old slit trench. Unfortunately he had a tin of detonators in his denim trouser pocket, and as he fell they were crushed and went off. I was ahead of him at the time and thought someone had thrown a grenade at us. He was pretty severely peppered in the groin. Another casualty, and we hadn't even begun the operation! My first objective was a group of farm buildings dominating the bridge over the canal. When secure, we were to signal this by playing the Troop tune on the pipes (we had the piper with us) and then press on to the second objective, which was to secure the bridge. It was dark as we approached the farm. When we were some 300 yards away, we got down off the raised roadway and made our way along the base of the slope hidden, I hoped, by the bank.

'We had just started to move again when there was a shout, a grenade went off, and there was a burst of fire (whose, I never knew). Next, two prisoners were hustled back. It appeared that my leading scout had fallen into an enemy advance post. He thought they must have been asleep, but one of them had thrown a grenade. No casualties at this stage, but our silent approach gambit was completely blown. Quickly I shouted the troop to spread out in line across the field to our left and charge the buildings ahead. This we did. I must admit it was exhilarating. Real "over the top" stuff. We had bayonets fixed and whooped in, screaming like dervishes. Someone appeared at an upstairs window and fired several bursts at us as we ran. I replied on the run with my ·45 and fired three shots – all of which went miles wide – and then I caught my foot in a hole, went over in a crash, and the ·45 spun out of my hand. I did not have a lanyard on it (they get terribly in the way) so I'd lost it. By no means a healthy place to hang about looking for it, so I scuttled after my chaps and ran into the farmyard. As I entered the yard there was what I can only describe as a God Almighty bang, and I was conscious of a great blast of air. As I dropped to the ground there was another great flash and bang, and to my horror I saw the barrel of what looked to me a most enormous gun just in front of me.

'In the flash I also saw Corporal Daniels of 4 Troop moving towards it. I then heard the characteristic whirr of an engine that wouldn't fire. I immediately thought that this was an enemy tank, and on the third flash-bang saw Corporal Daniels astride the turret, tommy gun in hand, shouting "Hande hoch – Raus, Raus" and out they came. It was not in fact a tank but an SP88 gun which, as we ran in, tried to get clear, and to put us off until they got it started, they fired at point blank range across the farmyard into an adjoining barn. We hustled the prisoners inside the building, found some Italian civilians sheltering terrified in the cellar, and I raced out again to see if we had in fact secured our objective. I ran round the buildings with Gunner Riddall, and as we approached an adjacent building, a figure appeared and fired a long burst of Schmeisser in our direction. I felt a terrific bang on the head, fell down and thought, "What a ridiculous way to die, right at the end of the war." I felt with my fingers for the hole I was sure was in my forehead, but then Riddall was shouting, "Are you all right, Sir? Your helmet's on fire!" I took it off. A bullet had struck the front rim, deflecting upwards, splitting the front of the helmet, and the spark had ignited the scrim and camouflage netting. A patch about as big as my palm was glowing brightly.

'Riddall had taken a shot at the guy, but we didn't proceed with that approach and returned, collected a few more chaps and assaulted the building from the opposite side. I happily gave the order to play the pipe tune, signalling our success, and I must add proudly that 4 Troop's piper was first. As the night wore on, one by one, the other Troops were heard playing their "on objective" tune. It was most heart-warming. At this stage I was, I think, actually the Troop Commander. Mike Long was called a Squadron Commander as he had two Troops under him. I've no idea where he was while all this was going on. I hadn't seen him for some time. We seemed to be a bit thin on the ground, however, and I found that we had three chaps wounded in the initial charge to the farm, including Lance Corporal Delaney from Ireland, whose claim to fame was that he had been in the Spanish Civil War. "Whose side were you on, Delaney?" I once asked. "Oh," says Delaney, "I was General O'Duffy's cook." O'Duffy, apparently, was the Commander of the Irish Brigade on Franco's side.

'We pressed on into phase two of the operation, to seize the bridge. George Bisset, our own RE chap, went forward to recce the area for booby traps, and to see if it was wired up to be blown. As we ran towards the bridge we came under pretty heavy fire, and suddenly there was a flash just beside me, and to my horror I saw Private Young on fire. A bullet, or maybe a bit of shrapnel (we were under mortar fire at the time too) had hit a 75 phosphorus grenade in his belt pouch. We stopped, tore his equipment and para smock off (all blazing) and pushed him down in the mud to try to put it all out. We didn't really succeed, and as he was in such great pain, I gave him a shot of morphine (all officers had a pack of five of these), and was just about to leave and carry on, when he gasped, "Is it all right if I have a fag, Sir?" It didn't really matter at all as his face was alight anyway. As I left him slumped against a wall, I picked up his steel helmet, put it on his head, saying, "You'll be all right, Young, the medics will get here soon," and ran off. I'd taken only about three paces when the whole earth erupted and I was blown flat on my back. The bridge had been blown. Had I not delayed those few minutes with Young, we would all have been on it.

'As I tried to make my way back to report to my wing, I had to crawl across an area under fixed line fire. It was pretty frightening as they were using tracer bullets. As I crawled and stumbled past a small building, a helping hand drew me in, saying, "Wait a minute laddie – what's going on?" It was Angus Ferguson, and he told me that Harry Kither had just been killed at that place. I reckon that helping hand saved me again too. Anyway, we withdrew to the safe(?) side of the raised roadway and awaited events. My troop was now at about half strength. As in most battles, I didn't know fully where everybody was. Gradually, as dawn came, we realized what was happening and where. It was decided that we would dig in and assault the canal that night, 15/16 April. We holed up all day and tried to sleep. The odd mortar bomb came our way but not too many. Later on, I was told that some REs would be bringing up assault boats with which we would cross the canal. All this happened, but unfortunately the assault boats had to be carried up and over the road. As the road was under almost continual fire, this posed problems. Each boat needed at least four men, better still six, to manhandle it. The REs who delivered the boats to us evaporated before I could press them into helping. What was left of 4 Troop tried, and we got two or three boats across the road, but took casualties and really did not have an effective troop left to do anything with. One of my stalwarts, Corporal Tanner, an ex-City of London policeman, was killed, and my two signallers, Lance Corporal Gardner and Signaller Brown were also killed. We had several chaps pretty badly wounded.

'At the height of all this, in the pitch dark, lit only by tracer bullets, I was in a hole trying to piece together what was happening when suddenly I saw a tall figure standing over me, quite upright, with a large map case at the ready. The figure had another person with him with a torch at the ready. "I say," said the figure, "are you an officer?" "Yes," I snarled, "who the hell are you?" "Oh, I'm the IO of 2nd Scots Guards," he said, "and we're going to take over from you tomorrow, and I was just having a look around first." "For God's sake get down before you get your head blown off," I said. "Oh dear," was the reply. "Is it really as bad as that?" I tried my best to enlighten him but it was difficult. At the time I had a Sergeant from another troop on a stretcher awaiting evacuation, and another of my chaps so badly wounded in the hands that the only place I could give him a shot of morphine was in the belly. I must say I was greatly impressed by the bearing of the Guard. His inability to recognize an officer was probably genuine. We did not wear pips on an operation like this. Section Commanders wore a piece of greenish rope on each epaulette. Troop Commanders wore two pieces. I think the CO and God wore three, but I never saw either of them close to at the time.

'My next memory is lying on a canal bank with Major Leslie Callf and Captain Mat Kennedy, awaiting the return of Lieutenant Mark Cloake of 4 Troop, who was sent to see what the chances were of getting across the canal without the boats. When he came back he was literally bubbling mud and ooze. "Mud," he said. "Mud, right up to here," indicating his chest. I had the remnants of 4 Troop with me on the bank, waiting, we thought, to lead the way across, then let other troops less decimated perhaps come through. However, it was not to be. A decision was taken to stay where we were till dawn, then re-assess the situation. As we lay there a rum ration came up. CSM Scott of 4 Troop enthusiastically dispensed the tots. As dawn lightened the sky, it was obvious that our present position was untenable as we were overlooked by high buildings on the far bank. It was decided to withdraw under cover of smoke to a wood about 200 yards to our rear. At the due time the smoke came down and back we went. When I got into the wood, I asked where Sergeant

Major Scott was (he was i/c the mortar smoke).
"Wounded, Sir," I was told. "Wounded?" How could he
be wounded, I wondered. We had not been fired on in the
withdrawal. It seemed that at some stage the two-inch
mortar firing pin had become so dirty and encrusted that
it had stuck in the "up" position. Scott, knowing we
needed the smoke badly, decided to try to fire it like a
three-inch mortar, i.e. drop the bomb in, then duck.
Unfortunately he hadn't ducked fast enough and collected
one on the chest. Out of my section of twenty-four men I
had seventeen casualties. Not all were killed or seriously
wounded, but seventeen were sent back one way or
another. Our padre, John Birkbeck, was a tower of
strength during this operation. His jeep with its two
stretchers for our dead and wounded used the open road,
and his presence was a great assistance. Later, back we
went to Marina de Ravenna, and that was the end of our
war in Italy.

Well not quite. There were awards. Leslie Callf sums
up:

'Totals awarded: 2 DSOs; 4 DCMs; 10 MCs; 16 MMs;
21 Mentioned in Dispatches. DSO: Lieutenant Colonel
R. J. F. Tod, DSO and Bar. DCM: Lance Sergeant J.
Thompson; CSM: G. Reace; Sergeant C. Scarle; Sergeant
L. Hopkins. MC: Lieutenant Colonel M. R. H. Allen;
Major R. A. C. Cameron; Major L. S. Callf and Bar;
Captain M. Long; Captain P. Bassett-Wilson; Captain E. J.
D'Arcy; Captain M. A. W. Davies; Captain H. Kither;
Lieutenant D. Long. MM: CSM F. Walsh; Sergeant H.
Jackson; Sergeant G. Wilkins; Sergeant G. McPherson;
Sergeant J. Wham; Private J. Farquhar; CSM H. Barton;
Sergeant G. Hughes; Sergeant J. Hodkinson; Sergeant W.
Waugh; Corporal T. Bostock; Private A. Scott; Corporal
R. King; Sergeant G. Wilson; Corporal J. Cramer; Lance
Brigadier S. Daniels.'

10

D-Day and Normandy, 1944

'Then forth, dear countrymen; let us deliver
our puissance into the hand of God,
Putting it straight in expedition.'

HENRY V

With the Second Front now looming on the horizon, No.
3 Commando, 280 strong, had returned to England on 4
January 1944 to join the Allied armies preparing for the
D-Day landings. Things had changed while they had been
away, and the Commando organization had expanded
considerably in their absence. By April 1943, two Brigade
Headquarters had been established, one in the UK, the
other in the Middle East. When Brigadier Laycock became
Chief of Combined Operations one of his first tasks was
to reorganize the entire Commando set-up, replacing ad
hoc arrangements with a more formal though flexible
structure. By 1944 there were four Commando (SS) Brigades: No. 1, preparing for D-Day in the UK; No. 2 in the
Mediterranean; No. 3 in or en route for the Far East; and
now forming, No. 4, also in the UK for D-Day and
consisting entirely of newly-raised Royal Marine units
from the old Royal Marine Division. These new Royal
Marine units caused – and to a degree still cause – some
heart-searching among the Army Commandos.

The root cause of this concern was that the Royal
Marine Commandos were not all-volunteer units. The
original Royal Marine Commando No. 40 had been

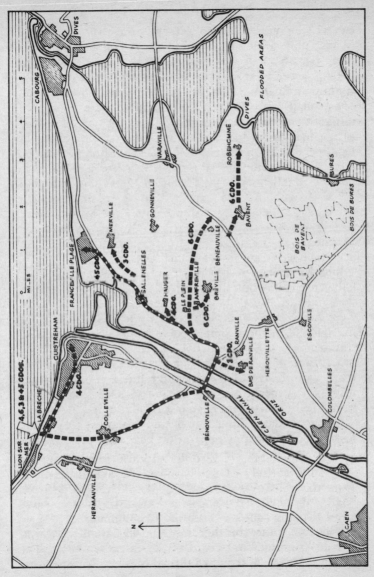

D-Day and Normandy

entirely composed of volunteers and the two Royal Marine units which followed, Nos. 41 and 43, had taken their fair share of the fighting in Italy and had been quickly accepted in the pressure of battle. The ones now training in England, Nos. 42, 45, 46, 47 and, from March 1944, 48 (Royal Marine) Commandos, were a slightly different proposition. Durnford Slater, for one, was dead set against them. He was now Deputy Commander of Commando Group which, under General Robert Sturges, controlled all four Special Service Brigades and the supporting establishments, and felt that 'units of conscripted Marines could not be expected to maintain the high standards achieved by volunteers'. His feelings were widely shared by other ranks of 3 Commando, who barred Marines from the pubs they frequented in Worthing, an act which led to a number of incidents.

John Kruthoffer of 40 Commando and 30 Assault Unit (30 Commando) found the Army/Marine conflict little to worry about. 'Most of the instructors I met in Scotland were Army types and absolutely first-class. They could not have been more helpful or encouraging to the RM Commando – the 'A' – in 1942. I can say the same about other units or individuals met in training or elsewhere; there was always cheerful banter but a lot of mutual respect. I suspect this was because we all suffered the same niggling criticism from our regular units.'

Durnford Slater soon found that his most important task was to promote co-operation between the old Army and the new Royal Marine units, who had in fact got rid of their unwilling recruits at Achnacarry or in the early training, and were now eager to play their part on D-Day. From his Mediterranean experience, Durnford Slater knew that the best way to promote comradeship was to brigade the units together. So No. 45 Commando was sent to Brigadier Lord Lovat's 1 SS Brigade, which then included Nos. 3, 4, 6 and 45 (Royal Marine) Commandos, plus the French Troops of 10 (IA) Commando, under Commandant Philippe Keiffer, attached to No. 4.

Peter Young also found few problems with inter-unit relations. '1st Commando Brigade – 1st SS Brigade, as it was then – was under Lord Lovat. 45 (Royal Marine) Commando was under Charles Ries, a good man and a good friend of mine. Ries also had a very good second in Nicol Gray, a very strong-minded soldier who later commanded the Palestine Police. A very good feeling existed between all units of 1 Brigade, later brilliantly led by Derek Mills-Roberts, a wonderful soldier.'

The second D-Day brigade, No. 4 (SS) Brigade, was under a Royal Marine brigadier, 'Jumbo' Leicester, and consisted of Nos. 41, 46, 47 and 48 (Royal Marine) Commandos. Action had continued through 1943 and early 1944, with the Small Scale Raiding Force, 12 Commando and 10 (IA) Commando mounting a series of raids down Hitler's Atlantic Wall from Norway to the Channel coast, but against steadily improving defences. The Small Scale Raiding Force, having lost many of its founder members, was disbanded in the summer of 1943, many of the survivors going to COPP (Combined Operations Pilotage Parties), and No. 12 Commando was gradually dispersed during the last six months of the year, most of the men transferring to 1 or 6 Commandos. During the early months of 1944 small-scale raids were carried out by Forfar Force, composed of troops from 10 (IA) Commando and 2 SBS, and until May by *Hiltforce*, commanded by Captain Hilton-Jones, largely comprised of men from 3 (Miscellaneous) Troop of 10 (IA), which carried out a number of raids onto the D-Day beaches to report on the shore defences.

For D-Day, the tasks facing the two Commando brigades were very different and since this book is primarily concerned with the Army Commandos, the tasks and actions of 4 (Special Service) Brigade can be dealt with swiftly. There was a difference between the two Brigades' tasks. No. 1 (Special Service) Brigade had to land, break through the German lines and link up with Sixth Airborne Division six miles inland, across and astride the Orne, then coming under the command of Sixth Airborne for the subsequent battles. The units of No. 4 (Special Service) Brigade were employed to extend and link up the flanks of the British and Canadian Divisions landing on Sword and Juno Beaches west of Ouistreham around the Bay of the Seine. Since many people think that Commandos always specialized in assault, it is worthwhile pointing out that on D-Day all the Commando units were in the follow-up waves and landed behind the assault divisions when, in an ideal world, the beaches would already have been secured. On D-Day itself, matters worked out rather differently. To begin with, all the assault units in every wave suffered during the crossing from the weather.

6 'Commando embarked at Spithead on 5 June and sailed for France at 20.00 hrs on a starry evening, with a good sea running,' recalls Phillip Pritchard. 'As the craft cleared the Isle of Wight, the Channel gale began to do its worst among the troops, many of whom were soon desperately seasick.'

1 (Special Service) Brigade were led ashore by No. 4 Commando, followed by Brigade HQ, 6 Commando and the two remaining units, 3 and 45. 4 Commando, with the French troops, veered to the east to attack Ouistreham, while the other units made all speed for the bridges of Bénouville, six miles inland across the Orne and the Caen Canal.

4 Commando, now commanded by Lieutenant Colonel R. W. P. Dawson, landed from LCAs at La Breche, a mile west of Ouistreham at 08.20 hrs on 6 June, advancing across beaches where the East Yorks Regiment of the 8th Infantry Brigade were still pinned behind the sea wall by rifle, mortar and machine-gun fire.

Private Farmborough recalls D-Day with 4 Commando: 'We sailed during the night of 5/6 June, and from the deck of *Princess Astrid* I saw a destroyer blow up and sink. It went down like a giant "V". Soon after this, we embarked in the LCA, were told to keep quiet, and headed for the shore. Suddenly all hell broke loose as we sailed close to a ship firing hundreds of rockets. The noise was terrific. We were crouched in our landing craft when a voice suddenly said, "A bloody racket out there and we've all got to keep quiet!" This made everybody laugh and the tension eased. As we beached, the front went down and out we poured. I had my left arm smashed by bullets before reaching the top of the beach. I found myself lying in front of a big gun emplacement. The gun was still firing when up the beach trundled a tank and put a shell through the aperture, knocking it out. I was between the pair of them and remember hoping that the chap in the tank was a good driver, otherwise I had had it. He couldn't see me, of course, but luckily he veered off to the right of the emplacement, missing me by about four feet. I must say I didn't realize how big a tank was. While recovering in hospital, I read that the tank commander received the MC for this action.' This tank was commanded by Captain Roger Bell of the Westminster Dragoons.

Colonel Dawson was wounded by mortar fire, and forty more of his men were lost crossing the beach before Colonel Dawson was hit again, this time in the head, and the command passed to the unit second-in-command Major Menday.

With the two French troops of 10 IA under Philippe Keiffer leading the way, No. 4 advanced towards Ouistreham, clearing snipers and machine gun posts as they advanced, overrunning a German strongpoint in the casino before moving on towards the Sixth Airborne perimeter at Hauger, on the eastern side of the Caen Canal. Meanwhile Brigade Headquarters with Lord Lovat came ashore, landing at 08.40 hrs with 6 Commando, followed by 3 and 45 Commandos, all heading for Bénouville and Pegasus Bridge across the Caen Canal, which a glider force had taken during the night.

Peter Young, then the CO of 3 Commando, recalls:

'Three of the landing craft were hit and a shell hit 6 Troop's supply of mortar bombs, which detonated, killing the troop sergeant major and a number of others. The first man ashore was the Unit Administrative Officer, Slinger Martin, who had served in France during the Great War.'

Sidney J. Dann of 6 Commando gives his account of D-Day: 'The crossing was very rough and I was very seasick. I took a blanket up on deck and crawled under a lifeboat and lapsed into a stupor. I awoke to a very big bang, which I realized was a shell exploding. A destroyer was burning furiously only a short distance away, and we were running into the beach. The troop were coming up on deck for the landing and my equipment was still below, but I made it in time.

'We were on the starboard ramp and Colonel Mills-Roberts and half of HQ Section were on the port ramp. The beach was covered in smoke with mortar bombs and 88mm shells dropping in. From a concrete blockhouse an MG 34 was spraying the area and buzzing noises were zipping past. Burning tanks, flails, bulldozers and other weird armoured vehicles lay at all angles. The East Yorks (8th Infantry Brigade) had been given the job of landing, holding the coast road and letting us through. They were still at the water's edge and digging in behind the derelict vehicles. Most of us had never seen a dead body before, so it was somewhat of a shock to see bodies floating in the water and others, minus head, limbs, etc., lying on the beach. We pushed through, formed up in order of advance, and with 3 Troop leading, headed inland to relieve the Airborne at the River Orne bridge, and then onto the high ground (which overlooked the landing area) at Bréville and Amfreville.'

Ken Phillott was in the Intelligence Section of 4 Commando on D-Day. 'During the war one of the tasks given to members of the Intelligence Section of No. 4 Commando was to obtain the billets etc. for the members of the unit every time they moved. Many unusual and interesting things happened. At one town I obtained a

billet for a real tough and robust Commando with an
equally robust type of young landlady. About a week later
he came to the office and asked to be allocated another
billet. He was reluctant to give his reasons, although he
admitted he was well fed and had a very comfortable bed.
He was duly given another billet. A few days later his
former landlady appeared at the office complaining that
"her Commando" had left her. She was assured she would
receive her billet money, to which she replied, "I don't
want your billet money. I want another Commando!"

'Anyway, having crossed the beaches, we then had to
cross a soft muddy area, and at one stage there was a dyke
full of green, stinking, muddy water to be crossed. At one
stage there were three of us attempting to get across. A
Marine Commando ahead of me was climbing the far
bank, another chap was in the middle of the water, and I
was sliding down the near bank. At this time a mortar
bomb landed in the middle of us. The Marine Commando
had ammunition in his pouches and this was hit, yet he
sustained only a slight body wound; I suffered no injury,
but the one in the middle was like a leaking sieve, blood
was coming out from shrapnel wounds all over his body.
We had to leave him to the medics and thought that was
the last of him. To our astonishment, some months later
we learnt that he had survived and was in a hospital in
England.'

Sidney Dann of 6 Commando again: 'We had our first
casualty some 200 yards inland, crossing a deep ditch
through a gap in a hedge which was covered by a sniper.
A lad called Adams, who had only joined us as a replace-
ment the day before we sailed, was shot in the head. We
were being strafed by a Nebelwerfer, a flat-backed lorry
with a battery of six mortars firing thermite bombs. We
were very pleased to have something to fire at, and he
scuttled off.

'We then had three pillboxes in our way, which were
defended. My section's pillbox was cleared by giving

covering fire to Jimmy Templeton, who carried our flame-thrower; a couple of quick spurts through the slit and no more Germans. Major Coade, our second-in-command, joined in the attack on the other two positions. He was hit in the face by a potato-masher grenade, and the CO's batman, Corporal Smith, was shot through the arm. He took the second-in-command back to the beach. We cleared the pillboxes and took two prisoners, our first sight of Germans close up.'

Peter Young again: 'The Germans were very keen to defend Ouistreham, but 3 Commando were not involved in that; our job was to get across the Caen Canal and the Orne. We reached the bridges and had a friendly reception from the Airborne, who were very glad to see us. I had been detailed for Cabourg but Lovat sent us to the Bas de Ranville and told us to defend it as a German armoured division would be along later. I wasn't too pleased as I had no weapons to hold off armour and, even worse, the inhabitants of Ranville had built their village in a rather alfresco style, ill-designed for defence by infantry sections.'

Sidney Dann continues: 'We reached Bénouville but found a small-scale battle going on there with Germans holed up in the church. We bypassed that as we were supposed to be at the bridge by mid-day. As we came out onto the road about 200 yards from the bridge, we could see a small group of men. There was a short pause while we tried to decide whose side they were on, and then a long cheer and much waving of Union Jacks – the agreed signal. Our OC 3 Troop, Captain Pyman, apologized for being two and a half minutes late to Brigadier Poett (5 Para) and Lieutenant Colonel Pine-Coffin (7th Para).

'Several versions of that historical meeting have been written. 3 Troop were first there and we carried straight on. As we crossed in extended order we were fired on from the roof of a hospital downstream towards Caen. So it was heads down and run like hell. We passed Ranville

from which came the noises of battle. Airborne and the
Germans were slogging it out. On up the hill to Le Plein
and to our position, a large house on the crossroads of
Béneauville to Bavent. We had been told in our briefing
that Béneauville was undefended. This was not quite so.
Two hundred yards from our position was a troop of four
German 105mm Howitzers and a 20mm dual purpose
gun. We were mortared and shelled for three hours and
lost twenty-two of our sixty-five men. Our Troop OC,
Captain Pyman, was killed by a sniper while trying to
attack the gun position.

'One incident worth a mention happened when I was
No. 2 on the PIAT (Projectile/Infantry Anti-Tank). This
fired a bomb with three-quarters of a pound of explosive
in the head. With Bert Lansdowne, No. 1 on the gun, we
were defending the main gate to the chateau. Soon after
digging in we heard the approach of a motor which could
only be a German, because we were the only troops on
the ridge. I dashed across the road, lay up behind a wall
and looked down the road. Coming at great speed was a
German staff car, complete with officer, driver, and,
facing the rear, two soldiers sitting to attention, rifles
between their knees. We had agreed that Bert would fire
when I dropped my hand. This he did but the staff car was
fifty yards up the road before the bomb passed my left ear.
I rolled over and was complaining that he had missed, and
noticed movement up the road. In an open window of a
house stood a German officer, and beside him sat a soldier
with an MG 34 and two others. The officer saw me at the
same time and pointed. The gunman fired and spattered
the wall behind me as I rolled over. I was soon back in
my slit-trench. Shortly afterwards we saw two people
deep in conversation, walking towards us. We kept well
down and as they passed I called out, "Did you know that
there is a war on?" These were two young German
officers, and they said afterwards that they were unaware
that we were so far inland (seven miles). They had been

told that we had not got past the beach. One spoke very good English and said, "This is all wrong – we are not your enemies. The Russians will be a bigger threat to the world than we will be. We should get rid of Hitler, sign a peace treaty, and sort out the Russians." This was in 1944!

'As all the troops in No. 6 had suffered casualties, instead of holding the whole ridge as originally intended we pulled back and dug in at Saulnier's Farm at Le Plein, a small blob on a large ridge. We brought back our walking wounded – the dead were left behind – and the more seriously wounded were left with villagers. We did a two-troop attack next day and recovered wounded and dead and destroyed the four 105mm guns and towed back the 20mm dual purpose. Our "Longest Day" was over but we had a long way to go.'

Peter Young: 'The Brigade established itself east of the Orne on the high ground from which, had they been able to hold it, the Germans could have aimed artillery fire onto the beaches and the offshore shipping, especially onto Sword Beach. We then had to edge down to the sea and retake the Merville Battery. We lost John Pooley there.'

Sidney Dann's friend, Philip Pritchard, gives another account of D-Day and the Normandy battle: 'Before the landings No. 3 Troop was located, I believe, off Langdale Road, Hove. From here we went on several warm-up exercises which consisted of leaving Newhaven by LCIs and landing (always wet) at a point between Lancing and Worthing. We got to know the LCI crews very well. In our crew was a three-badge AB, a fine seaman of the best type. We always referred to him as "Sergeant" because of his three red stripes (badges) and this made him mad at us as he had explained the difference on every voyage. From here we went in strict formation to the River Arun, as it passed through Arundel. We always chose a spot away from the bridge, and used rubber boats brought up by (I believe) No. 1 Troop (using bicycles) to cross the river in the dark. We then marched on for a further distance and dug in to await the dawn. Thereafter we returned to our billets. We did this on several occasions, each time carrying heavier loads over the distance, which was about twelve miles. This was supposed to equate to the type of ground, and distance we would have to traverse on the day of the assault. During one such exercise, a rubber boat overturned and Private White was drowned, his body being recovered several days later at the river's mouth.

'Our packs were of the Bergen type. As our supply lines were uncertain, we had been issued with the rucksack type so that we could carry a greater load than normal infantry. This was intended to give us a measure of self-sufficiency until our supplies caught up. My Bergen, which I weighed on a railway station weighing machine, together with my belt and Bren pouches, came to 96lbs. In addition, I carried a rifle – Lee Enfield Mk 4 (·303 in) – and bayonet which would put the average weight carried by any Commando soldier in 1 Brigade at well over 100lbs, which, I imagine, would make us the most heavily-laden foot soldiers of the war (possibly of any war!) We marched in a bent-over position, it being impossible to remain upright for long, and often had to assist one another to put on the pack.

'On the late afternoon of 4 June we made a final check of our kit and were issued with our combat rations. Each soldier received two twenty-four-hour ration packs which had been specially formulated for the invasion. The pack consisted of dehydrated meat with boiled sweets, chewing gum and blocks of sweetened oatmeal, together with a ration of "compo" tea (tea, sugar and powdered milk mixed together). Included was a round paper cylinder of eight hexamine (solid fuel) tablets and a small stove, the first I had ever seen. In addition to the two ration packs was the usual "iron ration", which as always consisted of a brass-coloured tin about the size of a flat tobacco tin with a thick bar of plain vitaminized chocolate. Embossed on the lid of the tin was a warning: *"This ration only to be opened on the order of an officer."* I should mention that none of us carried the useless entrenching tool, and in lieu we carried the general service shovel with one man in three carrying the general service pick (as I was!). In the early evening we paraded in full kit and went by Troop Carrying Vehicles to Warsash Cove, where we waited in a field near the landing where the LCIs were moored in pairs alongside each other. We kicked a football about and some of us caught a horse that was in the field and attempted to ride it. About 20.00 hrs we got back on the TCV and returned to camp where we were informed that the invasion was postponed for twenty-four hours. We thereafter saw a film called *Going My Way*, starring Bing Crosby and Barry Fitzgerald, which we were told had not yet been generally released in the UK, and that we were the first to view it. It was, I recall, a suitable film to take our minds off the coming assault. Not, I must admit, that I noticed anyone who was obviously nervous. Personally, I was looking forward to the great adventure, having seen very little real action up to that date. We were volunteers and our morale was always of a high order, and we were extremely proud to be Commandos, come what may. We came from every corps in the army and had no intention of letting either our regiment, corps, or No. 6 Commando down.

'On the next evening we boarded the LCIs. After a squeamish night due to a combination of the rough weather, rich fruit pudding and engine fumes, we were ordered on deck for the run in. I noticed many ships, including large rafts with vehicles on them. One was sinking and a small naval vessel like a corvette was alongside it, taking off survivors. I could not help noticing an LST with banks of rockets on the upper deck which was broadside on to the beach, and which had just let go a salvo with a great flash of flame. Once up on deck we fell into two parallel lines from bow to stern. As I was No. 2 on the two-inch mortar (Private Wally Hutton [Green Howards] was No. 1) and was, in addition to the load previously mentioned, also carrying eighteen two-inch mortar bombs (twelve HE and six smoke) at an approximate weight of 2lbs each, I was considered to have a heavy load and I was ordered, together with the No. 1, to the bow of the vessel (starboard side) so that we would be among the first off. The ramps were dropped and down we went into waist-deep water, about thirty yards from the beach. I can remember getting out of the water beside a D. (amphibious) tank and pausing behind it. In the rather grey and overcast weather I noticed sparks appear on the turret of the tank, caused, I imagine, by bullet strikes. I then went up the beach some 200 yards to the remains of some houses which had been demolished and cleared leaving only open cellars lined with concrete. Here my troop gathered and I bound up a slight hand wound on Trooper Jim Carrigan, who was our sniper. No. 3 Troop was not the leading troop, and we moved across a road with a tramline alongside it. We then moved over about 500 yards of open marshland intersected with several dykes which had evil-smelling muddy banks, and which we had to wade through or jump, until we reached a three-strand cattle-wire fence, over which we climbed. We noticed little yellow pennants with black skull and crossbones hanging from this fence and learnt later that this indicated a minefield. As nobody, to my knowledge, was injured during the crossing, I imagine this may have been one of those phoney minefields intended to deceive us.

'We assembled in a small wooded copse for an attack on some concrete pillboxes. I was in a ditch which lined the edge of a cornfield, firing at the pillboxes, and from here I was ordered forward through the corn after dumping my heavy Bergen rucksack, not before I had accidentally fired my rifle in the air, causing the TSM (Lofty) Rae

(South Staffs Regiment) to pass a caustic remark concerning my marksmanship. Lofty was originally in the Black Watch, and when in action wore their red hackle in his beret; otherwise, when in the UK, he wore the Stafford Knot. He had won the MM in North Africa and was much respected in 3 Troop. I seemed to spend most of this attack crawling through the waist-high corn until a light tank appeared and we were ordered back to our assembly area in the copse. Here we picked up our kit and moved on through a small village where some of the local people came out into the street. I was handed a bottle by a middle-aged Frenchman and having taken a drink, found it to be a strong, raw-ish spirit, which I later discovered was Calvados. We went through this village into open country, until we came to the canal bridges, which we doubled across as best we could with our heavy loads. I can remember the bullets striking the ironwork of both bridges, which were not too far apart. As I ran across one of the bridges, I stopped near a dead British officer who had a Colt automatic ·45 pistol attached to his neck with a lanyard. I broke the lanyard by putting my boots on it and secured the pistol in an inner pocket of my BD blouse. The pistol came in very handy later on. This officer was one of the glider party that had landed during the night and did such good work in capturing the bridges intact. I believe he was recommended for the VC but only received an MID.

'We moved very rapidly, and by about 14.00 hrs were in Bréville occupying a large house on the outskirts of the village. Here we dug in and I, with several others – Gunners Puttick and "Ginger" Smith (RA) were two I can remember – "looked through" the house, set in its own grounds of about an acre enclosed by a high brick wall. In one room we found a German Army leather pistol holster (empty) on a bedside table, and in a wardrobe in the same room a uniform coat. The evidence seemed to point to a hasty departure. In a chest we found a couple of pairs of neatly rolled socks made of some heather-coloured coarse mixture. I believe Gunner Smith put a pair on in exchange for his own. We had started to dig in when my subsection was ordered to accompany Captain Pyman, our troop leader, together with Lieutenant Colquhoun on a recce to find the enemy. We moved out from the rear of the house, and went into the garden of another quite large house nearby. Captain Pyman was lying on the other side of a hedge with Lieutenant Colquhoun, and the rest of us were lying in the garden behind the hedge. I was actually behind a large manure heap with marrows growing on it, next to Private "Lofty" Layton (RAOC) and Sapper Ron Pealing (RE). Captain Pyman said, "I can see someone waving a yellow air identification slip. I will wave back with one of ours. Who has one?" This was a fluorescent yellow cloth with loops sewn on, and was intended to be pegged out on the ground or attached to the back of the pack as an indicator to our aircraft. Naturally, very few were worn on the pack as it was considered an easy target for an enemy sniper. One was passed to Captain Pyman and he put it on the barrel of his rifle, stood up and waved it. There was a sudden burst of machine-gun fire, followed by a pause, when Lieutenant Colquhoun said, "Captain Pyman has been hit." Another pause. "Captain Pyman is dead."

The enemy then fired mortar bombs into the garden, wounding several, including Private Layton. As things were getting hot we moved to the front of the house. I managed to carry Private Layton plus his weapon and mine. After a short pause we headed back to the main house via various back gardens. I stopped in a laneway and laid Private Layton on the ground. An old French couple came out of a house adjoining the lane. They became very concerned about Layton, and asked us to put him into the house, which we did. His face was grey and his eyes appeared to roll up into his head. He seemed to be dying. The enemy started to press us and we moved back to the main house as quickly as we could, firing Brens to slow them down. Once there we started to dig in again. Several shells (105mm) then hit the house, causing many casualties, including my chum Gunner Puttick who was very badly wounded.

'About 19.00 hrs a jeep arrived and took some wounded, and we moved back to Le Plein where the main Commando was, carrying the remainder. I helped to carry Gunner Puttick. We placed him on a folded deckchair used as a stretcher, and carried him that way. He must have been in great pain as a shell had exploded virtually alongside him, shattering his right leg and arm. He made light of these injuries and cracked jokes when he could. Because of the "stretcher" we were forced to keep in the open and under constant enemy fire. Corporal "Taffy" John (RAVC) or Trooper "Pluto" Friend (RAC) fired a few two-inch mortar smoke bombs to cover the worst area, which was just after we left the house. On our way through Bréville back to the main Commando in Amfreville Le Plein, during one of many halts, some French people came out and gave a drink to Gunner Puttick. He made a joke about "Lips that touch alcohol will never touch mine," which caused us all to grin.

'I cannot speak too highly of the attitude of the local people, who gave us all the help they could. On arrival at Amfreville we put the wounded into the RAP, located in a large cider press which was part of a fine farm called, I think, La Grande Ferme. It was typical of the old Norman farms, consisting of a single large building surrounding a large courtyard. It had the look of a fortified building, which it probably was. By this time we had lost twenty-two killed and wounded out of the sixty-four present at the landing. I know this because I wrote it in the back of an address book I carried with me and which I still have. The survivors of 3 Troop, now under the command of Lieutenant Colquhoun, were ordered to dig in on the left flank of No. 6 Commando position in an orchard about seventy yards back from a crest adjacent to the farm. While we were digging, the roar of aircraft engines was heard and we saw hundreds of gliders, mainly Horsa, coming in to land between us and Caen. Flak was bursting among the aircraft and I saw one catch fire, dive steeply and then level off about 300 feet from the ground. This appeared to put out the fire but smoke continued to pour from the glider as it disappeared from view. We all agreed that "you would need to have your head read" to fly a glider to war – brave men indeed!

'We were soon dug in and a standing patrol was placed on the crest by the orchard, where there was a cornfield stretching about 150 yards to the enemy positions on the edge of a wood in Bréville. In this wood was a German four-gun battery of 105mm (horsedrawn) guns which had fired on us in Bréville and which was attacked the next day by two troops from 6 Commando. The wood was captured and my troop was sent in to assist with the removal of the guns. Lying about the gun area were many German dead and several horse wagons loaded with supplies. These consisted of 105mm ammo in wickerwork containers and some rations. I checked the ration wagon and found many postal packets of crispbread, unfortunately impregnated with caraway seeds (which I cannot eat), together with several sacks of sugar. I emptied a German pack and had filled it about half-full when I saw coming through the wood, some two to three hundred yards away, German infantry on cycles. They were in the process of dismounting and forming up for a counter-attack. I called out a warning to my section officer, Lieutenant Leaphard, and to another friend of mine, Private S. J. Dann (E. Surreys) who was looking through another wagon. As we hadn't been spotted, we prudently moved back to our main position, leaving one gun (less striker case) as the others had been removed. Apart from the half pack of sugar, which went to the RAP, we had gained an MG 34 complete with a beautifully made tripod, which we set up in our trench line. We had some trouble making this gun fire more than one round at a time until we discovered that the actuating arm in the breech cover could be assembled in two ways, one of which was incorrect. Later I heard that my friend, Gunner Puttick, had died of his wounds some two hours after we brought him in. I remember him as a fine friend. We continued to occupy the position in the orchard, and were shelled and mortared day and night.'

With 3 Troop of Derek Mills-Roberts' 6 Commando in the lead, 1 (Special Service) Brigade marched hard across country towards Pegasus Bridge, with individual troops peeling off to attack enemy pillboxes, artillery emplacements and strongpoints. The six miles from La Brèche were covered in three and a half hours, the first troops of 1 (Special Service) Brigade crossing the canal exactly two and a half minutes behind schedule. Once across, 6 Commando linked up with 9 Para to clear the village of Le Plein, while No. 3 occupied Le Bas de Ranville, and No. 45 moved towards Franceville Plage and Merville. No. 4 Commando came in to the perimeter later, after clearing Ouistreham.

By mid-afternoon the Brigade was across the canal and the River Orne and onto the heights around Ranville, with 6 Commando dug in around Le Plein. The rest of the Brigade was established in a line between Merville in the north, near Franceville Plage, and Bréville in the south, anticipating the enemy counter-attack. They were very relieved when the glider troops of Sixth Airborne came in to land that night, bringing heavy weapons, including more anti-tank guns. Many of the gliders landed in or around 3 Commando's positions.

On the morning of 7 June, two troops of 3 Commando were directed to re-take the Merville Battery, which had been overrun by British paratroops on the night of 5/6 June but reoccupied by the Germans later when the parachute soldiers had to withdraw. Major John Pooley, a veteran 3 Commando soldier, was killed in the assault, and among many other founder members, No. 3 Commando lost Lieutenant George Herbert. He and many other soldiers of 1 (Special Service) Brigade who were killed in the D-Day fighting now lie buried in the Ranville Military Cemetery.

S. J. Dann again: 'We had been briefed to expect the German counter-attack four days after landing, as they anticipated it would take the Germans in reserve on the French/German border that long to reach us. Facing us at the time was the 744 Infantry Regiment and expected was the 857 and 858 Infantry Regiment and elements of the 21st Panzer Div. However, three days after the landing, late in the afternoon, we heard – with some consternation – a number of tanks moving in our direction. These were reported as twelve Tiger tanks. Fortunately we had a capital ship – I believe it was the HMS *Rodney* – offshore as heavy back-up, and 16-inch guns *are* heavy. We plugged our ears and got down in our slit trenches as her shells came over, sounding like railway trains and shaking the earth even at two miles. This was followed by an RAF Typhoon strike and the Tigers were no longer a threat.

'During that night, 9/10 June, we could hear a lot of movement from the enemy as there was only a cornfield separating us. We could hear tracked vehicles – mobile 88mm guns we assumed. The night passed quietly and at dawn, after "stand-to", I was shaving when Derek Mills-Roberts came along and gave us the "Not a step back – fight to the last man and last drop of blood" routine. It looked like being a lousy day. He told us that the Germans were expected to attack at various points and exploit any weakness in defence. Our orchard was an expected target. At 08.00 hrs all was still and quiet, and then all hell broke loose – mortars, shells and machine guns – but all fell on the leading edge of the orchard. We held our fire and waited until we saw the glint of the sun on the helmets of the German infantry as they advanced through the corn. They came at a steady pace through the hedge and penetrated several yards into the orchard, where they stopped and looked about. By all the rules we should be defending the leading edge and looking down a forward slope to their positions. Instead the CO had us dig in at the back of the orchard and only have standing patrols along the front. Very crafty.

'On the given word, we opened up with everything. My own subsection (I was a lance-corporal by now) had a Bren, a Vickers "K" gun, a Browning and the captured German MG 34. The Germans were lifted off the ground by the weight of the fire. Some tried to crawl back and the second wave beat a hasty retreat. A period of quiet and then the next attack came in from our right flank, which was clever of the Germans as several of the troops had no field of fire. However, this was a weak affair and soon died out. Then, at approximately 11.00 hrs, it was our turn again, with a barrage of mortar and shells. This time their shelling was accurate; casualties mounted. Their infantry crawled through the corn and fired from the hedgerow, and when the enemy thought we were softened up enough, they charged. Of the whole day's activity, this was the crucial moment. They made half the distance between us before faltering and then retreating. Their next attack came from the right flank and there was a danger of a complete breakthrough. Our TSM came dashing along, saying, "Take one man from each slit trench and get across to 4 Troop. They are in trouble." To get to 4 Troop we had to go round a pond. This took us out into an open area. A stick of mortar bombs fell and the man behind me was killed and three others wounded. I was aware of a hot blast in my face and felt a bang on my head; blood and sweat ran into my eyes but as I was still running I knew I was alive. I dived into the first slit trench but got out a lot quicker. The two occupants had both been hit; one, from the Army, was very dead, and the other had a serious back wound. I was to meet him again thirty-five years later, still paralysed from the waist down.

'The attack died down but within minutes we were running again. German troops had infiltrated through houses and a small wood to our right, where a self-propelled 88mm gun was moving up the road from Ranville, and I could see Captain Powell with a section going after the SP gun on our left. We got behind a low wall and immediately were confronted with approximately ten Germans running towards us, using the gardens and walls of the houses as cover. We let them get half way and opened up. Our aim was poor but two fell with leg wounds and the others dived over a low wall.

'Then came one of my lasting memories of the war. I go back to Normandy each year for the D-Day Pilgrimage, and I relive these few minutes each time I walk down that road. We had a stalemate situation; we could not move out, and we were down to our last magazine for the Bren and could only keep the Germans' heads down with single shots. They were behind a low wall and could only pop up for a quick burst with rifle or Schmeisser. Then one stood up, jumped over the wall and charged up the road towards us, firing from the hip. He had fifty yards to go and stood no chance. A short burst stitched his chest and, arms flailing, he fell. There was no support from his comrades, so we moved down cautiously and I turned him over. He was a tall, blond, pure German, wearing an Iron Cross 2nd Class, the Afrika ribbon and several campaign ribbons. I thought what a terrible waste, what a way to finish his career and life. We picked up the two German wounded and flushed out a couple of poor specimens hiding in the bushes and returned to the farm.

'About 18.00 hrs the Germans had had enough and withdrew. Peace reigned over our little piece of Normandy. We had been engaged by three battalions, we were now about 350 in number, but I think we did a good job. We had about one-third of the unit as casualties.'

Peter Young recalls the counter-attack: 'They hit us with some division they'd brought over from Le Havre and some of their infantry got to within five yards of my HQ . . . very nice of them! Anyway, we beat them off and took forty-five prisoners. Then we went to the Bois de Bavent and on Operation Paddle, the advance to the Seine. I gathered that I was Derek Mills-Roberts' favourite CO, so he kept putting us in first; a fine way to treat a friend. Anyway, we didn't get lost, which was the main thing. 45 put a sharp volley into our rear as we moved off, but I don't hold that against them.'

Kenneth Phillott remembers one incident from this period: 'One of my tasks was to go down from Brigade HQ to the forward observation posts of the different Commando units and bring back the latest information. One day I passed a 6 Commando OP, which had two Commandos manning it, but after that point I saw no one, felt uneasy and decided to turn back. When I got to the OP I stopped, and one asked me where I had been going. I replied, "The forward OP. Why?" They told me that one of their jeeps had gone down that road earlier but had not returned. At a reunion after the war, I was talking to Cliff Bryen and he told me he was in that jeep with some of his men, got ambushed by the Germans and finished the war in a POW camp. A lucky escape for me, though.'

C. L. Bryen, the RSM of 6 Commando, takes up the story: 'I have no evidence which would implicate any German in obeying Hitler's order to eliminate Commando prisoners and I feel well qualified to discuss this. I was wearing a green beret and Commando flashes and the Combined Ops badge on each sleeve. These caused a little comment by the German Intelligence Officer who interrogated me at their Army HQ, but brought no illtreatment to the many other Army and Marine Commandos captured in Normandy. Indeed, when I came to Stalag IVB in Germany, where some 9,000 British troops were imprisoned, I was the only Commando still in possession of flashes and green beret. The rest had had theirs removed as souvenirs. My appearance provoked no comment from our guards or the SS with whom the camp was well supplied, though a green beret was still a novelty. Shortly before D-Day, I heard that the Germans had opened a special camp for Commando prisoners and I got accounts of it by hearsay, but never encountered it myself. Whether this was because the Germans knew they were losing and wished to whitewash themselves, I don't know. Personally, I doubt it, as they continued to shoot Russian prisoners on the slightest provocation.'

On 12 June Lord Lovat was wounded by a shell splinter, and Lieutenant Colonel Derek Mills-Roberts took over command of 1 (SS) Brigade. 45 Commando re-took France-ville Plage on the 7th but were driven out by a fierce mortar and infantry attack; 6 Commando launched an attack on the village of Bréville, which they captured, taking several prisoners, while infantry attacks came in almost daily on 3 and 4 Commandos' positions. All four Commando units suffered steady losses from mortaring, sniping and infiltration during the days after D-Day. On 10 June a troop of 4 Commando lost all its officers in one attack but stayed in position, commanded by a sergeant. On the 12th, 1 (SS) Brigade, supported by 12 Para Battalion, counter-attacked in Bréville and took the town, although 6 Commando suffered very heavy casualties from artillery. The Brigade then settled into defensive positions around Sallenelles, a small village overlooking the coastal marshes, where the men were plagued by mosquitoes and snipers, but kept the enemy occupied with fighting patrols while the armoured divisions fought over the plain around Caen to the south-west, striving for a breakthrough from the D-Day bridgehead.

Philip Pritchard takes up the story: 'Some two days after D-Day, we were briefed for an attack on the village of Bavent. We were reserve troop and once the attack had gone in we moved up and crouched in a ditch on the outskirts of the village. Here we met RSM Woodcock (South Staffs) who was a well-known figure to us all. He directed us forward and as my subsection passed him, he yelled out to Private Doug Underhill, who was carrying the Bren and about twenty full mags: "Get that top button done up, Underhill!" which caused all of us but Doug to grin. Actually we were not needed in this attack but were used almost immediately on reaching the objective to attack a small hamlet further on called Robehomme, where we started to dig in. We could see across a large flooded valley (Dives Valley) to some heights. We had grown used to digging in by now and had developed a pattern. Each slit trench was occupied by two men. We were given a location which we tested by checking on the field of fire from ground level, and once this was established we dug a trench five feet deep, generally "L" shaped. We then put overhead cover on either end, leaving the middle open for fighting. The cover was either doors from houses, or (if we could get them) 4·2-inch mortar ammo boxes, which were made of steel and which could be filled with earth. This afforded a modicum of protection from a direct hit by 81mm mortar; I fancy a shell would be a different matter. At Robehomme we used the doors from abandoned houses on a "first-in-best-dressed" basis. After a quiet day and night we were told that we were to move out that evening. A jeep and trailer arrived and as many as possible climbed on board. We had something like twenty fully-equipped men in one lift, and very soon all of 3 Troop was ferried down to the edge of the flooded area. We moved over this area via the remains of broken bridges, occasionally wading in the flood-water, until we arrived at a small hamlet, where 3 Troop were put into a large barn with huge cider vats, full of rough cider. Having spent quite a bit of my youth in Hereford-shire, I was one of the few who were familiar with scrumpy, but most of the lads found it too bitter for their taste.

'We were told to get what sleep we could and about midnight we were roused and moved out along an old railway track (no rails, I think) until we moved off to the left and up the ridge. We heard some firing ahead and then took the lead. As we were going up a country lane, a thundering of hooves was heard, and down the lane towards us came a German Army horse-drawn wagon towing a 20mm cannon, with two horses in the shafts and two men on the seat. A burst of Bren from Corporal "Taffy" John brought it to an abrupt halt. I did not have time to check the wagon but I understand it was full of ammo and women's clothes and shoes. We pushed on to the top of the ridge and all we saw was a field telephone in a ditch, still connected. One of our number cranked the handle and got an answer from the German at the other end, much to their mutual surprise. By this time it was quite light and we moved forward along the top of the ridge for a few hundred yards. 3 Troop were detailed to hold an area to the left of the road, while 6 Troop (Major Leaphard) held the right half. I was with my sub-section on the road which formed the boundary between the troops. By virtue of my exalted rank, I had acquired a Thompson sub-machine-gun, which was one of the original models with the claw-shaped foregrip. It had "Irene" carved on the butt. I obtained this from a pile outside the RAP back at Amfreville and it looked as though it had seen plenty of action. With half of my section I was ordered to move further up the road to some buildings, where we found a line of German packs in a neat row but no Germans. As I had only been ordered to check these buildings, I returned to our lines and continued to dig in by the side of the road, hanging my Thompson on a gate. The Bren group was also digging in and had the gun ready as always. Suddenly we heard the roar of a motor and down the road from the direction of the enemy came a staff car. I grabbed my tommy gun but the sling had caught on the gate. The Bren gunner grabbed the Bren, only to have the bipod collapse, and the car, which had seen us, could do nothing except speed up and try to crash through our lines. It was soon stopped.

'Not long afterwards we were heavily shelled. Fortunately for us the aim was too high and the shells exploded in 6 Troop area. I can remember seeing one poor devil blown up into a tree. In fact, I could actually see the German guns with the gunners loading the rounds from those wickerwork baskets. Our artillery were soon on the job and the enemy guns were silenced. In the meantime, quite an attack developed on our right flank, mainly against 6 Troop. Doug Underhill, who had the Bren, moved out of his trench with Gunner "Mog" Morris, his No. 2, to a position where he was able to enfilade the enemy, and he caused havoc in their ranks by firing along their exposed flank. They very smartly pulled out, leaving many dead behind. A lot of them were wearing their packs as if they intended to stay – a short-lived expectation!'

The Commando units around Sallenelles quickly settled into a routine, standing-to at dusk and dawn, sending out snipers and patrols to harass the enemy in the Bois de Bavent, digging their trenches a little deeper each day as the mortaring continued, getting what sleep they could between turns on sentry-go. This constant bickering with the enemy caused a steady stream of casualties. By D-Day plus four, No. 3 Commando had lost 125 men, including nine officers, and while the Holding Operational Commando at Wrexham was sending reinforcements out from the UK, all the units needed men. By the time 3 Commando received a much needed draft of fifty-two men, they had lost another sixty-two soldiers, but they continued to harass the enemy.

'A policy of "live and let live" is no good when you are fighting the Germans,' wrote Peter Young. 'If you leave them in peace, the next thing you know they will start beating up your own quarters.' On 1 August, 3 Commando left Amfreville and arrived at new positions in the Bois de Bavent, where they were greeted by a hail of mortar bombs. Heavy mortaring became a feature of their stay in this part of the line and on 6 August, no less than 120 mortar bombs of varying calibre fell on their front line positions, so Peter Young borrowed the mortars of 4 Commando on his right flank, and with eight mortars at his disposal, gave the enemy as good as he got.

By now the Commando units had been two months in the line. The declared intention prior to D-Day was that they would be withdrawn after the bridgehead had been consolidated but, here as elsewhere, the need for well-trained infantry kept them in the forefront of the battle. From time to time small parties would go to the rear or back to the beach to clean up or have a full night's rest. Patrols went out every night to dominate the no-man's-land between the two armies, but the fighting and the casualties went on until the break-out from the beach-head began on 18 August. As usual, the Commandos were in the van.

On 17 August, 1 (SS) Brigade were ordered to attack across the Dives. The enemy was believed to be pulling out units along their front and the Brigade was ordered to take the high ground to the east, far across the Dives. This was a night attack across open ground overlooked by the enemy, and began at 23.00 hrs with the Brigade advancing in single file, led by No. 4 Commando, followed by 6, 3 and 45. In this formation, the Brigade infiltrated through the enemy lines without detection, and the opening shot of the battle was fired when Lieutenant Pollock of 4 Commando killed a sentry outside a German HQ. By dawn 3 Commando had taken the village of Varaville and 1 (SS) Brigade were established on the heights behind the Dives, where they dug in to resist counter-attacks, beating off four determined assaults during the day.

In early September 1944, No. 1 (SS) Brigade returned to the UK, where they began to prepare for a move to the Far East. At the end of September, No. 4 Commando was detached from No. 1 Brigade and returned to the Continent to replace the much reduced 46 Commando in 4 (SS) Brigade, now preparing for the next great Commando operation of the war, the assault on Walcheren.

11

Walcheren to the Elbe, 1944–45

'For thy sake . . . thine uncles and myself,
have in our armours watch'd the winter's night.
Gone all afoot in summer's scorching heat
. . . and from our labours thou shalt reap the gain.'

HENRY VI, PART III: ACT V, SCENE VII

To continue their advance across Belgium and into
Germany during the autumn and winter of 1944, the
Allied armies needed a working port much closer to the
front line than those they had already captured during
their advance up the Channel coast of France. Of all the
ports available, the ideal was Antwerp, the second largest
port in Western Europe, the only one fully capable of
supplying food, ammunition and reinforcements to the
advancing Allied armies, which now numbered over two
million men. The 11th Armoured Division entered the
port of Antwerp on 4 September. It had been thoroughly
wrecked by the Germans, but work began at once on
restoring it to full efficiency, and within days it was
possible to unload small ships at some of the quays. As
usual, however, there was a snag.

Antwerp lies forty miles from the sea, at the inner end
of the Scheldt estuary, which widens out below Antwerp,
and divides into two parts, the East and West Scheldt,
which are separated by a long peninsula, South Beveland,
and two islands, North Beveland and Walcheren. These

three features had been fortified and were strongly defended by the Wehrmacht. Until they could be captured, the port of Antwerp was useless. The task of clearing the Germans away was entrusted to the 52nd (British) Division, the 2nd (Canadian) Infantry Division and No. 4 (SS) Brigade, which was specifically charged with capturing the island of Walcheren.

Walcheren had been very strongly fortified by the German Fifteenth Army, who had prepared an interlinking series of minefields, machine gun posts and heavy calibre coastal batteries set in concrete blockhouses. The island itself is triangular and largely below sea-level, the shores protected by dykes and sand dunes. The RAF bombed Walcheren thoroughly before the assault, doing little damage to the blockhouses but breaching the dykes and letting in the sea which flooded the centre of the island. For the assault on Walcheren, Operation Infatuate, 4 (SS) Brigade, still commanded by Brigadier 'Jumbo' Leicester, consisted of Nos. 41, 47 and 48 (Royal Marine) Commandos and No. 4 Commando, once again commanded by Lieutenant Colonel Dawson, recovered from his D-Day wounds. This force, with tanks, engineers and supporting units, amounted to about 8,000 men. To get them ashore and provide gunfire support, the Royal Navy provided 'Force T', which included the battleship *Warspite* and two fifteen-inch gun monitors, HMS *Erebus* and *Roberts*, plus a host of support craft, rocket ships and Landing Craft Guns (LCGs) which would help to quell the coastal batteries. Brigadier Leicester sent his three Royal Marine Commando units to capture the strongpoints at Westkapelle and No. 4 Commando to attack and capture the town of Flushing, the island's principal port. The attack took place on the afternoon of 1 November 1944, and our story will follow the fortunes of 4 Commando.

No. 4 Commando were to land on Uncle beach at the south end of the island, take Flushing and then advance along the dyke to join the Royal Marines advancing along

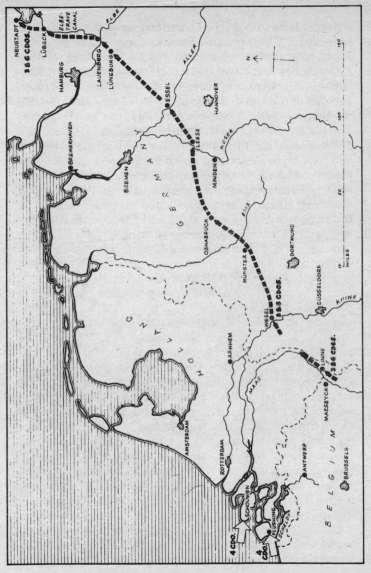

Walcheren to the Elbe

the coast from Westkapelle. Artillery support would come from Force T's ships and field artillery firing from the southern shore of the estuary. While the three Marine Commandos were battering their way ashore at West-kapelle, No. 4, accompanied by their two French Troops and part of the Dutch Troop of 10 (IA) Commando, landed on Uncle beach in three waves, starting at 05.45 hrs, covered by a fierce bombardment from the Allied ships and artillery. The first wave did not have an easy landing; one craft became impaled on an underwater obstacle but the troops scrambled up onto the 'Orange Mole' and were soon appearing among the enemy positions. With the first wave established, the second wave came in, landing at the same point, following the leading troops through the wire and into Orange Street, making at once for the German barracks and an arsenal. On the way they overran a 50mm gun, turned it round and used it for fire support, clearing pillbox after pillbox as they advanced. By 09.00 hrs the second wave of No. 4 were on their objectives in the town. Meanwhile, the third wave had come ashore, meeting an alert and aggressive defence which greeted them with machine gun and cannon fire. With all the unit ashore, work now began on winkling the enemy out of Flushing. This meant street fighting, house clearing, street by street, and the steady reduction of the many concrete pillboxes. Each man carried a special explosive charge and much of their progress through the town was made through the walls, from house to house, blasting a hole and passing through. Any strongpoint that proved too stubborn was reduced by rocket-firing Typhoon fighters called down from a 'cab-rank' in the sky. The bulk of the town was safely in 4 Commando's hands by nightfall, and that night they were joined by elements of the King's Own Scottish Borderers.

On the following day, No. 4 linked up with 47 Commando which had advanced along the dyke from West-kapelle, and the next two days were spent mopping up pockets of resistance and removing 3,000 prisoners to the mainland. The last resistance on Walcheren ended on 8 November.

After Walcheren, No. 4 (SS) Brigade which, like the other Special Service Brigades, became a Commando Brigade on 6 December, returned to Ostend to rest and prepare for the advance into Germany. But increased German activity and the Ardennes Battle of the Bulge soon saw it back in the line along the River Maas. The enemy were very active here during the Ardennes counter-offensive, putting great pressure on the Allies. During the winter of 1944-45 all the Commando Units of 4 Brigade made raids across the Maas. In mid-January half of 4 Commando raided German positions on the island of Schouwen, north of Walcheren, landing unde-tected, taking nine prisoners and killing sentries before withdrawing under fire. 4th Commando Brigade mounted forty separate operations against the enemy between 1 December 1944 and the end of the war in Europe on 8 May 1945.

1st Commando Brigade had left France in September and spent the autumn in England, absorbing new recruits and training for operations in the Far East. Lieutenant Colonel Peter Young was detached from his beloved 3 Commando, which passed to Arthur Komrower, and was sent to the Arakan as Deputy Commander of 3 Com-mando Brigade under Brigadier Campbell Hardy. In Janu-ary 1945, 1 Commando Brigade, under Brigadier Derek Mills-Roberts, DSO, MC, of the Irish Guards ('and a soldier if ever there was one', says Brigadier Peter Young, DSO, MC and two bars – no mean soldier himself) was ordered to return to the fighting on the Continent. Mills-Roberts insisted on high standards of training and disci-pline, and professional soldiering at all levels throughout his Brigade. 'If a morning exercise went well, the Brigadier might give us the afternoon off,' records one officer. 'If it didn't go well, then we did it again and again until we got it right. "Just good enough" wasn't good enough.' A fighting soldier, who led from the front, Mills-Roberts had the experienced units of his Brigade at peak efficiency when he led them back to the war.

Bill Sadler of 6 Commando continues the story: 'The Brigade had only recently returned to Europe to commence a second tour of operations, having previously been in action continuously for some three months after landing on the beaches of Normandy on D-Day. The Commando replacements and other troops travelled overnight from Tilbury to Ostend before being entrained for Brussels, a journey of some sixty miles, which took exactly twelve hours to complete, allowing ample time for some troops to flog their blankets from the carriage windows to the local villagers, who appeared to experience no difficulty in keeping up with the train as it thundered along. An occasional stop at a wayside station allowed everyone plenty of time to descend and explore, so very little of the currency gained actually left the area.

'After arriving in Brussels we spent two or three days at a staging camp awaiting transport to Brigade. Our enjoyment of the facilities for well-heeled soldiery was confined to the bistros. We eventually arrived at HQ 6 Commando and were given billets for the night in a partly-destroyed barn containing straw, but of course we had no blankets. Next morning Jim South received the full blast of RSM Woodcock's extreme displeasure, and later that of the CO, Lieutenant Colonel Lewis. Due to the intense frost overnight, Jim had slept in his trousers and battledress jacket, which did not improve his appearance on CO's orders. The proximity of the enemy would allow no diminishing of the general standard of turnout.'

Arriving on the River Maas, No. 1 Commando Brigade split up. 46 Commando was detached to guard Antwerp, 3 Commando went to Maeseyck, while No. 45 (Royal Marine) Commando and 6 Commando went into action along the Maas. On 23 January, 45 Commando attacked

St Joostburg and with 6 Commando, which had crossed the frozen Juliana Canal on the ice, occupied Maasbracht. Both units were soon engaged in the fighting round the Montfortbeek, where Lance Corporal Harden, RAMC, attached to 45 Commando, gained a posthumous VC for treating the wounded under fire.

Bill Sadler again: 'The final crossing of the Maas was the first operation after our arrival, a previous attempt to cross the ice-covered river having resulted in failure. I doubt if the success of this second operation was due to our recent arrival. As far as I can recall, 2 Troop occupied its position against little or no opposition.

'Each Commando was allocated a sector beforehand and each troop within the Commando given its respective task within that area, each troop being required to capture and hold its sector while the remaining troops passed through their position to extend the operation, a method of investiture and occupation which resulted in those initially at the rear becoming the foremost during action. If a troop experienced little or no opposition, it still occupied its own sector, leaving the continuation of the advance and expansion of the operation to the column moving up from behind.'

Philip Pritchard tells his story: 'In the mid-afternoon, my troop was detailed to go forward and take over the advance from 45 (RM) Commando. We were in a sunken road which was being shelled with large calibre shells from gun positions in the Siegfried Line which was not far away. We peered out of the sunken road and could see the shells exploding on either side of us. The fire was not accurate and we understood that this was because there was no observer and the guns were firing off the map. At the head of the road, where it came out into the open, we could see several hay and corn stacks burning, and behind one was a British tank firing its main armament. We got what cover we could near some houses, when we were ordered back down the sunken road into the town again.

Here we got a meal and moved into a house. This house had a small, narrow cellar with a stove in it. Straw was on the floor and we used this to sleep on, only to find subsequently that there was a teller mine in the stove connected by trip wire to the door. As no one had attempted to light the stove or close the door – it had been wired in the open position – we were lucky! That evening we were again briefed that we were to attack where 45 (RM) Commando had been held up the previous afternoon. Early next morning we were given a cup of compo tea, two pieces of cold Spam and four biscuits each, prior to moving into some old German trenches built World War One fashion, opposite a creek with a windmill on the far bank. The creek, which was lined with leafless trees, was about 300 yards away. Somehow my section had acquired an issue water bottle full of rum, which we passed along the trench. It had just reached me when we got the signal to go. We swept forward to the creek which was frozen over. The creek ran between fifteen- and twenty-foot banks, which afforded us some cover. After a short while in the creek bed we were ordered to take some buildings over to our right. These proved to be the remains of a condensed-milk factory with a large cellar, in which many Dutch people were sheltering. We took over some existing enemy positions which had been dug by the Herman Goering Parachute Division. Some of their dead were lying around. They were well clad in snow-suits, which was more than we were. We were still wearing brown and green camouflaged parachute smocks and brown leather jerkins, which stood out in the snow-covered countryside. There was a railway line nearby, and very soon I was ordered, together with the section, to go down this line and prevent some Germans from unloading a wagon.

'In the section at that time were Private "Inky" Penn (Dorsets), Sapper Hedges (RE), Sapper "Big Bill" Scott, Gunner "Mog" Morris (RA) and Private Ernie Crouch

(HLI) to mention a few. Sapper Hedges had the Bren and we originally opened fire from the railway track at 700 yards on some German infantry, only to notice that we were having no effect on them. We then left the railway and ran over an open field some 150 yards to the road. This road led down to a cluster of houses and we did a rapid search when suddenly we noticed a considerable number of Germans a hundred yards or so away converging on the houses. We started a lively fire (Bren and rifle) from the windows of the houses. In one such action Bill Scott fired his rifle through a window while "Inky" Penn played a one-finger version of *In the Mood* on a piano that happened to be there. Subsequently this was reported in one of the Northumberland papers as "Fishburn man fights to music", Fishburn being the home of Sapper Scott. It was obvious that we were outnumbered, so we fell back along the road, firing Bren to slow them up. Sapper Hedges was hit in the calf and I took over the Bren and kept it firing until we all got back to the factory area. Upon our return it was noticed that Private Crouch was missing. He was a great pal of "Inky" Penn, and they were both Londoners (despite their regiments). They went through the depot at Achnacarry together and were in the same billet.

'So far we had nothing to eat since our sparse breakfast, and I was told that a meal was on its way. During my absence someone had discovered a Kitchener type of fuel stove with an oven attached. It had been lit using brickettes of brown coal which were plentiful. I opened the oven door, sat down on a box and put my feet in the oven to dry my boots. Someone gave me a paper (*News of the World*) to read. While I was so occupied, I heard the familiar sound of an enemy gun firing but decided that as I was under the lea of the factory, the shell would either hit the other side, or go well over the top.

'Unfortunately I hadn't checked the roof, which was in fact only a bare shell, there being no tiles left on. The enemy shell came through the roof bearers much lower than I calculated and landed immediately behind me. I felt a sharp bang on my left elbow and dived for the dugout. There were several in the shelter and when I said I thought I was wounded there was a chorus of "You lucky bastard." Once the shelling had died down, I went over to the factory and down into the cellar, where our medic, Gunner "Darkey" Williams (RA) – half West Indian from South Shields and a thorough gentleman – took off my jerkin and smock and proceeded to cut along my left sleeve seam. Blood was pouring down my arm. I thought I had been hit in the elbow, only to find that I had been hit in the armpit. "Darkey" put a shell dressing on it. Meanwhile the Dutch were busy praying in front of a large crucifix and I assumed they were praying for me, which I appreciated. I then made a dash for the RAP, which was in a cellar beneath a barn some 200 yards to our rear. Here I descended a ladder into the straw-filled cellar, where there were many wounded. The cellar was lit by a Tilly lamp and our MO (Captain Keat, MC) checked my wound, replaced the dressing and wrote out the waxed envelope which he attached to my BD blouse pocket buttonhole. One of the medical orderlies (Corporal Taffy Eyles) who had been checking the dead said that he could identify all but one. This man had no apparent ID and the only positive thing was a silver ring with "Armentières" written on it. I knew at once he was Private Thomson (Black Watch) who was one of my section. The ring had belonged to his father who, I believe, was killed in the First War. Jock Thomson had been killed when a tiny splinter from the shell which got me entered his brain.

'It was dark by now and I was taken outside and put on a stretcher, which was strapped to the top of a jeep. This vehicle then took off back down the road to Maasbracht. As the German guns from the Siegfried Line were still shelling the road, the driver had to judge when the

shells were likely to come, so he waited until a salvo fell
and then, during the lull, went at full speed over the icy
road. As a casualty, lying on an open stretcher on the top
of the jeep, with one arm useless, you can imagine my
feelings. As my companion on the other stretcher was in
a bad way, I had to try and hold him as well as keep
myself on. I was very relieved when we came to the
Casualty Clearing Station. I was taken into a school room.
The desks had been piled in one corner and the floor space
covered with wounded. The long master's bench was
being used as an operating table and I was placed on it
under a portable light. The doctor told me that he had
been going since 06.00 hrs and that there had been such a
great influx of wounded that he had run out of anaesthetic
and apologized that he had only "local" left. He then
injected my left shoulder, and once it had gone numb
proceeded to remove sundry bits of shrapnel. I was then
given a penicillin injection, to be repeated every three
hours. Somebody had given me a blanket, which I was
beginning to need as my left arm was completely bare. So
far I had had no food or drink except water since breakfast,
well before first light, and I was really hungry. I did not
receive any food or hot drink at the CCS, and a couple of
hours after my operation I was put into a proper ambulance with three other casualties, one of whom was in a
bad way and who kept crying out at intervals, and sent
further down the line to an Advance Dressing Station
where, at last, I was handed a small enamel bowl full of
hot sweet tea. The bowl had no handle, which made it
rather hard to hold, but I managed to drink most of that
nectar of the Gods, or so it tasted to me. The Dressing
Station was in another public building, and I was laid in a
corridor with several others, mostly from the Brigade.
Next to me was a soldier from No. 3 Commando who had
a badly fractured knee. He was part of a section which
had been trapped in a house in a narrow street by German
tanks at either end. There was no way out except by the

door. They had only two-inch mortar smoke left, and he had fired the mortar by placing the baseplate just above his knee. This was the only way he could fire it so as to hit the wall of the house opposite. I seem to remember him saying that he fired at least two bombs. This enabled the section to blind the tanks and get away. It said much for his courage that he did this, and despite his injuries, he got away.

'Eventually I left in an ambulance, which took me to an ambulance train. This train, after many stops, finally arrived at Brussels and here we were met by ladies of the Red Cross, who checked with each of us if we had any immediate requirements. We were then driven to a large hospital in the centre of Brussels, the Hôpital Militaire Belgique, which had been taken over by the 110 British General Hospital. I was taken up a flight of stairs and placed in a bed. It was nearly dark and I could see out of a window a dark object, somewhat like a fighter plane, with an orange flame coming from its rear. I was told that it was a flying bomb (V1 rocket), one of many that flew over that area and which generally exploded at, or near, the site of Waterloo. As nobody seemed very much concerned, I decided that I would not be. The ward was full of amputees, which did not bode well for me as my arm had become very stiff and yellow. I was looked at by several surgeons, one of whom was a woman. She asked permission to try a penicillin drip on me together with a blood drip. This was carried out immediately and I was held captive in bed for two days or so. The Sister fixing the drip took several small pieces of shrapnel out of my left hand and fingers which had been overlooked at the CCS. After I had been taken off the drips, I used to go down each day to a room where my dressings were changed by a very nice looking VAD.

'Later I had an interview with the CO and persuaded him that I could find my unit if he would release me from the depot. I suppose he liked the look of me, as he immediately gave me permission. The next morning I picked up the necessary documentation and thumbed a lift on a truck that was going towards the front line, which took me nearly to Maasbracht. It was just getting dark when I was dropped off at a spot near Venray, where 6 Commando HQ was. I was told that 3 Troop was in a small town on the banks of the River Maas called Wells, and that a jeep was going that way. I found the troop spread out in the town with Troop HQ in a fine house, obviously owned (or occupied) before the war by a Dutch bishop. The house was in ruins and the HQ occupied what remained of the ground floor. My section was in a small cottage at the entrance to the town. We had a Bren post on the road. I was told that the enemy was in the habit of infiltrating over the river and appearing in the town, and the fact that we were in a rear area should not be regarded as a sinecure.'

45 and 6 Commandos, joined by No. 3, had beaten off repeated counter-attacks in freezing weather, and continued to advance from the Maas against aggressive German forces which now contained Parachute Troops, SS and Luftwaffe units, until the Brigade reached the Montfortbeek Canal near the town of Linne. 3 Commando tried to coax the enemy out of Linne with feint flanking attacks, but when this failed, No. 1 and 6 Troops stormed the town, roaring across the flat open ground on the back of Sherman tanks, and the enemy wisely withdrew.

Beyond Linne, the Brigade faced a strongly defended part of the Siegfried Line, and began to reduce it with fighting patrols raiding across the Maas, and tank-supported sweeps along the front; cold work in freezing winter weather. The fighting took a steady toll and the Brigade lost over 100 men in the next few weeks before a sudden thaw in February turned the ground into a quagmire, bringing the tanks to a halt and reducing offensive activity to infantry patrols.

On 6 March the Brigade withdrew to Venray on the

Maas, and began to train for their next major operation, the crossing of the Rhine into Germany.

The target of 1st Commando Brigade was Wesel, on the east bank of the Rhine. At this point the Rhine, a fast-flowing river, especially after the spring thaw, was some 300 metres wide and contained by high banks known as *bunds*, which varied in height from fifteen to twenty feet.

Brigadier Mills-Roberts' plan required 46 Commando to lead the assault in Buffaloes, accompanied by Brigade HQ, and secure a bridgehead on the Grav Insel, a flat area a mile west of Wesel. They would be followed by 6 Commando and 45 Commando in stormboats, with the veteran No. 3 Commando bringing up the rear in Buffaloes. Once across, they would wait until the covering air bombardment was over and then advance swiftly into the stricken town. 46 were to fight their way into the town centre, with 6 Commando following to mark a cleared route, and then the whole brigade, in single file as during the Normandy breakout, would enter the town. 46 would clear the town centre, 6 Commando would put in a flanking attack on the north-west suburbs, while 45 Commando would seize a large factory which overlooked the northern limits of the town, and 3 Commando would clear the surrounding area. If all went well, they would soon have a bridgehead across the river, through which infantry from the Cheshire Regiment, ferried across in Buffaloes, could reinforce them. Finally, the US 17th Airborne Division would drop north of Wesel and move south to link up with the Brigade. During the parachute drop no artillery support was considered possible, so the Brigade must hold Wesel for half a day without any gunfire support.

After a four-hour bombardment by artillery and RAF Lancaster bombers, the assault began at 21.30 hrs on 23 March 1945. 46 Commando's Buffaloes set off across the Rhine for the Grav Insel, and reached the far side in four minutes. B Troop of 46 Commando were the first British troops to set foot in Nazi Germany. 6 Commando crossed under heavy fire in their stormboats, and a number of men were hit or drowned when their boats were sunk. A number of other boats were swept away downstream when their outboard engines failed, but most of 6 Commando got onto the Grav Insel, and followed 46 in the advance to the now burning city, marking a route with white tape through the dark rubble-filled streets.

By midnight, two hours after landing on the east bank, 3 and 46 Commandos were in the town, 45 had captured the factory and No. 6 was in the northern suburbs, with No. 3 filling in the gap between 45 and 46. Enemy mortar and sniping began at dawn but the damage wreaked in the rubble-choked streets by the RAF prevented a counterattack developing, and by mid-morning the American Airborne and the 1st Battalion the Cheshire Regiment were arriving to expand the Commando perimeter. The troops gave themselves over to patrolling and sniping, in which 4 Troop of 3 Commando did particularly well, ambushing several German patrols, and dealing with snipers by drawing fire and then concentrating several Brens on the snipers' positions. By the evening of 25 March, the whole town was in Allied hands and apart from several hundred dead, some 800 German prisoners were being ferried back across the river. Professional soldiering also saves lives. The Rhine crossing and the capture of Wesel by No. 1 Commando Brigade was achieved at a cost of eleven men killed, sixty-eight wounded and seventeen missing.

Bill Sadler again: 'A general who has a clear idea of what he intends to achieve can dictate his requirements in detail to his staff before the battle, in full knowledge that the success or failure of his efforts will be analysed later with all the advantage of hindsight. But an individual in battle has only time to cope with what is at hand according to the extent of his responsibilities, so I have been obliged to add some details to my account gained from other sources. I have always been intrigued by accounts which state, quite clearly and in great detail, who shot who, when and how often. I was always more concerned that no one shot me.

'The successful crossing of the Maas resulted in the enemy's eventual withdrawal across the Rhine, and preparations now began for an assault on selected crossing points along the river. The Brigade used one of the estuaries of the Maas to perfect its movements and formations during and after the crossing, and continued to train daily until the Brigadier expressed himself satisfied with the standard achieved. The Rhine crossing was scheduled for the evening of 23 March. During the morning of the 23rd, all Commandos taking part in the crossing received a final briefing, being then issued with a toggle rope and a Mae West to add to the miscellany of kit already carried. As the positions to be taken up after the crossing were directly among those already occupied by the enemy, there could be no direct means of supply, and all rucksack and equipment pouches were therefore loaded to capacity.

'My personal extras included, among other things, a field telephone, a reel of telephone wire and HT batteries. I was fortunate in not possessing a rifle, being armed with a ·45 automatic slung at the hip, but the overall effect, when fully loaded, prevented me standing erect. On entering the boats later, I released the buckle of the webbing belt to which were attached the equipment pouches – each of which I believe also contained a packet of Army biscuits, an item quite capable of stopping a bullet – and unfastened the epaulettes of the camouflaged jumping jacket, which kept in place the carrying straps of the other items carried. This would allow me to instantly discard all the items carried if suddenly projected into the river during the crossing. I was a good swimmer, but not while still attached to a full and heavy rucksack, battle equipment, a 38 patrol set, a reel of telephone wire and a field telephone. I re-fastened the belt buckle and epaulettes only on stepping ashore.

'The morning programme prior to the crossing included the final briefing and an inspection requiring a full depot standard of turnout in both weapons and dress, all equipment being blancoed to perfection for the last time until after the war, when it would be scrubbed white. Highly polished brass would be dulled later for the crossing. We then enjoyed the last meal not out of a tin until the end of hostilities – half a chicken to each man – after which we were dismissed to rest in preparation for the night operation. Towards 17.30 hrs, however, at the time of the expected first raid on Wesel by 100 RAF Lancasters, we proceeded to high ground to witness the event, the town of Wesel being visible in the distance. Exactly on time, 100 Lancasters, flying line astern, approached from the rear. Veering slightly, and passing overhead, they flew directly towards Wesel, each plane on arrival dropping its ten-ton blockbuster bomb on the town before veering away and heading for home. The ack-ack fire was negligible, their positions having been heavily bombed on a previous occasion.

'Exactly at the moment the last plane dropped its bomb and headed for home, every gun for miles around opened fire, to begin a pattern of continuous firing which extended to the following day. The ground literally shook as every gun fired simultaneously. The cattle and horses in the nearby fields became crazed with fear, neighing and bellowing as they stamped and galloped around in a vain attempt to escape the noise.

'At 19.30 hrs, 6 Commando formed up in Indian file to join the column commencing its march to the river, the projected time for the commencement of the crossing being 21.30, with the entry into Wesel timed for 22.00 hrs. 46 (Royal Marine) Commando and Brigade HQ embarked in Buffaloes to head the assault, closely followed by 6 Commando, whose task it would be, on reaching the opposite bank, to lead the Brigade column to the outskirts of Wesel by laying a continuous white tape to indicate the route taken. Here they would await a second 100-Lancaster attack before leading the Brigade's entry into the town. En route to the river, the column passed through a number of heavily engaged artillery positions, and from then on the march was to the accompaniment of the crash and thunder of the guns and the sound of shells continually passing overhead, while the constant flashes of the guns assisted the groups of searchlights playing their beams onto the clouds, often obscuring the almost full moon to create their own artificial moonlight.

'After some miles' continuous marching, the packs and equipment began to assume twice their original proportions and weight, but shortly before reaching the river a halt was called to supply the column with some unexpected and welcome refreshment, the packs and equipment being left in a position to move off again, while each man collected his issue of tea, rum and sandwiches – the last bread we would see until after the war.

'Normally, when occupying the hole you had dug in the ground for the night, the RSM came round with the rum ration, each man receiving one dessertspoonful of the life-giving fluid. But on this occasion we were told to take as much as we wished from the large dixies of tea and rum standing at the roadside, with RSM Woodcock advising, "It will kill some of the noise later." Apparently we had so far only experienced the overture to later events, when we would be in close proximity to the ten-ton blockbuster bombs being dropped onto the town. I took a mug of half-and-half, and on return to the packs and equipment, picked them up and placed them on my shoulders with surprising ease, while the crack and thunder of the guns and the sound of shells passing overhead during the remainder of the march to the river began to resemble the opening movement of Beethoven's Fifth

Symphony or the more impressive parts of the 1812 Overture. I believe no one took enough of the refreshment offered to interfere with the efficient performance of his duty.

'En route to the river, the column passed close to the BBC commentator giving a running description of events. From the well-modulated tones of his voice, he had not yet resorted to the rum to offset the accompanying noise – in direct contrast to that slightly inebriated and later unemployed BBC commentator who had enthusiastically described an attack on a Channel convoy with the words, "The RAF are shooting the whole bloody Luftwaffe down?" or words to that effect.

'On arriving at the riverbank, 6 Commando began to enter the small powered boats, operated by Royal Marines, which had been under fire since appearing from their places of concealment further up the river. 2 Troop, commanded by Captain Peter Cruden, RA, initially consisted of three officers and forty-eight other ranks, but this number became somewhat depleted when the boats were hit during the crossing. The second-in-command, Lieutenant Hume-Spry, drowned with other members of the troop, although some were picked up, to return to the troop on later operations. The boat I was in completed the crossing successfully, but on arrival we discovered we had landed on an island so another short embarkation and landing was required, again without loss.

'2 Troop then formed up with 6 Commando, which would lead the Brigade column to the outskirts of Wesel where it would halt less than 1,000 yards from the town to await the second Lancaster raid. Pathfinder flares guided the approaching planes and almost as the last bombs fell the column moved forward to take up its positions. 2 Troop HQ's intended position was at a road junction immediately adjacent to a railway embankment. That was what was on the map. Now it was an area of complete destruction, pitted by large bomb craters and surrounded by shattered ruins, so that even the 38 set, finally positioned at a cellar window, looked down into an extensive crater. 6 Commando gained and took up their positions, and 3 Commando and 45 (Royal Marine) Commando passed through to extend the operation. 46 (Royal Marine) Commando, who had made the original crossing with Brigade HQ, now came up from the rear to complete the area of occupation, which had been selected to be held against all opposition until mid-morning the following day, when the 17th US Airborne Division were scheduled to arrive. It was quite a spectacular and colourful sight when they did.

'Operations throughout the night and the following day took care of a considerable number of the enemy, including the Wesel garrison commander, Major General Deutsche, who was shot dead on refusing to surrender to a patrol led by RSM Woodcock. The RSM was reputed to have had three boats shot from under him during the crossing. An attempted counter-attack by the enemy next morning was effectively broken up by directed shellfire, but another contact with the enemy made by 2 Troop resulted in the wounding of Lieutenant Barnes, which left Captain Cruden in sole charge of the twenty-five men now remaining in 2 Troop. One patrol reported that when a number of the enemy had approached them in apparent surrender, one of them had dropped down on his hands and knees with an LMG strapped to his back. The patrol were the ones to return, so they must have reacted swiftly.

'Although wireless silence was in force throughout the operation, a twenty-four-hour listening watch was maintained. Telephonic communication had been established to the rear from Brigade HQ, but such communication was hardly possible between the positions now held among the enemy. I never saw the field telephone and reel of telephone wire I had brought across again, for which I was extremely grateful. (Future operations were carried out in battle order only, using 38 patrol sets for communication.) Due to this wireless silence and lack of direct telephonic communications, I was at one time required to convey a message to Brigade. After checking the route on the map, I proceeded through the rubble and destruction to deliver the message. On return I halted momentarily to check my bearings. Most houses look alike after being knocked about by bombing and shellfire, but I soon discerned the route for my return, and also observed one which I thought would prove quicker. As I stepped off in the new direction, a bullet passed through the spot where I had just been standing, followed by the crack-thump of a rifle. The crack is invariably followed by a thump, a vibrating effect which can give a clear indication of the direction from which the weapon has been fired. It is not advisable to stop and look for this position right away, however, especially when the weapon has been fired directly at you, and between the crack and the thump I was back behind cover. Another bullet passing behind me caused me to make an instant decision. He could shoot a lot further than I could and would probably shoot first. He could also see what he was aiming at. Deciding that known ways were best, I returned to HQ by the previous route. Circumstances don't make a man a hero or a coward. They simply reveal what he already is. I was just being careful.'

Philip Pritchard picks up a point from this story: 'In a garden area of Wesel, a lance corporal was digging a grave. This seemed strange to us and we asked him why. It appears that he was one of a party searching through the cellars when he was confronted by a German officer. The lance corporal immediately said, "Hands up!" whereupon the German replied, "I am General Von Deutsch and I only surrender to an officer of equal rank." The lance corporal is supposed to have said, "Well, this will equalize you," and fired his Thompson gun at him with fatal results. The story was that the Brigadier was furious and

ordered the lance corporal to bury the General as a
punishment. Anyway, this was the gist of the story and
the unfortunate lance corporal said, "That's the last time
I kill a General!"'

On 3 April, once again under the command of their old
D-Day friends in Sixth Airborne, the 1st Commando
Brigade were on the move again, heading now for Osnabruck, which was seized by 3 Commando in a night
attack supported by 45 Commando. The town was in
their hands by dawn and the Brigade took over 400
prisoners.

Bill Sadler again: 'The Brigade entered the outskirts of
Osnabruck during the very early hours of a Sunday
morning, a tactic that would be repeated on later operations. The route laid down for the column required it to
cross thirty or forty yards of open concrete into a tram or
bus depot, which led to a number of casualties from
machine-gun fire. This resulted in the immediate Commando reaction, "Bash on regardless." The possibility of
the column being halted could not be accepted. Covering
fire for an encircling movement would give the enemy
time to reinforce its present solitary position. The attack
had to be continued, immediately, and was carried out by
groups of four, five or six, running straight across the
open space at irregular intervals, directed by an officer
crouched at an intersection, who selected a group from
the column as it edged forward under cover, then ordering
"Go!" The group took off at a speed guaranteeing instant
selection for the next Olympic Games. The Spandau
concerned was silenced by a well-placed Piat bomb from
2 Troop, the depositor later receiving one of the Military
Medals awarded for the action.

'Halfway across the open space, when one of my boots
actually made contact with the concrete beneath, I heard
a metallic clatter as the German entrenching tool I carried
on my belt fell to the ground. I considered the advisability
of its retrieval at a speed that would have given a modern

microchip an inferiority complex, and before the other foot touched the ground I said, "B * * * you – stay there!" and continued my forward progress according to orders.

'One of the most pernicious and useless items of equipment issued to the long-suffering infantryman was his entrenching tool. Encased in hard webbing and consisting of a wooden handle and a detachable iron head which insisted on remaining detached while in use, it was suspended by two straps across the buttocks. Unnoticed on the march, it became very much more evident on the run. I had replaced mine with the standard German issue, which had a shaped and polished handle, at one end of which was a ratchet that allowed the permanently attached head to be locked in position for use as a shovel, or at an angle for use as a mattock. With the head folded flat and locked against the handle, it could be carried quite comfortably slung on the belt.

'The column continued its progress into Osnabruck and completed the capture of the town by 10.00 hrs, except for one or two isolated pockets of resistance, taking 400 prisoners, including a number of Hungarians. The local area Gestapo chief was shot dead in his office by the Brigade field security officer, Major Viscomte de Jonghe. 6 Commando occupied its allotted positions in town and 2 Troop established Troop HQ and its signal station in the library of one of the larger houses, which also contained an extensive collection of classical, dance and military band records, together with recordings of rally songs, including "We march against England". Some of these accompanied us further into Germany, together with an excellent *Telefunken* portable gramophone, carried for us by the troop jeep, which always arrived shortly after a position had been taken. The jeep driver was also the cook, so his arrival was always welcome.

'The discovery of a garage showroom resulted in some of the cars being commandeered by those who had the rank to do it, but their possession ended with the occupation. However, I believe the 1000cc BMW motorcycle commandeered for Brigade use ultimately accompanied the Brigade back to the UK.'

Arriving at the next obstacle, the Weser, the Brigade found that the town of Leese on the far bank was in the hands of a depleted battalion of the Rifle Brigade, so 45 Commando were hastily ferried across to reinforce them crossing in assault boats under heavy fire from SS troops of the 12th Training Battalion, who gave the Commando soldiers and the riflemen a very testing time for the next twenty-four hours, until the rest of the Brigade could get across, which was managed about midnight on 7/8 April. The Brigade once again formed into that single file infiltration formation, encircled Leese and attacked the SS positions from the rear, while 2 Troop of 6 Commando stormed a gun position and captured four 20mm cannons, and 3 Commando seized a factory manufacturing V2 rockets on the northern side of the town.

Bill Sadler again: 'Some months previously, on D-Day, I had been safe in Southampton docks. I would now be among the first half-dozen or so heading the advance of the entire British Army into Germany. I can recall no regrets.

'As the crossing was to be made some distance down river from the town, the boats to be used were carried to the chosen spot on the shoulders of 2 Troop during the hours of darkness. What that distance eventually was I have no idea, but no halt was made to change shoulders. I came to the conclusion during the march that either I was the tallest man on my side, or I had got the heaviest part. It's quite likely that everyone else thought the same, as it was in addition to the battle equipment and weapons already carried.

'The crossing was carried out undetected and unopposed, in complete silence, and within minutes of arriving on the opposite bank, 2 Troop formed up to lead 6

Commando and the remainder of the Brigade on the all-night march, the responsibility of leading the column in the right direction, at the correct speed, to arrive at the correct place at the right time, being that of Captain Cruden, who would use map and night compass to negotiate unfamiliar territory. The march began an hour or so before midnight, and was timed to end with an attack from the cross-roads at the rear of the town, around 07.00 hrs the following morning.

'During the march, the column encountered ditches, hedgerows, woods, ploughed fields and marshland, returning to a metalled road shortly after crossing a railway embankment, its first success being a rush through the darkness to capture a surprised four 20mm gun crew, who were interrogated and handed over to field security. We were not immune to surprise ourselves, Captain Cruden later confessing to a few moments' unease when he had to resort to the use of a torch in a barn to check his position on the map. Normally, however, the strict silence maintained throughout the march, with all conversation reduced to a whisper and smoking forbidden, combined with the use of the silent Commando boot and the practice of approaching from the direction least expected, in Indian file during the hours of darkness, usually made the approach of the column difficult to detect until too late.

'Throughout the night march the artillery maintained sporadic periods of fire on the surrounding countryside, directed by the forward observation officer accompanying the column, so that the Brigade continually traversed around and eventually moved ahead of its own shells. 2 Troop led the column towards the crossroad selected for the commencement of the Brigade's attack, keeping close to the hedgerow on one side of the country road.

'While still approaching the crossroad a sentry appeared from behind the houses on the right, whereupon the column stood stock still. The sentry wandered out into the centre of the cross-road and looked down towards the town, where another shell had just fallen. He then turned and looked in our direction. Whether the camouflaged jackets and green berets against the hedgerow background were sufficient to conceal us is hard to believe, but he apparently failed to see us and turned back towards the town. It was then the realization of what he had seen suddenly hit him and he stiffened, to turn back with his arms slowly rising. On being made prisoner, the half-empty bottle of Advocaat in his right hand revealed the real reason for his slowness of recognition. He had not been shot on sight as that would have raised the alarm. In his present condition he might not have cared.

'Having led the all-night march, 2 Troop was now in position for first entry into the town. The Brigadier's ruse, employed some years previously by Hannibal against the Gauls, had apparently succeeded, the enemy still being contained at the riverside, convinced that this was the area that would be attacked. 2 Troop was thus able to occupy its own positions against little or no opposition, the remainder of the Brigade then passed through to successfully engage the riverside and other positions from the rear. 3 Commando captured a V2 factory, complete with its staff of scientists.'

The Brigade were then transferred to the command of the 11th Armoured Division and moved on again towards the Aller, crossing the river on the half-blown spans of a railway bridge to take the town of Essel by assault, 6 Commando charging the enemy position to the sound of hunting horns. Covered by fire from the Support Troop MMGs, 6 Commando cleared the enemy out of Essel at the point of the bayonet, advancing over a quarter of a mile, killing everyone who stood in their path.

Bill Sadler continues: 'The crossing of the River Aller involved the only road-bridge for miles in either direction, which was defended by the 2nd Battalion of Marine

Fusiliers (*Kreigmarines*). A direct assault would undoubtedly result in its immediate destruction, but a mile or so
north a railway bridge, now a mass of twisted rails and
girders, also spanned the river. Shortly after dark, the
leading troop of 3 Commando crossed the partly destroyed
bridge in stockinged feet and captured its defenders and
the demolition party preparing its final destruction at a
cost of five men wounded.

'The Brigadier then decided that where these few could
go, the rest of the column could follow, once more during
the very early hours of a Sunday, a day that would prove
fateful for Belsen, only a few miles away. The column,
headed by 3 Commando, crossed in Indian file, to move
around and behind the enemy positions in complete
silence, until 3 Commando and Brigade HQ engaged the
enemy in close-quarter fighting in the woods later in the
morning, an action which resulted in temporary stalemate as far as the objective was concerned. It was then
decided that the position had to be taken by storm by 6
Commando using the bayonet.

'6 Commando were withdrawn from the positions they
had dug during the night, in which they had only recently
experienced some searching mortar fire, and were
entrenched in line along the long dry ditch immediately
facing the open area they had to cover to reach the
enemy's position. Vickers machine guns from Heavy
Weapons Troop also extended along the line, then opened
fire for a predetermined period, completely lacerating the
enemy positions. The moment they stopped firing, each
man knew what he had to do. Lying there with bayonets
fixed, nine rounds in the magazine and one up the spout,
safety catches off, there was no time for the philosophical
introspection beloved by Hemingway and other authors
when describing such moments. The Commandos just
waited for the bullets to stop. The moment they did so, 6
Commando rose to its feet as one man, and with the

second-in-command sounding a "tally ho!" on his hunting horn, charged forward. This was carried out at an all-out run, firing from the hip whenever an opportunity presented itself. It made more sense to kill a man at a distance than to get close enough to use the bayonet. Doing it at the run shortened the time he had to shoot you.

'The enemy finally broke and ran, for which they couldn't be blamed, but not before they had left their battalion commander, two company commanders and the RSM among the many dead. On reaching the enemy position, my immediate opponent was already dead. I thought it was as well for me that he was. He was well over six feet and around sixteen stone. He was smiling serenely, as if enjoying a private joke, or having just solved a problem whose solution had eluded him. The bridge position was taken after a 400-yard charge across open ground and into the wood, but the enemy soon proved his mettle by staging an almost immediate counter-attack, shouting "Cease firing!" as they came back through the wood. We didn't, neither did anyone else, and the position held. We were then rewarded by the one concession made throughout the entire campaign – "No one need shave for the time being."'

On the following day, 45 and 46 Commandos expanded the Brigade bridgehead across the Aller, but met heavy resistance from fresh German troops. On 13 April they tried again, 45 achieving its objective and 46 Commando seizing the town of Hadensdorf after a very stiff fight in which Y Troop of 46 Commando lost all its officers and continued to advance under the command of Sergeant S. Cooper, MM, who led the troop until the town fell.

D. Blackburn of 6 Commando, tells of an incident that happened about this time: 'I have told this story several times but, quite frankly, I am sure many people do not believe it and think it's just a good "old soldier's yarn". You will recall that when we withdrew from the Battle of

Green Hill in North Africa we had to leave many wounded behind in the care of our section stretcher bearer, who volunteered to remain with the wounded and be taken prisoner. Well, after D-Day and various other campaigns, we returned to Germany for further action, and one of the tasks included clearing the vast area of forest, consisting of thick woods, shrubs and poor roads or dirt tracks. Large forest fires broke out from the continual shelling. We were lying up in the wooded areas, awaiting orders, when it was decided that it would be much more comfortable and safer to move into a large clearing away from the fires, which were being fanned by the breeze into roaring walls of flame with terrific heat.

'Having posted a look-out, the rest of the section stood down. After a short while, the look-out shouted, "Movement to immediate front!" and we saw what appeared to be two figures. One was in RAF uniform and the other wore khaki dress of some sort. We were very cautious, as many times on previous occasions the Germans had played tricks on units to expose their positions, with dire results. It was full sunlight and we lay very low as the two figures unsuspectingly approached, straight in line with our position. When they were within shouting distance, we hailed them. "Halt, who goes there?" The reply came, "British prisoners of war." We replied, "Advance slowly," and as they came towards me I could not believe my eyes. "Good God! It's Garth!" The stretcher bearer who had stayed behind two years ago on a hilltop in Africa had walked straight into his own section in the middle of Germany. Out of, I suppose, possibly one million British, American, French and Canadian troops, he walked into his own unit – incredible! His comrade was an RAF prisoner of war, and he couldn't believe it either.'

Philip Pritchard continues the story of 6 Commando in Germany: 'The enemy were in Leese and a small bridgehead had been created by British troops. We were briefed for a crossing further up the river and were due to go over in Folding Boat Engineers (FBEs). These were canvas-sided collapsible pontoons capable of holding an infantry section (ten men). There were eight paddles and therefore eight rowers with one man each at the bow and stern. They were excellent for silent crossing of small rivers and were highly portable. While having our evening meal we were joined by a number of Russian prisoners. One of them had several bottles of what he called vodka, but said by those who had tried it to be more like methylated spirits. One Russian was pointed out as being a colonel. He didn't look any different from the others and appeared rather young for his rank, apparently in his late twenties. At nightfall we all paraded in an assembly area, where we picked up our boats. These were carried to the river's edge and then in successive waves we crossed the river and moved along the opposite bank away from the town (our objective) for some distance until we all moved over the bank and into a very wet and swampy area where we made our way in a wide sweep round the town to enter the opposite end to the small British bridge-head.

'At one point we crossed a road upon which was the black outline of a tank. This proved to be a British Cromwell, apparently knocked out and abandoned. They must have got out of it in a big hurry because I could see through the open driver's hatch the red glow of the master switch light. Having passed the tank we were all halted. We could see, not far away over to our left on the outskirts of the town, a German gun firing with a long flash of flame from its barrel. I can remember seeing one of its crew actually remove a shell from the wickerwork container. One of our troops made a surprise capture of the gun. The attack on the town no doubt came as a complete surprise to the Germans and they had no idea that we were behind them. It was operations such as this that gave us such confidence in our Brigade Commander. To me he was a thinking soldier and during any action he was always well forward, generally with the leading Commando, and on occasions with the leading troop. We were never surprised to see him where the bullets were flying. In fact, if my troop was leading, we could be sure that he wasn't far behind. Indeed, it made us more conscientious as he was never known to suffer fools gladly, neither did he mince his words. He was thirty-six years old and had come from being a Lieutenant in the Irish Guards Reserve of officers in 1939 to a Brigadier in 1944. A fine effort indeed and in my book he was a true professional soldier and represented all that was best in the British Army.

'Once into Leese we started to get long-range machine gun and rifle fire from a railway embankment which had a few wagons still on the lines. The enemy were firing from behind these and even at that range (700 yards or so) managed to kill a Forward Observation Officer who was with us. One of our troops came in from a flank along the railway line and soon put paid to the Germans. We understood that a V-weapon factory had been captured. It was apparently very well camouflaged, being partly underground with trees and bushes growing over the buildings. I only saw it from a distance and unless I had been told I would have had no idea that a factory was there. We did not tarry long in the town. Long enough, however, for the RSM to have his teeth checked. Apparently the RSM (Woodcock) had some trouble with his teeth, and as we didn't have a dental officer he enquired if there was a civilian (German) dentist available. One was produced and the RSM is alleged to have sat in the chair with his ·45 Colt automatic pointing at the dentist. It appears that the treatment was successful, no doubt much to the relief of the dentist.'

On 19 April 1st Commando Brigade reached Lauenberg, passing the concentration camp at Belsen, coming under the command of the 15 (Scottish) Division, before preparing for what turned out to be their last operation, Operation Enterprise, the crossing of the River Elbe.

Bill Sadler takes up the story: '3 and 6 Commandos had been directly concerned with the capture and occupation of the bridge position, and remained there for some time afterwards, during which time 45 and 46 Royal Marine Commandos moved out to extend the bridgehead to the north and east, where they met another Kreigmarine Fusilier Battalion approaching to reinforce the position. An immediate all-out charge by the Marine Commandos caused these to eventually turn and run. One of their officers shot himself where he stood when he failed to stop them. The capture of the bridge resulted in the discovery of Belsen concentration camp later that morning. On returning from a visit to the camp, the padre attempted to give an account of what he had seen, but no one at that time could fully appreciate what he was attempting to describe. Later 6 Commando were ordered to proceed to Belsen to assist in the general clearing up, each man being thoroughly impregnated with anti-typhus powder. At the same moment as the trucks arrived to take us to Belsen, a message also arrived with instructions to accompany the armoured advance in the direction of the Elbe. We accordingly sped along an autobahn towards the Elbe without calling in at Belsen.

'After an hour or two of progress along the autobahn, a counter-order was received, halting the Division in its present position, possibly because an immediate crossing of the Elbe was no longer considered feasible. Armour extended along the autobahn in both directions as our trucks were guided onto the wide grass verge, where we halted to receive further instructions. On being told to jump down and stretch our legs, my oppo and I strolled over to the nearest tank, only a few yards away, where one of the crew was brewing up on a couple of petrol tins. Eventually, after consolidating at the top, 6 Commando moved out to capture the bridge over the Elbe-Trave canal.'

1st Brigade's task was to cross on the right flank of 15th (Scottish) Division to seize Lauenberg and the bridge across the Elbe-Trave canal. The assault began at 02.00 hrs on 29 April when the war in Europe had just nine days left to run.

6 Commando again led the way, crossing under fire in Buffaloes, two miles downstream from Lauenberg. The enemy had dug in on top of a 150-foot cliff and engaged the Commandos with rifle and machine gun fire and potato masher grenades, but the advance went on. Spreading out to the flank and covered by fire from across the river, 6 Commando swarmed up the cliff and beat the enemy back from the rim. Then 46, 3 and 45 Commandos came up, and having seized the high ground, the Brigade advanced to take Lauenberg. An advance patrol from 6 Commando reached the bridge just in time to stop a demolition party firing the charges. Near here, Field Marshal Milch surrendered his baton to Derek Mills Roberts, who, disgusted with the sights the Brigade had uncovered at Belsen and elsewhere, broke the baton over the Field Marshal's head.

Bill Sadler again: 'The Brigade continued north unopposed, to enter Lübeck and Neustadt, where they found the bodies of some 300 men, women and children, all clad in pyjama-type prison clothing, lying at the edge of the sea. All had been shot or drowned. The circumstances were never made clear. The Brigadier ordered the burgomaster to provide a burial party from the most elderly citizens, and they were buried in one mass grave. Some years later I read in an international paper that a mass grave had been discovered in the area. Apparently no one in the town had any knowledge of its existence or origin. A remarkable case of mass amnesia.'

Still advancing, 1st Commando Brigade reached Neustadt in early May, and brought their war in Europe to a close.

12

Burma,
1944–45

'Well have we done, thrice valiant countrymen.
But all's not yet done.'

HENRY V: SCENE VI

Peter Young was commanding 3 Commando in the Bois
de Bavent when General Robert Stuges arrived at his
headquarters and offered him promotion to full Colonel
and the post of Deputy Commander of 3 Commando
Brigade which was operating in South-East Asia. 'No one
has less objection to promotion than I have,' says Peter
Young, 'but I asked the General to defer my transfer at
least until the end of the Normandy campaign. I finally
arrived in Ceylon in the middle of October 1944.' 3
Commando Brigade under the command of a Royal
Marines officer, Brigadier W. I. Nonweiler, had been
dispatched to South-East Asia at the end of 1943, sailing
from Gourock for India on 15 November. This brigade,
the 3rd (Special Service) Brigade, which became 3 Commando Brigade in December 1944, consisted of two Army
Commandos, Nos. 1 and 5, and two Royal Marine Commandos, Nos. 42 and 44, plus the Dutch Troop of 10 (IA).
Both Army units had already seen service, No. 1 in cross-
Channel raids and in North Africa, No. 5 in the landings
at Madagascar, but the two Royal Marine units were new
formations raised from the battalions of the Royal Marine
Division.

On the voyage to India the Brigade suffered a severe

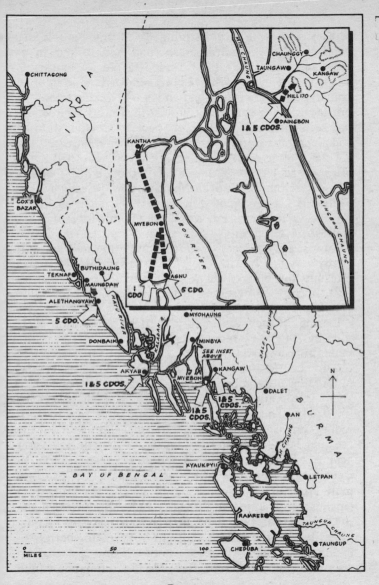

Burma

setback when the ship carrying No. 1 and No. 42 was bombed in the Mediterranean, and had to put in at Alexandria for repairs, but Brigade HQ, No. 5 Commando and No. 44 (Royal Marine) Commando arrived in India in January 1944. However, No. 1 and No. 42 did not rejoin the Brigade until September, by which time the other two units had seen some action and were back in Ceylon, training and preparing to return to the Arakan front in Burma.

Peter Young again: '3 Commando Brigade had some brilliant people in it and a very good staff; Douglas Drysdale from the Royal Marines was Brigade Major, Tony Pigot, a very good officer . . . it was a damned good Brigade. Of the units, I'd rate 42 Commando for steadiness and No. 5 for dash; 42 had a very good CO in David Fellowes, a good friend of mine. I rate him and Campbell Hardy very highly. However, I have to say that No. 1 was probably the best of them, a thoroughly good infantry unit, one which deserves to be mentioned in the same breath as 3 and 6 . . . and 2.'

During the previous January, even with half his Brigade missing, Brigadier Nonweiler soon had the two units under his command committed to battle. Their field was the Arakan, the coastal strip of Burma between the central mountains and the Bay of Bengal, a vast region of swamp and jungle, seamed with rivers, of which the largest is the Irrawaddy. The Arakan was the territory of the 15th Indian Corps and No. 44 (Royal Marine) Commando made the first landing behind the Japanese lines on the coast near Alethangyaw on 11 March 1944, going ashore in three waves from old, leaky landing craft. The Marines took Alethangyaw, enduring much harassment from Japanese snipers tied into trees, and after fighting through the village put two fighting troops across the chaung (river) behind the village and sent out fighting patrols to bicker with Japanese outposts, until the unit re-embarked after two days ashore to relieve No. 5 Commando which had carried out a similar landing at Maungdaw further north, closer to the main battle area.

Frank Atter of 5 Commando takes up the story: 'Alethangyaw was an operation where both Commandos involved went into action very much on their own without close support from either the Navy or the Air Force. The object was to take the strain off the main corps battle on the Maungdaw-Buthidaung road, and attract attention so as to divert Japanese troops who might have been used there. My opinion is that we did that efficiently enough. Alethangyaw was under very accurate Jap mortar fire the whole time. We patrolled quite a bit, but the village was our base, and we took quite a few casualties there.

'Then our CO, Colonel Shaw, MC, decided we should attack the mortars overlooking our positions. The exact sites of the mortars were not known, so he sent 3 Troop across open paddy fields to draw their fire. As I was in one of the leading subsections I can assure you this move did succeed. We went forward steadily, running forward and dropping when the bombs fell. Curiously, we took few casualties while we were moving. We reached a village across our path and were told to halt on the forward edge. We were a bit cramped, and my subsection commander agreed with me that I should move my Bren group to a depression on our right where there was a better field of fire. Having no sense of smell, I was not aware this was the village lavatory. As my group were complaining about the smell, a bomb hit the trees to our left and caused casualties, including one dead, so the complaints stopped immediately. It became quite obvious that without artillery or air support we could not continue. The largest mortar we had was a two-inch, so we were at a great disadvantage, and later we withdrew into a "box" (a defensive square) at Alethangyaw. That night we sent out a fighting patrol which clashed with a Japanese patrol on its way to attack the box. At the time we did not know what was happening, bullets and bombs whistled over our heads, and only when our patrol had seen off the Japs and rejoined us did the picture become clear. We had the best of it. I think we lost about ten killed, and several wounded. The Japs made no further attempts on the box apart from continual mortaring. They realized we were there to stay, and would only leave when our task was complete. Alethangyaw taught us valuable lessons. We had taken our Vickers guns into action instead of our three-inch mortars. We never did this again, and our Heavy Weapon Troop soon became really expert in the use of mortars in close country.'

Corporal John Wall, also of 5 Commando, remembers another incident at Maungdaw. 'We made a landing in the Alethangyaw area south of Maungdaw, where some fierce fighting was taking place. We made a box from which to make our forays on the Japanese communications. One night my troop was warned to prepare for a sortie and at sunset we left the box in a "T" formation. "Titch" Shoreman was at the extreme right of the leading line when something brought the whole formation to a standstill. At that moment a figure appeared in front of Titch and it was obviously a Jap; perhaps to the Jap, Titch seemed a comrade as he was short and stocky. But quick-thinking Titch was in a quandary as he was the grenade rifleman and the discharger was fixed to his rifle, which was only loaded with a cartridge. What should he do, as there was a long bayonet at the end of the foe's rifle? At that moment the Jap, obviously confused, jabbered at Titch, whose answer was an equally incomprehensible jabber. At the same time Titch waggled his left thumb to indicate that the Jap should proceed a few steps more to the left and find a convenient British bayonet. As the Jap walked to the left, the next man to Titch also waggled his thumb, thinking that Titch was OC the patrol! This thumb-wagging went on until the Jap reached the centre of the line, where he was conveniently shot. Titch was thereafter famous as the only man in the Commando who had carried on a conversation with a Japanese soldier!

'As soon as the Jap was shot all hell broke loose, for we had run into a large party of Japanese with well-sited machine guns. Our response had been to form a box with our Brens sited at the corners so that they could enfilade each side. However, we did not get away lightly as our Bren magazines were loaded with one-in-three tracer and automatically became the target for almost every enemy gun in the area. At the distances involved, grenades were largely ineffective, and the two-inch mortar had to be brought into action to silence the Japs. From this action we quickly learned how the Japs would shout in English something they had heard. One of our chaps, very badly wounded, was calling for his troop commander and the Japs would repeat the same shout in an effort to confuse and attract some approach towards them.'

Frederick Palmer of 5 Commando was wounded here. 'I was wounded on two occasions. First, when on patrol with No. 2 Troop of No. 5 Commando in the Maungdaw area — the village of Dopan — a bullet wound in my left leg which put me out of action for two months. I remember being carried on a makeshift stretcher by six Burmese for three or four miles to No. 5 Commando base HQ at the beach. Freddie Hoyle was the Admin Officer and Sam Hartley was RQMS. Nonweiler was the Brigadier at that time, and he was on board his command ship about a mile offshore. There were three or four wounded already on the beach. There was a lad in Commando HQ Admin named Fred Musson, a regular soldier who joined as a boy just before the war; he fastened a rope around his waist and swam out to the Brigadier's ship, a small fishing boat. Using this rope, the wounded were pulled from the shore to the boat and then taken to a field unit at a place called Nela. After a short stay there I went on to Chittagong, strapped to the wings of a Moth-type plane. I didn't know

331

about all this until it was over as they had given me a jab to put me out.'

Denis Crowden was also at Alethangyaw. 'Our first joust with the Japs was on the edge of Alethangyaw, not far from the beach, where we dug in in the traditional box formation on the grounds that you never knew which way the Japs would come, and they always came. The villagers dug in too. One night when one of our troops went out to look for Jap long-range guns which had been giving us hell, they walked right into the Japs advancing on three sides of our box. Battle commenced and among our wounded was one chap who had been wounded thirteen times and lay there groaning all night until we could retrieve him at first light. Both sides suffered heavy casualties. I had to lead my section to bring in the dead and wounded. I shall never forget how the order was passed verbally round our box then stopped at me. Some of the dead had already stiffened and looked grotesque. In my ignorance, at twenty-three years of age, I tried to straighten out their limbs, but the only way to do that was to break them, and I wasn't going to do that to my friends. A few dead Japs were there too. They usually took them away but in this case the Japs had had enough too and didn't waste any time. But they did sever one or two arms from their dead to remove forms of identification. When we pulled out, my troop had to stay another night in another location. We were plied with rum for our rearguard, so we were trigger-happy and nearly wiped out a herd of cattle in the dead of night.

'We were exhausted but before we could return to an area of safety we were called upon to rescue some gunners who had been cut off by the Japs. They took us over swampy land in two amphibious vehicles, called DUKWs. Lieutenant Noble took his section in while the section I was in formed a bridgehead. Those who went in were badly cut up. A particular friend of mine was wounded and unfortunately tried to sit up and was shot again. He was pulled out but seemed to have no will to live. He had lost both legs. Lieutenant Noble pulled out three of the wounded single-handed, under fire. He was very brave. When they returned to our bridgehead they came through at the point I was covering. Lieutenant Noble couldn't speak, he was in shock and the wireless operator who was with him, although not wounded, had all the webbing holding his equipment shot away. One saw some strange wounds, such as a groove under the bottom lip, or a neat hole in one cheek and a much bigger hole where it came out through the back of the head.'

Victor Stevenson of 1 Commando also recalls the conditions of soldiering in Burma. '"Old men forget," as Henry V said, but at the time it was a matter of great pride to be a Commando, though alas the word has now been appropriated by the media to describe half the murderous brigands of the world. Anyway, certain things made South-East Asia so different ... solid bamboo jungle, mosquitoes, leeches. The first cut you to pieces, the others ate you alive. We all had malaria, dysentery, rotten jungle sores. I suppose we complained but I don't remember it. These were the occupational hazards of everyone caught up at the sharp end in Burma, quite apart from the daring of the Nips.'

Nonweiler's half-brigade returned to India to be based at Silchar, where No. 44 Commando had elephants on the unit strength, and then moved to Ceylon where the other two units, Nos. 42 and 1, arrived to join them in September. Charles Hustwick of the Signals was there. 'From Bombay we went by train to a tented camp just outside Poona, which was to be our home for a little while to become acclimatized. At long last we were all together; the other Commandos, No. 5 and No. 44 (Royal Marine) Commandos were already encamped. This was the first time I had made any contact with Marine Commandos. They were not volunteers like us and their outlook on life generally was quite different. Still, after a while both the Army and Marines buried their differences and got on remarkably well. The battles which took place later in Burma proved that. After a period of acclimatization we moved south by road to Belgaum near the border with Portuguese Goa for jungle training. We camped astride a river which at night was alive with water-snakes, though few, if any, took any notice, for everyone enjoyed the swimming – in fact we had a gala. We had a chap called Ron Roberts, an ex-London policeman and Olympic swimmer, so we won most of the events. Learning to live in the jungle was hard; one had to learn how to deal with the mosquitoes, snakes (which were abundant), scorpions, leeches, in fact, anything that moved. I recall one interesting story. A head hunter had killed a twelve-foot python which had just eaten a calf, and we could see the shape of the calf within the tightly stretched skin of the python. The hunter told us to be on the lookout for the python's mate, as they usually worked in pairs. This did not please me one bit, especially as the hunter's parting words were, "Don't worry, this is tiger country, we don't normally get large snakes in this area." I don't think many of those who heard this got much sleep that night.'

By November 1944 the units had begun raiding again along the Arakan coast, with all units participating in a series of attacks. Half a troop of 42 Commando went ashore on Elizabeth Island, south of Akyab, on 30 November, charged with the task of taking one prisoner of war (if possible) for the Japanese soldier was notoriously reluctant to surrender, and would often kill himself rather than fall into Allied hands. The 42 patrol killed ten Japanese soldiers who charged into their position, shouting and firing, and withdrew with the loss of one man. On 10 November, Nos. 1 and 42 began nightly patrols down the coast from their base at Teknaf and by the end of the month had been ashore eleven times.

John Ferguson went on these raids with 5 Commando. 'In Teknaf Peninsula about thirty of us used to embark in

two ALCs about 02.00 hrs every morning and get into a
position just behind the twelve-foot swell where the huge
breakers thundered down. The ALCs anchored just this
side of the breakers and we jumped in and made our way
shoreward and carried out an unopposed landing. How
nobody was drowned in the breakers is really incredible.
After the landings we made our way back to base, about
five miles. Our clothes soon dried in the sun later in the
day. This was carried out every morning for a week, and
we took it to be part of our normal training. Not so! A
few weeks later our small party was kitted up and we
went to the southern tip of Teknaf and embarked in two
MTBs, where to my great surprise and pleasure we met a
raiding party of SBS. The Japanese had erected thirty-foot
bamboo watchtowers for hundreds of miles down the
coast of Burma, and recent aerial photography showed six
towers in our area. An SBS reconnaissance party found
them to be guarded by a company of Japanese, and our
task was to dispose of the towers. The SBS went ashore in
Folboats and myself and some others of our party were
selected to go with them in some spare craft. We also had
a Carley float fitted with explosives and charges to repre-
sent all manner of fire – machine gun, rifle, mortar etc. –
when it was detonated. This float was to be a diversion
while the towers were being disposed of. Anyway, we set
off about 02.00 hrs in our Folboats, aiming for a break in
the surf which goes all down the coast. The advance party
of SBS got ashore and put the Folboats under cover, but a
recce showed that the towers were defended by a whole
battalion of Japanese, not a company as was first thought.
After discussion it was decided to call off the raid as we
could not have got anywhere near the towers with so
many defenders to contend with. Anyway, it was back to
the MTBs, where we launched the Carley float and set it
off, the MTBs travelling away at speed. As we passed
offshore, we opened up on the Japanese with all our
armaments and they, of course, replied and passed on

information to their other towers, who in turn opened up on us as we sped north . . . an exciting but abortive raid.'

On 29 December 1944, command of the Brigade passed to Brigadier Campbell Hardy, DSO, of the Royal Marines, who had a considerable reputation among the Commando forces. Alf Pimblett remembers the Brigadier. 'One of the things that comes to my mind is his composure and guts. We were pinned down on a hill on the Myebon Peninsula in the Arakan when he crawled up beside me and said, "Are you all right?" I said, "Yes Sir, scared stiff." Bullets were flying all about us, but he stood up and said, "Follow me," and away the troop went over the top of the hill. We killed twenty-four of the enemy in the next half-hour and never had a casualty, thanks to the guts and calmness of a fine soldier and gentleman. I had occasion to meet him again at Kangaw on Hill 170; some of the Indian troops were firing at our chaps on the hill, and I and an officer, Lieutenant Allen Davies, were told to get to them and point out where the Japs were. We both ran like hell across open ground, and lo and behold the Brigadier turned up. We had just lost our Colonel, shot in both knees, and I said to the Brigadier, "The bastards have got our Colonel." Then realizing I had sworn at him, I said I was sorry for the language, but he put his hand on my shoulder and said, "It's all right, son, heat of the battle." That's the type of man he was. We would have died for him.'

With the Japanese in retreat, 3 Commando Brigade now expanded their operations, moving on from coastal raids to all-out assaults, beginning on 3 January 1945 with a landing on the island of Akyab. The largest amphibious lift ever seen in Burma was assembled for this operation, but when an RAF reconnaissance plane overflew the island early on the 3rd, the pilot reported back that the place seemed deserted. 3 Commando Brigade and 26th Indian Division landed unopposed, though Captain 'Chips' Heron, MC, of 5 Commando managed to overtake the retreating enemy at Pauktaw and killed six of them.

On 12 January 3 Commando Brigade went ashore again, on the Myebon Peninsula. A COPP reconnaissance had revealed that the beach had been fenced in offshore, but after a gap had been blown, the landing craft could pass through. Supported by a naval bombardment the Brigade went in to land against light opposition from artillery. 42 went ashore first, covered by a smoke screen, losing a few men to mines and a shell that hit a landing craft. They were followed in by No. 5, who passed through the 42 Commando beach-head and into the jungle, advancing to a hill feature, codenamed Rose, where they met more machine gun fire and, as usual, snipers.

Frank Atter again: 'At the time, I described Akyab in a letter to a friend, as "a tactical exercise without Japs", but despite the anti-climax, the occupation of Akyab was a very necessary part of the campaign with its good harbour and airstrip. At Myebon we were opposed, but the enemy were surprised. 5 Commando was in the second wave, and passed through 42 RM Commando to advance up the peninsula. We were lucky, because although the tide was going out, we merely waded our way ashore easily, while those who followed found thick mud. We were lucky also on the beach, which was infested with mines – not the usual kind, but primed aircraft bombs – just below the surface, and the slightest touch would set them off. My troop did have casualties, with at least one killed, but afterwards when we saw the Engineers making the mines safe, we realized how fortunate we had been. Myebon was a good, carefully planned operation, an example of how true co-operation between Services should be. At Brigade level, both Brigadier Campbell Hardy and Colonel Young provided the sort of cool, efficient leadership soldiers respect. The support of three tanks of the Indian Army was also much appreciated.'

The other two units, No. 1 followed by No. 44, landed on a beach to the left of the first landing, and the tide was now falling. The landing craft grounded ever further offshore, giving the second wave a long exhausting slog through waist-high mud. Some of troops took three hours to cover the 400 yards from their craft to the firm beach, and staggered ashore exhausted. 'What would have happened if the Japs had stuck in an attack or even started mortaring us then, God alone knows,' said one of No. 44 Commando. 'Fortunately they didn't.'

Dr J. K. Paterson was then a Signals Officer in No. 1 Commando. 'I was the only officer in the Brigade who spoke Urdu; the result of this was that I was on every "outing" we had from then on. Very exciting and full of entertainment, but this is not the important thing about my time with 1 Commando. It was simply that this was a very special unit, from the CO, Colonel (later Brigadier) Kenneth Trevor; the second-in-command, Major Jim Davis; the Adjutant, Ian Carrell; right through to my troop funny man, Cockney ex-copper, Fusilier Stan Burden. Some are now dead, but some I continue to meet, year after year, at reunions, run ever since 1948 by No. 1's orderly room Sergeant Major, Henry Brown. The Commando Association owes an enormous debt of gratitude to this man. He has literally made and preserved the most remarkable ex-service organization this country has ever had.

'Three entertaining episodes remain in the forefront of my memory. First was the time when I was plodding along a jungle path in company with Major John Turnbull. We were sniped at by Japanese hiding in trees. After a few minutes' fruitless peering into the undergrowth, John put down his rifle, rolled onto his left side, put his hand in his pocket and said, "I can't see the buggers – have a sweet." The second was when Stan Burden fell into a chaung, carrying a large wireless set on his back. Any ordinary mortal would have drowned or jettisoned the set. Burden came scrambling up the bank, saying loud and clear, "Blimey, I've been playing bleeding submarines!" I hope the Japanese laughed as loud as we did. Just before this, though, there was the problem of getting ashore when we had been put out a trifle early by the Royal Indian Navy. I was up to my chest in water, carrying almost exactly one hundredweight. I have little feet, size 5½, and with my weight and my load, this meant taking more than seventeen stone on a small boot. The mud was sticky and mighty thick, and I was making very slow progress. The worthy Burden came splashing past me, all fourteen stone of him with feet well suited to a London copper. He burst out laughing and called to a friend, "Look at the boss, he's bleeding sinking!" Little did he know. I suffered coronary pain shortly after, in spite of having a perfectly normal heart and being extremely fit.

'Perhaps the funniest episode was when I accompanied a small patrol down the coast, looking for signs of Japanese. We came to a village where I was assured by the locals that the Japanese were not far away, but in numbers too great for us to tackle. So we trudged back fourteen miles to raise reinforcements, rather than alert them by using our radio. Within minutes I was on my way again, with twenty-eight miles to my credit that day. After forty-two miles, I led the patrol straight into an ambush! We had to get out before regrouping to deal with the problem. I followed my last man, Private Jones, ran my fastest over 100 yards to a sort of hedge, got stuck and finally fell down the far side of it. Picking myself up, I ran on, only to find that my precious green beret was missing . . . it hung in the hedge. So back I went, quite oblivious to the rather aggressive acts of the Japanese, pulled my beret out of the hedge and donned it solemnly before running to cover.

'This last tale has a sequel. After the war I married a sailor's daughter. My father-in-law, Captain Berry, was sunk three times; on the third occasion he was convoy Commodore in the Mediterranean when he was bombed. All hands were off ship when he turned to his First Officer, saying, "Hang on a minute." He slid down a very sloping deck to his day cabin, collected his beautiful new white cap, braided in gold, and put it on before jumping into the sea.'

John Ferguson continues: 'For our landing at Myebon our ALC took us to within 200 yards of the beach and as we got out the sea came up to our chests, but the lower three feet was all thick slime. As we got to the beach some of our comrades were killed when they stood on mines laid just under the surface. We pushed forward and took up position to clear the Japanese from their holes on a ridge. Our troop officer was wounded as he was preparing for the attack. The order was given for covering fire as one section advanced, then the covering party moved up. All this time the Sherman tanks were firing, when suddenly, out of the undergrowth on my left, a young boy and girl both about twelve years of age and holding hands, came forward, looked at me, smiled in a startled sort of way, and made their way to the back of our lines, realizing that way meant safety. I often wonder what became of these two youngsters. While all this was going on, the headman of one of the villages came running forward to say that some of the villagers were badly wounded half a mile away. We just could not hold up the advance at that moment, so pressed on up the hill as some of the Japanese came out of their foxholes with hands up, although one could never be sure if they had a grenade in a clenched fist, ready to lob at us. Wherever we went there were scores of dead Japanese lying around, but you never knew if they were booby-trapped. Even going over ground or through bushes recently evacuated was a risky business; there was always the possibility of a counter-attack.'

The Commando landing was supported by tanks of the 19th Lancers which, unable to land across the mud, were put ashore even further up the coast, and it took hours of work by Engineers before they could rejoin the Brigade around the *Rose*, a feature which was attacked and taken at dawn on 13 January.

42 Commando then led the advance to Myebon village, which was found to be unoccupied, and the Brigade moved on to drive the enemy from the small hills which overlooked the village. During these operations, Lieutenant Colonel Fellowes of 42 Commando was wounded and borne off to the rear, shouting, 'Carry on lads, I'll be back.' That night, 13/14 January, passed quietly. On the following day, the Brigade began to send patrols forward, with No. 1 Commando getting into one sharp fight which required tank support before the Brigade moved on to the village of Kantha. No. 1 Commando, supported by the tanks of the 19th Lancers, took a hill, Point 200, overlooking Kantha, and the Japanese then withdrew. At Myebon, 3 Commando Brigade could chalk up a successful operation, driving the enemy off with 150 killed for the loss to the Brigade of four men killed and twenty-eight wounded.

Frank Atter recalls one incident at Myebon. 'No. 5 Commando was in the second wave, and although the landing was somewhat sticky, the tide was not right out, and we were not bogged down in the mud as those who followed us were. We led the advance, and then paused while the Brigade and supporting tanks joined us. Then Brigadier Campbell Hardy planned a series of advances up the peninsula. It was obvious he knew his job, and so we were confident. I remember at this time, Campbell Hardy noticed Peter Young (our Deputy Brigadier) walking around near us dressed in khaki and wearing red tabs. Campbell Hardy urged him to go to the rear, because if he himself was a casualty, his deputy should be ready to take over. But most of us expected to see Colonel Young up where he always was – where the action was.

'My troop had to advance down a short slope and take a hill on the forward ground. We did so fairly easily. There was a certain amount of fire directed at us, but we moved very quickly through thick cover. The Japanese left the position and we arrived at the top. Here the situation seemed uncertain. Fire was coming at us from in front and behind. Our Troop Captain, John Heron, MC, stood calmly on the summit looking around while we took up firing positions lying down. He waved a hand towards the front and rear and said, "This, gentlemen, is the 'Fog of War'." He was not acting a part nor trying to impress us, he was merely being himself. Cool and utterly collected. The firing from the rear was quite obviously from our Garands, not Japanese, so we bellowed for them to stop and this was done.'

Harassed intermittently by enemy infiltrations and snipers, the troops had three days' rest before re-embarking on their landing craft and sailing right round the Myebon peninsula to cruise up the Daingbon Chaung and land on the Burmese mainland. The landing went well, the Brigade getting ashore without opposition and then advancing quickly upon the town of Kangaw, a small place overlooked to the south-east by a long low hill codenamed Hill 170.

Peter Young gives a thumbnail sketch of the great fight at Kangaw: 'Our task was to cut the lines of communication of the Japanese Army attempting to retreat to the south. We moved in landing craft up a chaung, landed in a mangrove swamp, took Hill 170 with No. 1 Commando, and then gradually unrolled, taking further hills. Eventually the Japs got fed up with us and counter-attacked. They attacked one end of 170 which was held by one troop of No. 1 Commando, which was cut off from the rest of the Brigade by a re-entrant, and this troop behaved quite brilliantly. They massacred the Japanese but they were massacred themselves as well. We had a hundred casualties in one long and tedious day, wounded men being carried past constantly, and the following morning we changed 1 Commando for 5 Commando to get fresh troops into the line. I visited Robin Stewart of 5 to ask how he was getting along, and he said, "I think if we give them another shove, the Japanese will go." I said, "Well, you know Campbell Hardy has given the order for no more counter-attacks – we've done six already. However, if you do it, I shall support you." He was one of those chaps who didn't give a bugger so, without thinking of his commission, he gave them another shove – and they were all dead. There they were, all lying on the ground, dead. You couldn't step on the ground without treading on dead or dying Japanese. I've never seen anything like it, ever. They had great gashes in them, great head wounds. We had killed over 300 and found only two or three with enough breath left to croak. I captured one Japanese soldier, the only one we took alive, the only one remotely human. He only had his heel missing, but we got him back to hospital. He survived, although the Sikhs wanted to cut his throat. We took one prisoner at Hill 170 and the battle went on for days. Afterwards, we got a nice letter from "up top" saying we had won the decisive battle of the Arakan campaign, but of course it's all forgotten now. Nobody knows what happened in Burma.'

What happened in Burma was one of the great Commando battles of the war. No. 1 occupied the lower, southern slopes of Hill 170 before being held up by machine gun fire. 42 Commando then came up and took the land between 170 and a small chaung, while 44 Commando advanced past 170 onto another hill feature, codenamed Pinner, which they occupied without difficulty. This done, 44 failed to dig in adequately and were unprepared when the Japanese put in a furious series of counter-attacks, preceded and interspersed with artillery fire from field guns manhandled close to the Commando lines and fired at point-blank range. 44 took heavy casualties before the Japanese withdrew, after which 44 Commando pulled back behind Hill 170, which had now fallen to No. 1 Commando. The Brigade stayed on or around 170 for the next ten days, while the Japanese continued to shell it intermittently and infiltrate their positions each night with small, aggressive, probing patrols. The more experienced Commando soldiers could sense that something was building up in the dense jungle to their front, but the relative calm continued until 06.00 hrs on 31 January, when the Japanese hit 170 with everything they had.

Charles Hustwick recalls the landing and what followed: 'We landed on 22 January on the side of the chaung. The shore consisted of four-foot vertical mudbanks with a good strip of mangrove swamp and thick bush. Inland the scrub was thin and the ground full of spikes of mangrove roots, nine inches high, all close together. One had a job to get a foot between them. Beyond that, leading to Hill 170, were paddy fields, swamped by tides for a distance of half a mile. At this stage there was no tank or gun support. There was no opposition on the beach itself and No. 1 Commando passed through and advanced towards Hill 170 and cleared the southern end. The enemy, from their pocket on the hill, made a fierce attack on No. 1 Commando, who fought bravely in hand-to-hand fighting. Shelling was continuous. There were many casualties within the whole Brigade. Many shells fired by the Japs failed to explode, the lads getting up and cheering at each dud. Some tanks did appear on the 26th, but the ground was far too marshy for them to be of much use to us.

'Having held the line for some ten days, we were about to be relieved when a heavy artillery concentration was put down on Hill 170, and so began the fiercest battle of the campaign fought for twenty-four hours in an area of about one hundred square yards. The loss to the enemy was well over 300 killed and goodness knows how many wounded. The hill was finally cleared the following day. The back slopes of the hill were covered with enemy dead. They were dwarf-like and armed with long rifles and French-style long bayonets – really ugly creatures. It was here that Lieutenant Knowland, a reinforcement from England, won a posthumous VC; he was last seen firing a two-inch mortar from the hip. Casualties in our Commando were heavy among the Bren gunners. Twelve men were hit behind one vital Bren. By the evening, after about twenty-four hours' hectic fighting, which at one time involved the Headquarters of 1 Commando, the enemy onslaught ceased. A strike by Thunderbolt aircraft inflicted heavy casualties on the now retreating enemy. Several dead Commandos were found well forward, among the Jap dead. Many ruses were made by the enemy, one even wearing a green beret. I have no idea what 1 Commando's final casualties were, but the price of victory had not been small.'

Henry Brown recalls Hill 170: 'I was the Senior Administrative Warrant Officer, and just as I had done in North Africa, in order to carry out one of my tasks, the sad business of reporting casualties and collecting their effects, I had to stay as close to the action as possible. Consequently, I went into Kangaw and set up a small base, just me and my typewriter, on the lower slopes of Hill 170, along with Dave Reid of the Orderly Room staff. From our position, low down on the hill, we could see several incidents, and one I will never forget was the sight of a Jap, running naked along the field in front of the hill where all the action was then taking place. As we discovered a few moments later, he was carrying an explosive charge round his waist and dived under one of the three tanks which had struggled through the paddy to the forward slopes of the hill. They could advance no further because of the marshy ground. The Jap blew himself up and put the tank out of action. We had all heard of Japanese suicide squads and had now seen them at work. The battle of Hill 170 lasted many days, but on the night of 31 January/1 February, they made their last great attack, and casualties were indeed heavy. Our Bren gunners on the hill spotted the new Jap attack and commenced firing. This stopped the Japs in their tracks but they then decided to come across the fields directly in front of my small hovel, so there I was, in front of the troops (by mistake, I might add), and wondering quite vividly, what my fate would be. Fortunately, the Bren gunners were spot-on and the attack was halted halfway across the field. I breathed easily once more. Kangaw was certainly some battle and our success prompted the Corps Commander, Lieutenant General Christison, to issue a special Order of the Day, praising the action of 3 Commando Brigade.'

Des Crowden of 5 Commando continues the story: 'The hill was known as 170 because it was that height in feet. It was also known as Brighton, but it was nothing like Brighton. The whole Commando Brigade was earmarked for this one with sundry other troops, plus Air Force and Navy. The beaches and surroundings were hit by American bombers from Ceylon and shelled to hell by the Navy. The landing craft were lowered and circled round the mother ship until every one was down, then they formed up in line abreast and headed for the shore. Before long the water was spouting up around the landing craft. I comforted myself by thinking it was our naval fire falling short, but of course it was the Japs. They had survived the bombing, or some of them had. Anyway, the Navy's gunners were more accurate, as we were to discover later. Our Commando was the second to land. The beaches out there are steep and we were up to our armpits in water. Mines and small arms fire harassed us as well as the load we had to carry – all our usual equipment plus ammo, grenades, extra food, as well as petrol cans full of drinking water. Once ashore, you had to scramble through the mangrove swamps. By then the first casualties were coming back to the beach, much envied. We reached the hill and the first task was to dig in again in box formation. The ground was very hard. At least one chap was shot dead. Food varied between bully beef and tinned soup, and we had solidified smokeless fuel in portions, which we lit in the bottom of our trench or foxhole. The Medical

Corps set up on the same hill and did all kinds of wonderful things while the battle raged all round them. Patrols were sent out to nearby hills. Jap long-range guns continually shelled us unless one of our spotter planes was in the air – they were a godsend.

'The Japs decided that they liked this hill and they attacked us in strength and overran about an eighth of the hill. By the time they were forced to retire they had lost over 300 men and many more were wounded. The night before they finally retreated, my troop, No. 4 of 5 Commando, were at the sharp end, almost shoulder to shoulder in a box and under attack, but none of the Japs got through. The following morning, one of those ridiculous things happened; mail arrived on the hill from the UK, and two hard-boiled eggs apiece. We looked through this pile of mail, took out our own and passed the rest on, knowing that several letters would never be claimed. The support from the RAF and the Navy was fantastic. The RAF were bombing and strafing with Hurricanes, and at one point I thought they were dropping leaflets, but one of our planes had been hit with small arms fire, had blown up and was dropping in small pieces. We got plenty of Jap souvenirs on this trip and I understand that a Jap officer's sword was sent to the family of the pilot of this plane. The Navy were shelling the enemy through the trees above our heads; their OPs were on the hill with us and their direction was magnificent.

'Then we were ready to finish it off. One of our sergeants took some men along the foot of the hill while the rest of us crawled towards Japs along the top. One Sergeant-Major filled up a native's basket with hand grenades and did a solo attack. He was badly wounded but was dragged out and lives to this day. He was decorated. An officer of No. 1 Commando with a machine gun had, the day before, fired on the Japs till he was killed; he got a posthumous VC. Progress anywhere along the hill had to be in single file, and the one up front was usually killed or wounded. When it was my turn to lead, I saw a group of Japs retreating, carrying their wounded. I let fly with my tommy gun and signalled my colleagues to move up. It was looking better now and soon it was all over. The trenches we approached were full of dead or wounded; dead Japs wearing green berets they had taken from our dead. We found a wounded naval OP officer who, it turned out, had been seconded to us when we were in Madagascar. I should think he was glad to see the back of us. We suffered a lot of casualties and were glad when Indian troops moved in to take over. Every month for the past three months, a draw had taken place in each troop, and the winner's name went into the hat. When not in action the whole Commando were on parade to watch the final draw, for the outright winner got a month's leave back in Blighty. Believe it or not, the final draw took place on this bloody hill. The winner, who was in my troop, had to run across open ground to reach a landing craft on the nearby chaung and head home.'

Frank Atter of 5 Commando: 'Kangaw was our biggest operation, and a proper Combined Operation. I remember going up Daingbon Chaung, and landing in what appeared to be a mangrove swamp, then climbing up a long hill, which was 170. 1 Commando were in possession, and we dug in on their right. Although other hills were occupied, 170 was the dominant feature, and the key to the beach-head. Until the last Japanese attack, most of the danger was from very accurate shellfire. At first we thought the attack was for a short spell just after dawn. Their guns, mostly 75s, were brought very close to the hill, and a really massive barrage was directed at us. I know the guns were close because the two explosions of detonation and the explosion of the shells seemed almost simultaneous. Later, the barrage continued at a greater distance, but still with the accuracy that Japanese artillery were noted for, and the 75s were joined by heavier guns. Our own 25-pounders gave excellent support, as did the tanks, which

were in territory unsuitable for them. Water was not in
plentiful supply, apart from salt water from the chaung.

'Then 5 Commando moved forward to a hill in front.
Nothing happened there except the occasional shelling,
until one night we heard the noise of a real battle. This
was the big attack on 1 Commando, and it was obvious it
was serious. We were told to make our own way to 170
by subsections, and we went back to our old positions. I
can tell you very little about the battle. My only real duty
was to take ammunition up to those who were involved.
I never realized before how fast you could run carrying
heavy ammunition boxes, but when you are being shot at
you do concentrate somewhat.'

The tactics employed against 44 — intense close-range
artillery fire, followed by massed infantry assaults — were
repeated on a rising scale of violence against No. 1
Commando on 170. The main Japanese infantry assault
came in against 4 Troop of 1 Commando, holding the
north edge of 170, and reinforced when possible by troops
from 42 and 5 Commandos. No. 1 Commando fought for
their position on 170 throughout the day with counter-
attack following counter-attack. On 1 February the Japanese destroyed three tanks which had become bogged in
the marsh below the western slopes of 170, and then
mounted a second major offence against No. 1, overrunning the first line of trenches before they were stopped.
British Commandos and Japanese infantry were locked in
battle at close quarters, much of it hand-to-hand, bayonet-
to-bayonet. The Japanese manhandled their artillery
pieces forward to pound the Commando trenches over
open sights, the Commandos engaging their gunners with
Brens and mortars. At one Bren position, twelve gunners
were killed or wounded one after another, but another
man always came crawling out from cover to take up the
fight, while men in nearby trenches lobbed over full
magazines to keep the Bren in action.

Ted Coker was a Bren gunner in 6 Troop, No. 1

Commando. 'There was the grim day when we finally knocked them off the hill. I remember moving up a track to relieve some of our troops (there were seven troops in No. 1 – I was in No. 6). We met our blokes being led and carried out, looking absolutely shell-shocked, and I remember thinking, this is one we won't get out of. Anyway, we managed to get to our forward positions. I had a No. 2 on my Bren with me, but after about an hour he was killed and I understand mine was the only Bren to keep going. Funny what you remember about your thoughts at the time. I kept thinking, thank Christ for 1st and 2nd IA. When I was training on the Bren, the instructors were forever drumming into us our 1st IA and 2nd IA. IA is Immediate Action, and I used to think, how the hell can you have 1st and 2nd IAs? But on this day, on Hill 170, I was so glad I had done both blindfolded in training, as it no doubt saved my life and helped 6 Troop take part in that particular victory. I was lying in a shallow trench, and an officer and some others were managing to get magazines to me to keep me going, and I thought, why must they keep hitting me in the back, throwing those mags at me? To give you some idea of the ferocity of that day, our people counted over 370 dead Japs the next morning and we had lost far too many bloody good blokes. You can't describe it properly, you can't make anyone who wasn't there understand what it was like.' Ted Coker won the Military Medal on Hill 170.

By mid-afternoon, the heart of the fight had settled round the twenty-four surviving men of 4 Troop, now commanded by the newly-commissioned Lieutenant George Knowland, late of 3 Commando. They beat off one attack by 300 Japanese infantry, Knowland leaving his trench to move about the position, throwing grenades, sharing out the remaining ammunition, cheering his men on, taking over the Bren when yet another gun-crew were shot down. He then engaged a second attack firing into the advancing Japanese line with a two-inch mortar and a

Bren, picking up a rifle and then a tommy gun to spray their still-advancing ranks, now only thirty feet away. He was killed just before this attack petered out, when another desperate counter-attack by 4 Troop, aided by gunfire from the support craft on the chaung, beat the Japanese off yet again.

The fight for 170 went on all that day, and well into the night. The Japanese clung to that part of the hill they had captured, digging in and bringing up machine guns. Counter-attacks by 3 Troop of No. 1 and reinforcements from 5 and 42 Commandos failed to shift them.

John Ferguson: 'We had been moved to the forward edge of Hill 170. There were hundreds of Japanese at the base and about 3,000 more coming in through the swamps. While throwing hand grenades, I could hear them shouting, "Cease fire, don't shoot," and thought "I'll give you bloody cease firing." Later, during the grenade throwing, a burst of gunfire at close range severely damaged my left shoulder and put my arm out of action, but somehow it was possible to carry on throwing grenades. Later, a further burst hit me in the chest, and down I went, pole-axed, with blood flowing over my chest. There is still a bullet close to my heart. I got another grenade out and tried to get up again but all strength had gone. The last thing I remember was saying to someone, "Make sure that the pin is still in position," then oblivion.'

The Indian Navy sloops anchored in the chaung, the last surviving tank from the 19th Lancers and even strafing aircraft came in to help No. 1, but this was an infantry battle, fought with machine guns and rifles and bayonets and grenades, by exhausted men on either side hauling themselves up and forward for one more effort, one more attack, across ground already littered with dead and wounded. As darkness fell on 1 February, the battle spluttered out, fading into occasional bursts of machine-gun fire, the crump of mortar bombs, a splutter of rifle shots. That night the Japanese withdrew, and at dawn, as

Peter Young has related, No. 5 Commando were allowed to advance and take possession of the ground.

CSM Joe Edmans of No. 1 Commando gives his account of Kangaw. 'This new type of enemy we were now fighting was different from the half-hearted Italians and the methodical Germans we fought in North Africa. The Japs had snipers tied in trees, used wounded men to draw you into the open, also shouting in English "Johnny," or "Joe, where are you?" or "Help, help, I am wounded over here," hoping you would go out to pick him up. Can one imagine dense jungle, pitch-black, and every now and then these voices coming out of the dark. The least little movement outside your foxhole, a snake, or some other jungle creature moving around, and you thought, "Here they come, crawling towards me." We had to be fully alert and on top of our form with a steady nerve. Having had several brushes with the Japs, at Myebon we now had two days' rest and on 22 January, the Brigade re-embarked in the landing craft and set off for our last battle with the Japs. Little did we know it but in this last fight we were going to lose a lot of men.

'Eventually we reached Hill 170 and consolidated our position, dug in, and there we stayed.

'Every morning, just before it got light, we had stand-to, which meant everybody would get in their slit trench or foxhole, in case the Japs made an attack. On 31 January the shelling started earlier than usual, so we surmised that something was up and at once got in our trenches. I shared mine with Private Beaney, and being a Corporal I ensured that all my section were in their trenches. The northern end of the hill was held by 4 Troop with No. 1 Troop and the rest of the Commando spread along the top. My troop, No. 6, was next to No. 4. At the bottom of the hill was HQ, and along from them were two support tanks. Private Beaney and I were crouching in our trench, looking through the morning mist to see if we could see anything moving. Suddenly, there was a terrific explosion

from the bottom of the hill. I found out later that this was
our tanks being blown up by a Japanese suicide squad.
Then from out of the trees across the paddy fields came a
Japanese officer, waving his sword and running towards
us. He did not get far and was soon brought down. An
officer of 42 Commando at the bottom of the hill dashed
out to try and get the sword, but was hit in the leg and
had to get back to his trench. Another lad tried and he
was more successful. At the northern end of the hill the
sound of the firing became fierce. Then we got the news
that 4 Troop at the northern end had been overrun.

'Our section was then ordered to go down the right-
hand side of the hill to clear any enemy, so off we went –
Sergeant Roberts, Beaney, Dearden, Ruffell, Sweeney,
McFall, Hobbs – all in single file, with bullets whistling
through the trees. Keeping very low, we were moving
down the side of the hill now and the fighting to our left
was getting fierce. Suddenly, Dearden, who was in front
of me, was fatally wounded. We carried on down the hill
and Sergeant Roberts was hit, but he crawled back up the
hill. We consolidated our position and Sweeney and
McFall set up the Bren facing up the hill in the direction
of the Japs. Just a short distance from the bottom of the
hill, in the paddy field, was a bamboo hut. On seeing this,
Hobbs ran across the open ground to the hut (from the
other side of the hut you see round the other side of the
hill). Hobbs disappeared from view but we heard a burst
from his tommy gun. Then he came running back to say
that he had killed four Japs who had been hiding, probably
waiting for us. He then dashed across the open ground to
go back to the hut, but a Jap sniper had seen him, and as
he ran back across the paddy field he was hit in the jaw.
He came dashing back, holding his jaw which was pouring
with blood, and went up the hill to the medics.

'Our Bren team was giving the odd burst towards the
Japs, then down came a grenade which failed to go off,

but a couple more came down, and one went off, wounding the two Bren gunners. We realized that we were at a disadvantage being at the bottom of the hill, so we started on our way up, when we heard a moaning sound. Looking back towards the hut we saw Beaney had been wounded and was lying in the open. A couple of lads went back but as soon as they stepped into the open, all hell was let loose. Beaney kept on shouting, "They have gone now," and a burst of fire would come down. We tossed a couple of smoke grenades but as soon as the smoke came, down came the automatic fire. We tried several times but to no avail. We sent word back to HQ and were informed not to try any more as the casualties were heavy.

'A Royal Marine sergeant came down to see if he could help but the fire being put down by the Japs in front of Beaney was fierce, so we went up the hill to place ourselves in a better position. On reaching the top we heard that Sergeant Lander, who had been with No. 1 since 1940, had been killed by a sniper. At the top of the hill we got in our trenches and waited, while at the northern end, 2 Section of 6 Troop, under Captain Evill, were given the job of trying to clear the Japs off that end of the hill. Suddenly, the Japs charged up the hill, yelling and shouting, and we let them come up so far, then we gave them everything we had. 'We must have been outnumbered twenty to one. We used Bren gun, tommy-gun, American semi-automatic rifle, Colt ·45, and tossed quite a few grenades. After several attempts they gave up. By this time we had been reinforced with some of No. 42 and No. 44 Royal Marine Commandos.

'Then, coming through the trees down the bottom of the hill, was No. 5 Commando, who were in reserve and had the job of knocking the Japs off the hill. Lieutenant Colonel Pollitt, who was in command, used to be our Troop Captain and was a great officer, getting us out of a few tight corners while we were in North Africa. They came along the bottom, fanned out, firing as they went.

Suddenly one of the lads was engulfed in smoke and came
running up the hill. A bullet had hit one of his phosphorus
grenades and he was in agony. The fighting carried on for
some time, then eventually it died down and things went
quiet. We stayed in our trenches till the next morning in
case they decided to make another attack, but they never
came, and we were relieved by an Indian Division. While
the troops were moving to the boats, I went round the
hill, first to the side that we went down, and once again
further down, to where Beaney lay; he had been killed
with a bayonet. All the bodies were brought to the bottom
of the hill and a short prayer was said before they were
buried. We were then taken out of the line to a rest camp.'

No. 5 found hundreds of the enemy dead carpeting the
slopes of Hill 170 before the trenches of 4 Troop, and the
Brigade lost forty-five men killed and ninety wounded.
Lieutenant George Knowland received a posthumous VC
and Lieutenant General Christison, commanding 15th
Indian Corp, issued a special Order of the Day:

> 3 Commando Brigade, for indifference to
> personal danger, for ruthless pursuit in success
> and for resourceful determination in adversity,
> has been an inspiration to all their comrades-in-
> arms. The battle of Kangaw has been the
> decisive battle of the Arakan campaign and was
> won due to the magnificent courage shown by 3
> Commando Brigade on Hill 170.

Kangaw was the last Commando battle of the war. 3
Commando Brigade withdrew first to Akyab and then to
India, where it began to train for Operation Zipper, the
invasion of Malaya. Then, on 6 August 1945, the US Air
Force dropped the first atom bomb on Hiroshima. Three
days later another bomb fell on the city of Nagasaki, and
on 15 August the Second World War came to an end.

Epilogue

'God and the soldier, we alike adore
In times of trouble, not before,
Troubles past, both are alike requited,
God is forgotten, and the soldier slighted.'

FRANCIS QUARLES
1592–1644

When the Second World War ended, the Commando soldiers began to come home. 1 and 4 Commando Brigades stayed on in Germany for a while after the surrender, helping to restore order during the early days of the occupation before 1 Commando Brigade returned to Sussex in July 1945, where they began to train for operations in the Far East. 2 Commando Brigade had arrived from Italy a few weeks earlier, in mid-June, and 4 Commando Brigade finally came home in November.

After the Japanese surrender, 3 Commando Brigade were sent to Hong Kong, where they arrived on 12 September in time to take the formal surrender of the Japanese garrison. Meanwhile, the future of the Army Commando units was already being discussed in high places, and the decision was announced to the men of 1 Commando Brigade by General Robert Laycock on 25 October. After recounting their exploits and passing on the thanks of Higher Command, he concluded:

> It has fallen to my lot to tell you, the
> Commandos, who have fought with such
> distinction in Norway and the islands of the
> north, in France, in Belgium, in Holland, and in

356

Germany, in Africa and Egypt, in Crete and
Syria, in Sicily and Italy, on the shores and
islands of the Adriatic, and in the jungles of the
Arakan and Burma . . . it is, I repeat, with great
regret that I must tell you today, that you are to
be disbanded.

Disbandment began the following month. Many
soldiers returned to civilian life, while the professional
soldiers returned to their parent units to continue their
careers. The Headquarters of the UK-based Commando
Brigades were gone by the end of the month, and the other
elements of the wartime Commando structure, the Basic
Training Centre at Achnacarry, and the Holding Operational Commando at Wrexham, soon followed, the Holding Operational Commando being finally disbanded in
early 1946. Since the ending of the war in Europe, the
Holding Operational Commando had been receiving back
Commando soldiers released from prison camps and hospitals, and getting them fit and retrained before they
returned to their units.

Before the end of 1945, it was decided, at the instigation
of Lord Louis Mountbatten, that the British Forces would
retain a Commando Brigade, drawn, somewhat to the
chagrin of the Army Commandos, from the ranks of the
Royal Marines. This Brigade, No. 3 Commando Brigade,
Royal Marines, began to form in Hong Kong in the
autumn of 1945, while the wartime 3 Commando Brigade
began to break up. No. 1 and 5 Commandos lost a steady
stream of demobilized men and were combined into 1/5
Commando, which finally disbanded in January 1947.
The long march of the Army Commandos seemed to be
over.

It is notoriously difficult to keep good men down, and
the Army Commandos of the Second World War have
stayed together down the decades since the end of hostilities, gathered under the umbrella of the Commando

357

Association, formed at Achnacarry by Lieutenant Colonel Charles Vaughan in 1943 and, although time is thinning their numbers now, the Association is still alive and vigorous. Henry Brown, of the Independent Companies and 1 Commando, has been their Secretary for over forty years.

3 Commando Brigade, Royal Marines, has carried the Commando tradition on since 1945, serving with distinction in every operational theatre. Their history records only one year from 1945 to the present day when men or units of this Brigade were not in action somewhere in the world. Nor was 1945 the end of the fighting role of the Army Commandos. At the end of the 1970s, Army Commando units from the Royal Artillery and the Royal Engineers were raised to support the infantry of 40, 42 and 45 Commandos, and these Army units sailed with the Brigade to retake the Falkland Islands in 1982. As this book is written, over 1,000 soldiers of the British Army wear the green beret.

'Old men forget,' as Shakespeare wrote, a line many of the Commando soldiers quoted in their contributions to this book to explain any lapse of memory. It is a quotation that we might continue . . .

> Old men forget: yet shall not all forget
> Yet he'll remember with advantages,
> What feats he did that day; then shall our names,
> Familiar in their mouths as household words,
> Be in their flowing cups freshly remember'd.
> We few, we happy few, we band of brothers.

BIBLIOGRAPHY

Commando Crusade Major General T. Churchill
(William Kimber, 1987).

The Watery Maze Bernard Fergusson (Collins, 1956).

The Oxford Book of Military Anecdotes Ed. Max
Hastings (Oxford University Press, 1985).

Raiders from the Sea Rear Admiral Lepotier (William
Kimber, 1954).

The Campaign in Italy Eric Linklater (HMSO, 1951).

The Marines Were There Bruce Lockhart (Putnam, 1950).

The Miracle of Dunkirk Walter Lord (Allen Lane, 1982).

March Past Brigadier the Lord Lovat, DSO, MC
(Weidenfeld & Nicolson, 1978).

Commando Brigadier J. Durnford Slater, DSO & Bar
(William Kimber, 1953).

The Commandos 1940–46 Charles Messenger (William
Kimber, 1985).

*By Sea and Land: The Story of the Royal Marines
Commandos (1942–82)* Robin Neillands (Weidenfeld
& Nicolson, 1987).

The Greatest Raid of All C. E. Lucas Phillips
(Heinemann, 1958).

Commando Denys Rcitz (Faber & Faber, 1924).

Clash by Night Brigadier Derek Mills-Roberts, DSO, MC
(William Kimber, 1956).

Dieppe – the Shame and the Glory Terence Robertson
(Hutchinson, 1963).

The Attack on St Nazaire Commander R. E. D. Ryder,
VC, RN (John Murray, 1947).

The Green Beret Hilary St George Saunders (Michael Joseph, 1949).

Norway, the Commandos, Dieppe William Seymour (Sidgwick & Jackson, 1985).

Storm from the Sea Brigadier Peter Young, DSO, MC & 2 Bars (William Kimber, 1958).

INDEX

By Sea and Land
The Story of the Royal Marines Commandos

Robin Neillands

Foreword by Major General Julian Thompson CB OBE

This is the story of the Royal Marines Commandos, one of the world's elite fighting forces, from the bloody baptism of 40 Commando on the beaches of Dieppe in 1942, when they saw their Colonel die in his blazing landing craft, to the day when 45 Commando yomped into Stanley at the end of the Falklands War in May 1982.

In the forty years between, the Royal Marines have been constantly in action somewhere in the world. In major conflicts and countless small, half-forgotten campaigns, the Royal Marines were there – at Suez, Aden, Cyprus, Malaya, Borneo, Korea, Northern Ireland and the South Atlantic.

Here, told in the words of the commandos themselves, we see the battles through their eyes. The result is an extraordinarily vivid view from the sharp end of what it's really like to wear the legendary green beret, in peace and war.

FONTANA PAPERBACKS

Fontana Paperbacks
Non-fiction

Fontana is a leading paperback publisher of non-fiction. Below are some recent titles.

- ☐ All the King's Men *Robert Marshall* £3.50
- ☐ War Papers *Virgil Pomfret* £10.95
- ☐ The Boys and the Butterflies *James Birdsall* £2.95
- ☐ Pursuit *Ludovic Kennedy* £3.95
- ☐ Malta Convoy *Shankland and Hunter* £2.95
- ☐ We Die Alone *David Howarth* £2.95
- ☐ The Bridge on the River Kwai *Pierre Boulle* £2.95
- ☐ Carve Her Name With Pride *R. J. Minney* £2.95
- ☐ The Tunnel *Eric Williams* £2.95
- ☐ Reach for the Sky *Paul Brickhill* £3.50
- ☐ Rommel *Desmond Young* £3.50

You can buy Fontana paperbacks at your local bookshop or newsagent. Or you can order them from Fontana Paperbacks, Cash Sales Department, Box 29, Douglas, Isle of Man. Please send a cheque, postal or money order (not currency) worth the purchase price plus 22p per book for postage (maximum postage required is £3).

NAME (Block letters) _____

ADDRESS _____

_____

_____